A HISTORICAL GUIDE TO
Joseph Conrad

A Historical
Guide to Joseph Conrad

EDITED BY
JOHN G. PETERS

UNIVERSITY PRESS

2010

OXFORD
UNIVERSITY PRESS

Oxford University Press, Inc., publishes works that further
Oxford University's objective of excellence
in research, scholarship, and education.

Oxford   New York

Auckland   Cape Town   Dar es Salaam   Hong Kong   Karachi
Kuala Lumpur   Madrid   Melbourne   Mexico City   Nairobi
New Delhi   Shanghai   Taipei   Toronto

With offices in
Argentina   Austria   Brazil   Chile   Czech Republic   France   Greece
Guatemala   Hungary   Italy   Japan   Poland   Portugal   Singapore
South Korea   Switzerland   Thailand   Turkey   Ukraine   Vietnam

Copyright © 2010 by Oxford University Press, Inc.

Published by Oxford University Press, Inc.
198 Madison Avenue, New York, New York 10016

www.oup.com

Oxford is a registered trademark of Oxford University Press.

Library of Congress Cataloging-in-Publication Data
A historical guide to Joseph Conrad / edited by John G. Peters.
p. cm.
Includes bibliographical references and index.
ISBN 978-0-19-533277-3; 978-0-19-533278-0 (pbk.)
1. Conrad, Joseph, 1857–1924–Criticism and interpretation.
I. Peters, John G. (John Gerard)
PR6005.O4Z7442 2010
823'.912—dc22   2009011652

1 3 5 7 9 8 6 4 2

Printed in the United States of America
on acid-free paper

For my aunt, Ruth Snider

Acknowledgments

I would like to thank the contributors to this volume, Cedric Watts, Mark Larabee, Joyce Piell Wexler, Andrea White, Chris GoGwilt, and Allan H. Simmons, for the insights they provide on Conrad's life and works. Their knowledge has benefited me greatly. I would also like to thank Shannon McLachlan of Oxford University Press for her support of this project and Brendan O'Neill of Oxford University Press for his help with the various details in putting together this book. Furthermore, I would like to thank The Beinecke Rare Book and Manuscript Library at Yale University for permission to reprint the majority of the images reproduced in this volume, the Rare Books Room at the Willis Library of the University of North Texas for providing me with the images of *A Set of Six* and *Under Western Eyes*, the office of the Vice President of Research at the University of North Texas for a grant to aid in the proofreading and construction of this essay collection, and my Research Assistant Tanner Chase O'Brien for proofreading and regularizing the manuscript. Finally, I would like to thank my family for their support.

Contents

Abbreviations

Unless otherwise specified, all references to Conrad's works are to the Doubleday, Page & Co. (1925) uniform edition and are abbreviated as follows:

AF	Almayer's Folly	RE	The Rescue
AG	The Arrow of Gold	SA	The Secret Agent
C	Chance	SOS	A Set of Six
I	The Inheritors	SL	The Shadow-Line
LJ	Lord Jim	S	Suspense
MS	The Mirror of the Sea	TH	Tales of Hearsay
NN	The Nigger of the	TU	Tales of Unrest
	"Narcissus"	TLS	'Twixt Land and Sea
N	Nostromo	TOS	Typhoon and Other Stories
NLL	Notes on Life and Letters	UWE	Under Western Eyes
OI	An Outcast of the Islands	V	Victory
PR	A Personal Record	WT	Within the Tides
RO	The Rover	Y	Youth and Two Other
ROM	Romance		Stories

A HISTORICAL GUIDE TO
Joseph Conrad

Introduction

John G. Peters

Naturally, all authors are products of their cultural and historical circumstances, but if ever there was an author who was a product of the historical and cultural circumstances in which he lived, it was Joseph Conrad. Far more than any of his contemporaries, Conrad's background was utterly cosmopolitan. Born Józef Teodor Konrad Korzeniowski in a Polish region of Ukraine during the time of the partition of Poland, Conrad's life was particularly molded by the historical events unfolding at the time. As a young boy, he accompanied his mother and father into exile as a result of his father's conviction for seditious activities against the Russian rule of Poland. After his parents' death, which resulted from their time in exile, Conrad was raised by his maternal uncle. At the age of seventeen, Conrad left Poland behind to pursue a life at sea. He trained for this profession for four years in France before joining the British Merchant Marine service at the age of twenty-one and speaking no English. The next fifteen years of his life were spent predominantly in the East, serving on numerous ships and eventually working his way up to ship's captain. In the mid 1890s, he abruptly gave up his sailing career, permanently settling in England and beginning a career as a writer. Conrad's varied experiences in Poland, Russia, France, England, and the East would profoundly guide the direction of his writing and would significantly set him apart from his contemporaries. As a result of his unique background, he produced a surprisingly varied literary opus, everything from drawing room dramas, such as "The Return" (1898), to the exotic fiction of the East, such as *Almayer's Folly* (1895), to political fiction, such as *Nostromo*, to historical fiction, such as "The Duel" (1908). In producing his body of literary works, Conrad had the opportunity of writing as both an English insider and outsider, and his cosmopolitan background allowed him to see the world from various perspectives at once. The settings for his works are equally varied from the East to Africa to England to South America to Russia to the European continent. This remarkably varied output is best understood only when considered within the equally varied historical, cultural, and social context in which he wrote.

From the beginnings of Conrad's literary career, his work was a unique blend of elements. He has often been typecast as a writer of sea fiction or adventure fiction geared toward a male audience. This resulted partly from the way his publishers marketed his works and partly from the subject material that found its way into his works. To be sure, Conrad was adept at employing the adventure tradition. One need look no further than the storm scenes in *The Nigger of the "Narcissus"* (1897) or "Typhoon" (1902) to appreciate his uncanny ability to place the reader within the action of an event such that the reader experiences an event in the same way and typically at the same moment as do the characters. To see Conrad as primarily a writer of adventure fiction (particularly sea fiction) or solely as a writer of male literature, however, is to miss much that Conrad had to offer to those of his time and to those of our own time. Instead, his contributions to psychological fiction, political fiction, modernist fiction, and literature in general far transcend his contributions to the adventure tradition, as he consistently showed himself to be an innovator in the vanguard of the literary movements of his day.

Conrad's unique position inside (or perhaps more accurately outside) English society provided him with the opportunity to produce fiction far different from that of most of his contemporaries. He was perhaps the first to take the elements of the adventure tradition of writers such as H. Rider Haggard and transform such material into serious literary works. At a time when much of the serious fiction being written in England was concerned with social issues, Conrad was investigating the nature of the self and its relationship to society. In the process of such investigations, he focused on individual psychological and moral struggles. Before Freud's work in psychology began to find its way into the work of literary figures of the early twentieth century, Conrad was already exploring the permutations of individual psychology. Conrad's "Heart of Darkness" (1899), for instance, is as much about the individual psychology and morality of Marlow and Kurtz as it is about the colonial exploitation of the Congo in the late nineteenth century. Even in his earliest fiction, such as "The Lagoon" (1897) or "Karain" (1897), we find individuals who must struggle within themselves with their moral choices and must accept the consequences of those choices.

This same kind of innovation appears in the political issues that find their way into his fiction. Despite a generally favorable view of the colonial enterprise that permeated the Western world of the time, Conrad often appears as a particularly strong critic of colonialism. In such early fiction as *Almayer's Folly, An Outcast of the Islands* (1896), "An Outpost of Progress" (1897), and "Heart of Darkness," as well as in later fiction such as *The Rescue* (1920), which was actually begun quite early in his literary career, Conrad consistently questions the justifications behind the colonial endeavor. In a different but equally original way, his more strictly political fiction (e.g., *Nostromo* (1904), *The Secret Agent* (1907), *Under Western Eyes* (1911), "Gaspar Ruiz" (1906), "An Anarchist" (1906), and "The Informer" (1906)) once again is unlike most other political fiction in that despite the prominent role that politics plays in these works, particularly his political novels, Conrad's emphasis is largely elsewhere. Other political writers typically view their works as something of a vehicle for disseminating a particular political view. Conrad's political fiction functions otherwise. Woven within the fabric of the politics of these works are the lives of individuals, and Conrad's sympathies always lie with the individuals. As a result, he consistently rejects politics, whether revolutionary or conservative, because he sees all politics as treating individuals as means rather than ends. Ironically, the result is a body of political fiction that largely rejects politics and political activities.

Conrad's relationship to the modernist movement in literature, with which he is often associated, is similarly unique. While modernist writers, such as James Joyce and Virginia Woolf, were experimenting with narrative techniques in the 1910s and 1920s, Conrad was already experimenting with narrative forms as early as 1899 if not before. He began by making minor alterations and augmentations to traditional narrative techniques such as flash back (*Almayer's Folly* and *An Outcast of the Islands*), point of view (*The Nigger of the "Narcissus"*), and frame narratives ("The Lagoon" and "Karain"). Before long, however, Conrad began to take these minor augmentations of traditional narration much further, transforming them into something truly innovative. Beginning with "Youth," Conrad began to employ a technique that has since come to be known as "delayed decoding" (first coined by Ian Watt) in its most productive way. This technique first appeared in 1896 in "The Idiots" (Conrad's earliest published short story), but it is in "Youth" (1898) that we see its full effect, as Conrad uses it to represent point of view, provide immediacy of experience, and also place the reader into the place of the character such that the reader experiences what the character does at the very moment and in the very way in which the character does. For instance, without warning, we as readers encounter the following passage:

I perceived with annoyance the fool was trying to tilt the bench. I said curtly, "Don't, Chips," and immediately became aware of a queer sensation, of an absurd delusion,—I seemed somehow to be in the air. I heard all round me like a pent-up breath released—as if a thousand giants simultaneously had said Phoo!—and felt a dull concussion which made my ribs ache suddenly. No doubt about it—I was in the air, and my body was describing a short parabola. But short as it was, I had the time to think several thoughts in, as far as I can remember, the following order: "This can't be the carpenter—What is it?—Some accident—Submarine volcano?—Coals, gas!—By Jove! we are being blown up. (*Y* 22–3)

We as readers are just as much in the dark about what is occurring as is the character Marlow, and we discover what is occurring as if we were sitting alongside Marlow when the deck of the ship explodes.

Even more radical will be Conrad's experiments with narrative time and sequence. In novels such as *Lord Jim* (1900) and *Nostromo*, he so fractures narrative temporal sequences that readers coming to these novels for the first time often find themselves bewildered. These fragmented narratives, however, are not simply narrative experiments on the part of Conrad but instead an attempt to represent the complex and fragmented world in his fiction. It would be over ten years after the publication of *Nostromo* before another author of note would attempt this same kind of narrative fragmentation when Ford Madox Ford published *The Good Soldier* (1914). Thus the narrative disjunction that is so often associated with the fiction of Virginia Woolf and James Joyce, for instance, had its origins significantly earlier in the works of Joseph Conrad. The same is true of the stream-of-consciousness narrative technique so often associated with Woolf, Joyce, and Dorothy Richardson. When one carefully considers the narrative of Conrad's "Heart of Darkness," for example, it becomes apparent that Marlow's seemingly chronological narration of his journey up the Congo River is anything but chronological and progresses not according to the sequence of the events but rather according to the sequence of Marlow's thoughts. Similarly, at one point in *Lord Jim*, Marlow tells his audience that he had recently been involved in loading cargo, which he refers to as an occupation without glamour, the only other less glamorous occupation being that of an insurance salesman. This causes Marlow to remember that Bob Stanton had once been an insurance salesman, which leads him to remember Bob's death aboard the *Sephora* trying to save a lady's maid. Individually, none of these individual thoughts have much to do with one another, but together they form a kind of stream of consciousness, as one thought leads not logically but rather psychologically to the next (*LJ* 149–51). Such narrative experimentation becomes a proto stream of consciousness that heralds the more fully developed stream of consciousness of Woolf, Joyce, Richardson, and others.

Perhaps the most remarkable way in which Conrad anticipates modernism is in the view he projects of the world around him. It has become almost cliché to remark the indifferent universe that appears in the works of Ernest Hemingway, William Faulkner, F. Scott Fitzgerald, Woolf, and others, resulting from the devastation of the First World War. For Conrad, however, this indifferent universe appeared from the outset of his fictional works. Even more surprising is that Conrad's vision of such a universe appeared in stark contrast to so much of what was going on around him. Western civilization of the latter part of the nineteenth and early twentieth centuries was marked with an emphasis on the idea of progress. The atmosphere of this period was largely one of considerable optimism toward what the future might hold. This is not to say that many were unaware of the numerous social ills that existed at the time, only that there was a permeating belief in a bright future. In the midst of this atmosphere was the voice of Joseph Conrad almost alone in his questioning of the ultimate benevolence of the universe. Instead, he saw a fragmented and absurd universe in which human beings could neither control their existence nor find any ultimate meaning in their lives or in the world they inhabited. For him, meaning was not transcendent but constructed, just as it would be for Woolf, Hemingway, and so many who would follow Conrad. For Conrad, though, it would not take the onset of the First World War to come to the conviction of an indifferent universe. Instead, his wide-ranging and cosmopolitan experience would result in this view of the world long before his fellow modernist writers would come to a similar conclusion.

Conrad's view of an indifferent universe is also tied to his views of Western civilization, and once again he anticipated views that would become commonplace after the First World War. Even in his earliest novel, *Almayer's Folly*, Conrad was already questioning the privileged position that Western civilization held in the world. The colonial endeavor was based upon the view that Western civilization was founded upon absolute truths that should be disseminated to the non-Western world. In *Almayer's Folly, An Outcast of the Islands*, and "An Outpost of Progress," and other early works dealing with colonialism, Conrad consistently questions the value of disseminating Western civilization to the non-Western world. In the case of "An Outpost of Progress," in particular, not only does colonialism come into question but also the very idea of civilized progress cannot stand up to Conrad's scrutiny. In "Heart of Darkness," Conrad goes even further, demonstrating at each appearance of Western civilization in the African wilderness that it is either out of place, absurd, or actually detrimental. Similarly, in *Lord Jim*, the failure of Western romantic ideals in the novel undermines the authority of Western civilization. The resulting view of Western civilization is one in which it becomes a system of convenience for reasonable social interaction but without any transcendent basis. In fact, all of Conrad's most frequently studied works in various ways demonstrate his skepticism toward Western civilization. In addition to those works noted above, *Nostromo*, *The Secret Agent*, and *Under Western Eyes* reveal this same sort of skepticism. In *Nostromo*, Conrad focuses on the negative effects of Western capitalism and political influence in South America. The resulting Western-dominated government and society of Sulaco that arises at the close of the novel is of questionable merit, and, despite the tenuous political peace achieved, the people have become spiritually dead, as they have become increasingly fixated upon the silver of the mine. Conrad's skepticism occurs differently in *The Secret Agent*. Given his general scorn of the anarchists and revolutionaries in the novel, it may be easy to miss Conrad's equal scorn of the established government authorities. From Mr. Vladimir's cynical plan to have the Greenwich Meridian Observatory blown up, to the police cover-up of Verloc's murder, to the political infighting of Chief Inspector Heat and the assistant commissioner, to the silliness of Sir Ethelred and his secretary Toodles, Conrad's authorities come off little better than their revolutionary counterparts. In the end, Conrad affirms neither the revolutionaries nor the authorities, and one is left to wonder about the state of Western civilization and its future in this novel set in London, the very epicenter of Western civilization. In *Under Western Eyes*, Conrad also critiques Western civilization through questioning both revolutionary and established politics, as well as questioning Western values from yet another angle when he emphasizes the Western blind spot toward anything that is not

Western. In addition, Razumov's plight, in which he suddenly finds himself in the midst of an absurd existence where he can make no sense of things and where he has no real control over his life or circumstances, runs counter to the traditional Western view of an ordered and meaningful universe. All of these works appeared long before the beginning of the First World War and demonstrate as skeptical an attitude toward Western civilization and its projected progress for the future as do any of the post-war literary works of Conrad's contemporaries.

The future of Conrad studies looks bright, the number of new studies on Conrad's life and works continues to grow at a rapid rate. While some authors go in and out of favor according to changing critical emphases, the complexity of Conrad's works seems to provide material for whatever critical trends have arisen since Conrad first began writing. Throughout the history of literary criticism of the twentieth and twenty-first centuries, Conrad studies consistently followed the trends of new and current ideas in literary criticism, as Conrad's works continually reveal themselves to be fertile ground for investigating innovations in criticism. Initially, Conrad's unique and remarkable personal history was a particularly fruitful source for the biographical/historical criticism that permeated the majority of literary criticism that was written during the first forty years of the twentieth century. The concurrent *belles lettres* tradition of the early twentieth century found much in the literary quality and human themes in Conrad's works of which it could approve. Similarly, the New Criticism, which recognized Conrad's emphasis on moral dilemmas and the profound ambiguity of his works, was instrumental in propelling Conrad into the forefront of twentieth-century fiction writers. The contemporaneous psychological criticism that flourished from the 1940s to the 1970s also recognized the significance of the deep psychological struggles of so many of Conrad's characters and found ample material for comment in the pysche of such characters. The post-structuralist commentary that followed the New Criticism found in Conrad's complex narrative methodology, linguistic experimentation, and relativist truths a powerful resource for investigating the effect of language on meaning and for questioning the privileged position of Western metaphysics.

Post-colonial criticism has continued to see in Conrad's Eastern, African, and South American settings, politics, and cultures much that is relevant to issues of colonialism and post-colonialism. As a writer with elements of both colonialism and post-colonialism in his works, Conrad is a perfect subject for post-colonial commentary. In fact, not only post-colonial commentators but also many writers of post-colonial fiction have written direct responses to Conrad's colonial works.

The more recent emphasis on gender studies and the continuing interest in post-structural and post-colonial infused criticism show no signs of exhausting Conrad's fiction as resources for commentary. As is true of post-colonial commentary on both Conrad's colonial issues and post-colonial issues, gender criticism has found a wealth of material for discussions of issues of masculinity in Conrad's works as well as material for discussions of issues related to feminist interests. In the end, Conrad's works have provided seemingly endless materials for comment, whether biographical/historical, psychological, post-structural, post-colonial, or otherwise.

In his chapter on Conrad and the maritime tradition, Mark Larabee considers the relationship between Conrad's experience with the maritime tradition and what appears in his literary works. Despite the fact that Conrad increasingly came to dislike being thought of as a writer of literature about the sea, Larabee argues nevertheless that Conrad's experience with the maritime tradition molded much of his thinking and significantly influenced his literary output. Rather than focusing on the biographical associations between Conrad's life and his fiction, Larabee highlights the core values Conrad absorbed from his maritime career. In particular, he considers issues of trade, fidelity, and the craft. In so doing, Larabee shows how the exigencies of the trade affect the nature of the fiction Conrad wrote, from the cargoes transported to the routes taken to the loading of ships. Even more significant for Conrad's works is the idea of fidelity that he took away from his maritime experience. Attention to tradition, professional competence, one's shipmates, and the ship itself led to Conrad's views on loyalty, fidelity, and so many other values that find themselves so frequently in the foreground of his fictional works. Related to the idea of fidelity is that of the craft itself. Larabee argues that the idea of the craft leads to Conrad's emphasis on the importance of a job well done both aboard ship and also at his writing desk. Along with his discussion of Conrad's relationship to the maritime tradition, Larabee also provides readers with an understanding of the tradition itself.

Joyce Piell Wexler chronicles Conrad's relationship to the publishing industry, arguing that Conrad tried to negotiate a middle ground between maintaining his artistic principles and reaching a broader reading public throughout his career. She further argues that he sought this broader audience not only for financial reasons but also because he felt that it was important to reach a larger group rather than merely a small coterie. In her essay, Wexler also outlines the publishing landscape in which Conrad found himself. The publishing world of that time was an evolving one, a period in which literary agents had only just begun to enter this world and a world in which authors were struggling to transform the business from the Victorian model that still overshadowed the industry. Conrad benefited from the patience and help of both his early publishers, T. Fisher Unwin and William Blackwood, and from his friend Edward Garnett's knowledge of the publishing world. Wexler also notes the difficulty Conrad had in meeting the many unrealistic deadlines he would set with publishers. Typically, he would be unable to meet these deadlines when works such as *The Secret Agent* and *Under Western Eyes* would grow from Conrad's original conception of them as stories as he would become more and more engaged in their subject matter. Most important, however, Wexler demonstrates how Conrad was able to master the literary marketplace such that he was able to reach a wider audience while still remaining true to his artistic principles.

Allan H. Simmons gives an overview of the historical and political context in which Conrad wrote. He begins by outlining the important European historical events of the nineteenth century, particularly as they related to the plight of Poland and thus affected Conrad's early life and choices. These influences formed Conrad's political thinking, especially regarding his attitudes toward his Polish heritage and nineteenth-century European nationalism. Simmons then considers British politics and history of the time, such as colonialism and the Boer War, as these affected Conrad's attitudes about England and entered his fictional works. Simmons argues for an astute political sense in Conrad's works that was greater than that of many of his contemporaries and also argues for political elements in much of Conrad's fiction, not just in his overtly political novels, *Nostromo*, *The Secret Agent*, and *Under Western Eyes*, although Simmons also gives extended readings to these novels as well. He concludes with a discussion of Conrad's response to the First World War and comments on Conrad's late fiction and political writings.

Chris GoGwilt outlines how Conrad's works were written as a response to the colonial politics of his day. These works also continue to provide an indispensable guide to colonial history. The colonial settings for Conrad's fiction reveal a view from the sidelines of the main economic, political, and cultural realities shaping and reshaping the twentieth century. Although Conrad rearranges and fictionalizes historical facts, which makes his fiction an unreliable vehicle for such facts, the official colonial archives are themselves unreliable, and so Conrad's work becomes useful for evaluating the biases and distortions of colonial history. GoGwilt concludes by considering Conrad's use of English and how it is based upon a fundamental contest of colonial perspectives. As a result, Conrad's work will continue to serve as a guide for future debates about the historical significance of colonial history.

Andrea White, in her essay on Conrad and the modernist tradition, lays out the literary and intellectual landscape upon which Conrad's fictional works appeared. In particular, she notes the influences of Walter Pater and Henry James in the movement away from the realism and naturalism of the late nineteenth century. This atmosphere led to the impressionism and stream-of-consciousness narration of the literature of the late nineteenth and early twentieth centuries. One of the clearest manifestations of this turn in literary methodology was the rendering of consciousness. White notes the increased appearance and emphasis on perspective, multiple narrators, free indirect discourse, and other similar narrative devices that emphasized the subjectivity of human experience and revealed an epistemological skepticism underlying this approach to literature. Related to the rendering of consciousness is the appearance of modernist space and time. Contrary to the space and time rulers and clocks measure, modernist time and space reveals the subjectivity of human experience of both. Influenced by the philosophy of Henri Bergson and the physics of Albert Einstein, modernists investigated the relativist nature of space and time in the literature that they wrote. Not surprising, given the emphasis on subjectivity among the modernists, White suggests that both readers and critics play a role in the construction of meaning in modernist texts, and Conrad played a significant role both as innovator and influencer on those modernists who were to follow him.

Joseph Conrad's Life

Cedric T. Watts

In 1968, Roland Barthes published the influential essay entitled "La Mort de l'auteur" ("The Death of the Author"),[1] a satiric attack on the old-fashioned notion that critics of a text should disregard the life of the author of that text. The satiric intent should have been obvious, for Barthes took care to sign his essay, to claim authorial copyright for it, and to cite biographical information within it. Numerous academic readers nevertheless took the piece literally and assumed that Barthes was espousing the position which logically, he could only have been assailing. Perhaps they were stupefied by what Jacques Derrida has astutely termed "an ethic of [...] a purity of presence."[2] Fortunately, the true reading was then decisively expounded by the Belgian reader-response critic, Carlier,[3] who, aptly enough, had been slain in Conrad's tale "An Outpost of Progress" (1897). Resurrected by postmodernism, a dead character gallantly vindicated the life of the author. Carlier thus forcefully reminds us that anyone who doubts the value of a biographical approach to literature should study the life of Conrad. Only when we understand Conrad's situation as a Pole and a seafarer can we begin to appreciate the immensity of his achievement as a fiction writer in English. His life, in any case, resembles a novel in which the hero struggles for decades against great obstacles to achieve an eventual triumph.

Indeed, his creative career repeatedly erodes conventional boundaries between fact and fiction.

Joseph Conrad, originally Józef Teodor Konrad Korzeniowski (coat of arms Nałęcz), was born on 3 December 1857 at Berdyczów in the Polish Ukraine. At that time, however, Poland no longer existed on the political map of Europe. In a series of partitions (1772, 1793, 1795) the nation had been engorged by imperialistic powers: by Prussia to the west, Austria to the south, and Russia to the east. Polish patriots maintained their resistance, but repeatedly their uprisings were crushed. The nation, however, preserved its cultural identity and its aspirations to freedom, so that the Polish state would be reborn between the two world wars, and, eventually (having survived the Nazi and Communist oppressors), a fully autonomous Poland would emerge in the 1990s. The liberated nation would commemorate Conrad as tutelary hero in diverse ways: processions of schoolchildren would lay wreaths of flowers before his monument at Gdynia; scholars would hold conferences; films and plays based on his works would be produced; and his face and writings would appear on postage stamps.

Conrad's father, Apollo Korzeniowski, was a member of the *szlachta* class, the landowning gentry-cum-nobility; but tracts of the Korzeniowski lands had been taken from them during political turbulences. Apollo was first and foremost a dedicated patriot. His poem to commemorate the young Conrad's christening is headed, "To My Son Born in the 85th Year of Muscovite Oppression," and includes the words:

> Baby son, tell yourself
> You are without land, without love,
> Without country, without people,
> While *Poland—your Mother* [—] is entombed.[4]

In addition to religiously inflected patriotic poems, Apollo wrote two satirical comedies (*Komedia* and *Dla miłego grosza*) and translated works by Shakespeare, Dickens, Victor Hugo, and Alfred de Vigny. His wife, Ewelina (or Ewa) *née* Bobrowska, who came from a prosperous landowning family, shared her husband's

patriotic ardour and Roman Catholic faith. Their son's Chris-
tian name "Konrad" (by which the boy's father referred to him,
and which, anglicized, was to serve as the novelist's pseudonym)
was evidently chosen for its literary and political associations. In
Adam Mickiewicz's drama *Dziady* (*Forefather's Eve*, 1832), the hero
changes his name from "Gustavus" to "Conradus" on recognis-
ing his destiny to free Poland from Muscovite tyranny; while in
Mickiewicz's historic poem, *Konrad Wallenrod* (1828), the eponymous hero deceives the German oppressors into a disastrous
campaign.

Apollo advocated the liberation of the serfs, the rights of Ruthe-
nians and Jews, and an uprising to secure national independence.
He inaugurated the underground National Government. In 1861,
however, in Warsaw, he was arrested and imprisoned, and both
he and Ewa were sentenced to exile for their subversive activities.
The four-year-old son accompanied them on the dreary trek to a
settlement for convicts in the Russian province of Vologda. Partly
as a result of the privations of exile, Ewa, who suffered from
tuberculosis, died in 1865 at the age of thirty-two. Meanwhile,
the Polish uprising of 1863 had been bloodily suppressed. Apollo
became a brooding, melancholy figure. He wrote about Conrad:
"The little orphan keeps clinging to me, and it is impossible not
to worry about him constantly. [...] I teach him all I know [...],
and the little mite is growing up as though in a cloister; the grave
of our Unforgettable is our *memento mori* [...]."[5] Even before
then, at the age of five, that "little orphan" had acquired a proud
sense of patriotic identity, for he had written on the back of
a photograph: "To my dear Granny who helped me send pastries
to my poor Daddy in prison—grandson, Pole-Catholic and szlach-
cic [nobleman], KONRAD."[6] Upon Apollo's death in 1869, Conrad
(a "reading boy") became an eleven-year-old orphan. He followed
his father's coffin through the streets of Kraków in a procession
which was also a great patriotic demonstration. It is not surprising that Conrad's eventual works would be preoccupied by the
themes of loneliness, tragic death, self-sacrifice for a noble cause,
and beleaguered solidarity. They would also explore the ideas that
loyalty to one cause may entail treachery to another (as when a
man's political commitment damages his family) and that there

can be conflicts between honor, law, and love. Conrad would eventually become the most astute of political novelists, acute in his analyses of imperialism and its consequences. He transmuted private suffering into public wisdom. Master of metapolitics, he was *fully* political because he saw *beyond* the political, observing the ephemerality of human endeavours when contrasted with the immensities of space, time, and death.

Conrad's education was irregular, taking place in a variety of locations, and being overseen by a succession of guardians. He may have attended a school in Kraków, and probably in 1873–74 he attended the seventh class at a *gymnasium* (high school) in Lwów; he was also taught by private tutors. An acquaintance commented: "Intellectually he was extremely advanced but disliked school routine, which he found tiring and dull."[7] He had soon become fluent in French; and his schooldays had crucially nurtured a love of geography, which he regarded romantically as the exploration of exotic regions by heroic individuals, among them Captain Cook, Sir John Franklin, Mungo Park, James Bruce of Abyssinia, Richard F. Burton, and John Speke.

By far the most important and constant of his guardians was an uncle, Tadeusz Bobrowski, a prosperous landowner, who proved conscientious, wise, and patient in his guardianship. Repeatedly Bobrowski warned his young charge to beware of the "Korzeniowski" side of his temperament, which the uncle defined as romantic, idealistic, and impractical, and to pursue the course of prudence and diligence, depicted as the "Bobrowski" legacy.[8] (Bobrowski saw his own form of patriotism as one of compromise and appeasement, to preserve the family's fortunes through adverse times, whereas such militancy as Apollo's had been costly to the family in various ways.) Tadeusz Bobrowski had himself experienced lacerating griefs of his own: he had been a widower since 1858, when his wife had died giving birth to a daughter, Józefa; and Józefa died in 1871. Conrad became his surrogate son.

The adolescent Conrad insisted on choosing seafaring as a career, even though Adam Pulman, a congenial tutor, was charged with the task of dissuading him from his romantic ambition. In October 1874, at the age of sixteen, Conrad boarded a train for Marseille and the Mediterranean. His choice of the sea was probably influenced by his early reading, which included maritime adventure tales by Captain Marryat and Fenimore Cooper, as well as such travel books as Sir Leopold McClintock's *Voyage of the "Fox."* He later said that he had been introduced to sea literature by his father's translation of Hugo's *Les Travailleurs de la mer*, in which a seaman battles heroically with the elements. In any case, as he was legally a Russian citizen and the son of a convict, Conrad was liable to conscription into the Russian Army for many years. His choice of odyssey combined romantic aspiration and shrewd foresight. Although Conrad suggested that quixotism and "the inexplicable" accounted for that choice, there was also a guiding precedent: around that time, thousands of Poles emigrated to Western Europe and America.

In the 1870s, Marseille was a bustling port and a lively city, with its theatres, opera houses, fashionable restaurants, and waterfront taverns. Conrad mixed socially with the high and the low, with wealthy royalists, with artists and with sturdy Provençal seamen. From here he made his first oceanic voyages on sailing-ships: initially as a passenger, next as an apprentice, then as a steward. He sailed to the West Indies in the leaky *Mont-Blanc* and subsequently in the *Saint-Antoine*, both being three-masted wooden vessels. In later years he hinted that during his voyages in the *Saint-Antoine*, he had smuggled arms, possibly to insurgents in Colombia. His volume of memoirs entitled *The Mirror of the Sea* (1906) also claims that in the charismatic company of Dominic (or Dominique) Cervoni, a bold, broad-chested Corsican seaman, he had joined a syndicate that smuggled weapons along the coast to Spanish Carlists, Legitimist Royalists who supported the Pretender, Don Carlos. This adventure (which, predictably, has so far resisted scholarly verification) would also be mythologized in the late novel *The Arrow of Gold* (1919), which is set mainly in Marseille.[9]

Just as he was adapting to maritime life, Conrad found that the Russian consul would not prolong his passport, so that he could no longer serve legally on French ships. He proved unable to join an American squadron at Villefranche; and he also gambled and lost some borrowed money. The outcome was that, early in 1878, he attempted suicide with a revolver. According to the long-suffering Bobrowski, who traveled to Marseille to supervise Conrad's treatment and pay the debts, the bullet went straight through the young man's chest "without damaging any vital organ."[10] Bobrowski told a friend: "My study of the Individual has convinced me that he is not a bad boy, only one who is extremely sensitive, conceited, reserved, and in addition excitable. In short I found in him all the defects of the Nałęcz family. He is able and eloquent [...;] very popular with his captains and also with the sailors [...]. In his ideas and discussions he is ardent and original."[11] After Conrad's recovery, it was agreed that he should voyage to England ("where there are no such formalities as in France") to join the British merchant navy.

Conrad reached Lowestoft in April 1878 on board the steamer *Mavis*, in which he was unofficially apprenticed. On 11 July, he joined the crew of *Skimmer of the Sea*, nominally as an ordinary seaman with a wage of one shilling per month (when even the ship's boy received twenty-five shillings). *Skimmer* was a humble three-masted schooner that carried coal from Newcastle to Lowestoft. After Conrad left her, she foundered at sea, drowning some of his former shipmates. Later, he recalled her nostalgically: "In that craft I began to learn English from East Coast chaps each built as though to last for ever, and coloured like a Christmas card. Tan and pink—gold hair and blue eyes with that Northern straight-away-there look!"[12] After *Skimmer*, he soon found a berth as an ordinary seaman in the wool-clipper *Duke of Sutherland*, which plied between London and Sydney. (Conrad's early maritime career was subsidized by funds from Bobrowski's estate.) During the subsequent sixteen years, with numerous voyages on vessels ranging from elegant three-masters to rusty tramp-steamers, Conrad acquired experience and qualifications: third mate, second mate, skipper. Struggling with the English language, he passed (sometimes after repeated attempts) the successive inquisitorial examinations; and, in 1886, he not only gained his master's certificate but also took British nationality. Bobrowski was delighted by the double achievement, for he had long urged his nephew to relinquish Russian citizenship and become "a free citizen of a free country."[13] Conrad himself would refer to that "liberty, which can only be found under the English flag,"[14] and vicarious patriotism for his adopted country would inflect various subsequent literary works, notably *The Nigger of the "Narcissus,"* "Youth," and *Lord Jim.*

Repeatedly voyaging between London and Australia, Conrad gained ample knowledge of numerous eastern locations that would feature in his novels and tales: Bombay, Singapore, Bangkok, and Borneo, for instance. He visited regions where the civilized confronts the supposedly primitive and the familiar meets the alien, and he was led to consider whether the differences between them were profound or only skin deep. He also came to know intimately the maritime world. "It provided a surrogate family of 'brothers' whose corporate life turned upon values of fidelity and solidarity, a hierarchical society, and a code of time-honoured traditions and working truths symbolized by the Red Ensign."[15]

His life at sea entailed sometimes sheer hard toil, sometimes endurance in the face of adverse weather, sometimes the loneliness of command and the burden of responsibility for the costly vessel and the lives of its crewmen. It was a risky career: ships were frequently lost at sea. (Conrad's son Borys once told me that his father could not swim.) The *Palestine*, in which Joseph Conrad served as second mate in 1881–82, not only was damaged in tempests but also later smouldered, exploded, and burned, blazing in the tropical night, so that the crew had to abandon ship in the Bangka Strait and row for Muntok in lifeboats: the basis of the vivid tale "Youth." Conrad commanded the beautiful iron barque *Otago* on voyages between Siam, Australia, and Mauritius, and his experiences were transmuted into three of his finest works: *The Shadow-Line* (1917), "The Secret Sharer" (1910), and "A Smile of Fortune" (1911). This was the last great era of sailing-ships, for gradually they were being superseded by steamships. Conrad, who worked in both, would become the great celebrator and obituarist of the sailing vessel and her crews. As ocean-going steamships prevailed and became larger and more efficient, senior posts proved increasingly elusive, and remuneration could be disappointing. Conrad's final maritime appointment was as second mate on the *Adowa*, an iron steamer, in 1894.

The *Adowa*'s voyage being canceled, 1894 proved to be an important transitional year for Conrad. He had begun his first novel, *Almayer's Folly*, in 1889, and, although until 1898 he would make attempts to return to sea, he became increasingly dedicated to a second career, also very risky in its own way: that of a full-time fiction writer. His uncle Tadeusz died in 1894, and the knowledge that he would inherit a substantial sum from him helped Conrad to effect the transition. *Almayer's Folly* was completed in the same year and submitted to T. Fisher Unwin, a Liberal publisher. When the novel appeared in 1895 (dedicated to "T. B."—Tadeusz Bobrowski), it was widely and, on the whole, favorably reviewed. The second career of Conrad had been launched.

At Fisher Unwin's, *Almayer's Folly* had been read and recommended by W. H. Chesson, who described himself as "Mr. Unwin's receiver and weeder of MSS." "The magical melancholy of that masterpiece submerged me," he alliteratively recalled.[16] The work was also read by Chesson's colleague, Edward Garnett, a keenly perceptive critic, who commented, "Hold on to this."[17] Garnett was to be influential in advancing not only Conrad's career but also the careers of John Galsworthy, W. H. Hudson, R. B. Cunninghame Graham, Dorothy Richardson, D. H. Lawrence, H. E. Bates, and Henry Green. Politically left-wing and a midwife of modernism, Garnett was the foe of sentimental, conventional, derivative fiction, and a keen advocate of vivid, frank, original writing, of sharp-eyed realism and keen irony. By her labors as a translator, his wife, Constance, brought before the British public numerous volumes of fiction by such major Russian authors as Dostoyevsky and Turgenev.

Conrad's first novel was certainly an uncompromising work: bleak, skeptical, profoundly ironic, and politically bold in its depiction of a protagonist of European descent who is out-maneuvered by the diverse inhabitants of the remote Bornean region where he lives with his beloved daughter. The story of Almayer's decline and defeat is clear in its outlines, but Conrad also employs covert plotting, so that it may only be at a second or subsequent reading of the novel (if at all) that the reader perceives exactly the machinations by means of which Almayer has been defeated by the wily Abdulla, his Muslim trade rival. Of course, in that late Victorian period, there was a market (exploited by Kipling, Stevenson, and others) for works set in exotic locations, featuring

Europeans obliged to encounter a diversity of local challenges; and the early reviewers often compared Conrad with Kipling and Stevenson. Nevertheless, Conrad's fiction repeatedly displayed that subversive, ironic quality, so that conventional assumptions about the superiority of Western ways were repeatedly challenged. Predominantly, in *Almayer's Folly* and a range of subsequent works, Conrad would be, by the standards of his times, a boldly anti-imperialistic and anti-racist writer. Almost inevitably, there were some exceptions and ambiguities; but, when the works are judged in their appropriate context, their skeptical shrewdness is remarkable.

Alice Meynell, a fellow novelist and critic, had complained that literature of exotic outposts was "decivilised."[18] Conrad replied in an essay which, though it did not appear in print until 1920, was intended for publication in *Almayer's Folly* in 1895. He argued that the differences between Europeans and distant peoples were only skin deep: "I am content to sympathize with common mortals—no matter where they live [...]. Their hearts—like ours—must endure the load of the gifts from Heaven: the curse of facts and the blessing of illusions; the bitterness of our wisdom and the deceptive consolation of our folly."[19] This brief manifesto is true to the novel, which stresses that whatever the color of the person's skin, similar ambitions and dreams prevail. Indeed, the eventual downfall of Almayer is clearly related to his failure to overcome his own racial prejudice. Had he been able to do so, he could have joined Nina and her lover, Dain, in their new life across the seas. But prejudice prevails, and Almayer sinks to a lonely drug addict's death.[20] He evades "the curse of facts" in suicidally seeking "the blessing of illusions." Almayer's "folly" is threefold: a useless building, a dream of wealth, a failure to adapt.

Conrad's linguistic achievement is hard to overestimate. He was writing not in his first language (Polish) or his second (French) but in his third, English. With his early fiction, he may have received a little editorial help from his friends Edward and Helen Sanderson and Edward Garnett; but, from the outset, his prose was courageously adventurous and distinctive. It was characterized by a diversity of effects. Notably, there were descriptive set pieces that were romantic and poetic in their richness and rhythmic momentum. There were passages of macabre black comedy. His syntax, even when complex, was sturdily logical: translation, whether conscious or unconscious, eliminated vapidity. He explored various ways of rendering in dialogue the tones and accents of different nationalities and peoples. Already he was exploiting the technique of delayed decoding.[21] Thematically dense, his keenly ironic narratives cumulatively established a region in which humans could be seen now as magnified by the rendering of their inner selves, now as dwarfed by the invocation of the might of nature, the vastness of the encircling forests and oceans, and the daunting extent of evolutionary time. The individual could be seen both as the vital center of experience and as "more insignificant than a drop of water in the ocean, more fleeting than the illusion of a dream."[22]

Certainly, *Almayer's Folly* shows signs of being a first novel. The exposition is slow and cumbrous, the style sometimes all-too-elaborately stylish. The analyses of emotions can occasionally seem melodramatic, as when Nina Almayer gives her lover "one of those long looks that are a woman's most terrible weapon; [...] more dangerous than the thrust of a dagger [...]."[23] Often we sense that French is Conrad's second language, for, though writing in English, he sometimes uses terms in their French sense (e.g., "nothing pressed"—from *rien ne pressait*—for "there was no hurry"[24]), and, in a stylistic mannerism that would burgeon in subsequent works, Conrad likes to put a series of adjectives or adjectival phrases after the noun that they qualify.

Conrad's education may have been irregular, but, by the time of writing *Almayer's Folly*, he had acquired not only an exceptional range of geographical and cultural experience but also a rich grounding in literary and philosophical works. Polish literature had provided familiarity with romantic idealism, while, from Pyrrhonism, Schopenhauer, possibly Nietzsche, and an immense range of British, French, and classical authors, he had drawn reinforcements for his own temperamental pessimism and skepticism: indeed, a trait of the fiction of his first ten years as a novelist would be his tendency to apply the term "illusion" to a very wide range of entities (including love, virtue, and principles). Famously, however, he would declare: "Those who read me know my conviction that the world, the temporal world, rests on a few very simple ideas; so simple that they must be as old as the hills. It rests notably, among others, on the idea of Fidelity."[25] Although his writings often upheld traditional values (such as love, loyalty, duty, courage, kindness, and sympathy), he could submit them to a baptism in the fires of skepticism. To R. B. Cunninghame Graham, he wrote: "There is no morality, no knowledge and no hope."[26] He particularly admired the writings of Flaubert, Anatole France, and Maupassant, all three being skeptical in outlook; and Almayer has been deftly described as "a Borneo Bovary," being a self-destructive romantic dreamer, like Flaubert's doomed heroine, Emma Bovary.[27]

Almayer's Folly was reviewed widely, often at considerable length. A few reviews were curtly hostile; some were mixed; but high praise predominated. The main emphasis was placed on the emergence of a distinctive and powerful new writer. In the *Weekly Sun*, the editor T. P. O'Connor, an Irish nationalist who would later serialize *Nostromo* in *T.P.'s Weekly*, praised this "startling, unique, splendid book." The *Spectator* prophesied that Conrad might become "the Kipling of the Malay Archipelago."[28] (Given Kipling's prestige and popularity then, this was meant to be high praise; but Conrad, though also writing with personal knowledge of the East, differed critically from Kipling's outlook.)

Even before the publication of *Almayer's Folly*, Conrad had begun his second novel, *An Outcast of the Islands*, which appeared in 1896. This was, in effect, the second part of the "Lingard Trilogy" dealing with the adventures and defeats of Tom Lingard. The trilogy, which, conforming to Conrad's interest in *hysteron proteron*, appeared in reversed chronological order, would be completed twenty-two years later by *The Rescue*.[29] Again, although some complained of its prolixity (so that Conrad later made substantial excisions),[30] the reviews of *An Outcast* were predominantly laudatory. Conrad had established a strong identity as a writer of exotic, adventurous fiction who brought to the material a sophisticated, ironic, skeptically reflective mind, keen political insight, thematic orchestration, and distinctive stylistic virtuosity. He could even write what he termed "Conradese," idiosyncratically stylish prose, which would later be wittily parodied by Max Beerbohm in *A Christmas Garland*, 1912. His recurrent themes were now predictable: human isolation (even within a close-knit group), beleaguered solidarity, the vanity of romantic aspirations, the myopia of racial prejudice, and the recognition that some forms of loyalty may entail treachery. Repeatedly, aestheticism alleviated the thematic pessimism: his verbal vistas combined beauty of expression with sheer scenic beauty.

On 24 March 1896, Conrad married Jessie Emmeline George (1873–1936), who worked in the City for the American Writing Machine Company; her father was a warehouseman. According to Jessie's recollections, Conrad assured his prospective mother-in-law (who had "a strong prejudice against a foreigner"[31]) that "he hadn't very long to live and [...] there would be no family [i.e., children]."[32] Nevertheless, two sons duly appeared: Borys, born in 1898, and John, in 1906. Jessie, although fifteen years younger than her highly strung and temperamental husband, proved to be resourcefully supportive to him, but her subsequent memoirs provide glimpses of his sometimes neurotic, irascible, and demanding conduct. (Lady Ottoline Morrell described Jessie as "a good and reposeful mattress for this hypersensitive, nerve-racked man."[33]) Conrad, in turn, was generously loyal to his wife, engaging the best surgeons when she suffered a series of crippling ailments, and providing funds for members of her family. His own health was sapped by gout and particularly by pervasive depression.

In 1896–97, Conrad published in magazines the highly uneven quartet of tales ("Karain," "The Lagoon," "The Idiots," and the satiric masterpiece "An Outpost of Progress") which, with the cumbrously analytic but feminist story "The Return," comprises the award-winning volume *Tales of Unrest*, issued in 1898. Probably influenced by Ibsen's *A Doll's House*, "The Return" is a tale in which an alienated woman eventually makes the agonized declaration of her selfhood: "I've a right—a right to—to—myself."[34] (Eventual film adaptations of "The Return" would include the remarkable *Gabrielle*, 2005, directed by Patrice Chéreau.)

Conrad's friends and acquaintances during this first decade of his literary career included not only Edward and Constance Garnett but also Edward Sanderson, H. G. Wells, Stephen Crane,

John Galsworthy, and Ford Madox Hueffer (who changed his surname to Ford in 1919). A particularly sustaining friendship was with R. B. Cunninghame Graham, the aristocratic socialist, convict, adventurer, and writer. (He founded both the Scottish National Party, originally the Scottish Home Rule Association, in 1886 and Britain's first Labour Party, the Scottish Labour Party, in 1888.) William Blackwood, the Conservative proprietor of *Blackwood's Edinburgh Magazine*, proved to be a crucially generous publisher: he serialized "Youth," "Heart of Darkness," and *Lord Jim*, paying Conrad handsomely and showing remarkable patience when *Lord Jim*, expanding from a tale into a full-length novel, extended through numerous issues of the magazine. As Conrad's payment in such periodicals was usually related to the number of words produced, expansion (which occurred on numerous occasions) had financial incentives.

The timing of Conrad's career as a fiction writer in the entertainment industry was fortunate. At the end of the nineteenth century, there was a large, literate international English-speaking public; publishing houses were multiplying; numerous magazines sought tales and novels for serialization. Technological advances had made books (even their paper) cheaper to produce, while commercial advertising and publicity had become widespread. International copyright agreements (notably, in the United States, the Chace Act of 1891) guaranteed payment for books published abroad. Repeatedly, Conrad would be paid several times over for the same piece of work: serialization in Great Britain and America would be followed by book publication on both sides of the Atlantic; eventually there would be collected editions and perhaps the sales of manuscripts, and, sometimes, film rights. Initially, however, Conrad struggled to make a living, and his debts accumulated. He endeavoured to maintain the lifestyle of a gentleman, and this was costly.

He wrote to a Polish friend: "Homo duplex has in my case more than one meaning."[35] "Homo duplex": the double man. In its original context, one of the meanings of the phrase is that he was both English and Polish. He was also a romantic and an Augustan, a Don Quixote and a Hamlet, a moralist and a skeptic. When writing fraternally to Cunninghame Graham, he could declare: "There is no fraternity except the Cain-Abel business"; and he could even remark, "I respect the extreme anarchists."[36] Garnett describes thus (again as "homo duplex") the Conrad of the 1890s: "My memory is of seeing a dark-haired man, short but extremely graceful in his nervous gestures, with brilliant eyes, now narrowed and penetrating, now soft and warm, with a manner alert yet caressing, whose speech was ingratiating, guarded, and brusque turn by turn. I had never seen before a man so masculinely keen yet so femininely sensitive."[37]

Numerous critics would agree that Conrad's major phase as a writer extends from 1897 to 1911. It begins with *The Nigger of the "Narcissus,"* his first great maritime work. This marked a great advance from his previous novels, for now Conrad could be concise, mobile in perspectives, vividly graphic, subtly symbolic, thematically more crafty. (This text does, however, have some racist features: the eponymous James Wait is, homophonically, a "weight" or burden to the ship, and, homonymically, he causes it to "wait," delaying it.[38]) At least one critic associated the work with the impressionism of *The Red Badge of Courage*, by Stephen Crane, who would become a friend of Conrad. Conrad, however, usually regarded impressionism as a superficial mode. When, in his preface to *The Nigger*, he declared, "My task [. . .] is, before all, to make you *see*,"[39] he meant by "see" not only "visualize" but also "gain insight." In its advocacy of dutiful uncomplaining solidarity and its hostility to sentimental bonding (seen as vicarious self-pity, a threat to maritime and social order), in its patriotism and its contempt for Donkin, the pseudosocialist, the novel's morality chimed—quite deliberately—with that of W. E. Henley, militant Tory editor of the *New Review*, the prestigious periodical in which the novel was first published. Famed for poetry that included the lines, "My head is bloody, but unbowed," and "I am the master of my fate: / I am the captain of my soul,"[40] Henley advocated staunch patriotism and stoical heroism. Conrad's depiction of the ship's battle with the storm remains one of the most vivid descriptive sequences in fiction, with such alliterative and assonantal details as these: "Out of the abysmal darkness of the black cloud overhead white hail streamed on her, rattled on the rigging, leaped in handfuls off the yards, rebounded on the deck—round and gleaming in the murky turmoil like a shower of pearls."[41]

That major phrase continued with "Youth," "Heart of Darkness," *Lord Jim, Nostromo, The Secret Agent,* and *Under Western Eyes.* Conrad displayed mastery of delayed decoding, janiformity, covert plotting, and transtextual narration.[42] "Heart of Darkness" alone would, in its vividness, subtlety, and complexity, have ensured Conrad's place in literary history: it has influenced numerous subsequent writers, ranging from William Golding to George Steiner, James Dickey and Sven Lindqvist, and has been adapted as drama for radio (twice by Orson Welles), for the stage (numerous times), and for screen, notably as Francis Ford Coppola's spectacular film, *Apocalypse Now.* Orson Welles's own film adaptation, in which Marlow's observations were represented by the camera's, was never completed. In 1988 appeared a "comedy reverse-gender version," charmingly entitled *Cannibal Women in the Avocado Jungle of Death.*[43] Meanwhile, Kurtz was reincarnated in Graham Greene's "The Third Man" and the Carol Reed film based on it.

Loosely based upon Conrad's traumatic journey through the Congo in 1890, "Heart of Darkness" was first published as "The Heart of Darkness" in *Blackwood's Edinburgh Magazine* in 1899: then Queen Victoria still ruled the British Empire, and the Boer War had yet to begin. The tale became a center of controversy when, in 1975, the Nigerian novelist Chinua Achebe denounced it as "an offensive and totally deplorable book" while declaring Conrad "a bloody racist."[44] In fact, by the standards of its time, "Heart of Darkness" was bold in its satiric denunciation of the cruelty and hypocrisy of colonialism in Africa generally and, in particular, in the "Congo Free State," a region where the Africans were virtually enslaved and cruelly maltreated in the quest for rubber and ivory. As Marlow says, "The conquest of the earth, which mostly means the taking it away from those who have a different complexion or slightly flatter noses than ourselves, is not a pretty thing when you look into it too much."[45] (His ensuing attempt to find a redemptive feature in some great "idea" is then mocked sardonically by his own subsequent narrative.) After the publication of "Heart of Darkness," there arose an international outcry against the cruelties

of King Leopold's Congo (that vast region being the private property of Leopold II, King of the Belgians). Roger Casement, whom
Conrad had met there in 1890, and to whom the author sent
encouraging letters, published in 1904 a damning report on the
matter for the British parliament. Casement had read and praised
"Heart of Darkness," and consulted Conrad during the preparation of his report. Soon after that appeared, the Congo Reform
Association was founded by E. D. Morel to protest against Leopold's exploitation of the Africans. Morel remarked that "Heart
of Darkness" was "the most powerful thing ever written on the
subject."[46] Via Casement, Conrad supplied to Morel, for his campaign, a statement condemning forthrightly the Belgian regime
in the Congo. Conrad's statement included the following words:
"It is an extraordinary thing that the conscience of Europe, which
seventy years ago has put down the slave trade on humanitarian
grounds[,] tolerates the Congo State to day. It is as if the moral
clock had been put back many hours [...]. [In the Congo,] ruthless, systematic cruelty towards the blacks is the basis of administration[.]" Conrad's denunciation was published, as agreed, in
Morel's book *King Leopold's Rule in Africa* (1904); and the London
Morning Post, in a laudatory review of the work, quoted Conrad's
words again, saying that the denunciation came with particular
force from a writer who had actually lived in the Congo.[47] The
campaign helped to bring about reforms that improved the treatment of Africans there; and the campaigners' goal of seeing control transferred from King Leopold to the Belgian parliament was
achieved in 1908. Thus, Conrad had played a significant part in an
important anti-racist campaign. Near the end of his life, Conrad
described European imperialism in Africa as "the vilest scramble
for loot that ever disfigured the history of human conscience and
geographical exploration."[48] Even Achebe, we may think, could
not have made the point more scathingly.

Various feminists deemed "Heart of Darkness" sexist, demean-
ing to women.[49] They seem to have underestimated its ironies.
Certainly, Marlow claims that women are out of touch with
realities: "They live in a world of their own";[50] but he is there
ambushed by his own account. He is dependent for a job on the
very aunt whom he patronizes, as she has friends in high places:

so she is not so "out of touch" after all. (In a later work, *Chance*, Marlow would contradictorily assert that women see the truth, whereas men live in "fool's paradise."[51]) In any case, one large feature of the tale is markedly pro-feminist: characteristically virile activities—empire building, war waging, aggressive trading—are made to seem absurd and virtually deranged. The virile appears less than puerile. As we can thus infer from the tale, Conrad was a supporter of female suffrage. In 1910, he signed an open letter to the British Prime Minister, Herbert Asquith. It advocated votes for women. Conrad's signature appeared alongside that of May Sinclair, Sarah Grand, and other radicals and feminists. A copy of that letter was published in *The Times*.[52] So, in a period when it was politically incorrect or controversial to do so, Conrad was courageous enough to join a campaign for women's voting rights; and that was eight years before women were first permitted to vote at British general elections.

Among those major works of Conrad, *Lord Jim* (1900) also proved abundantly influential, even though some contemporaneous reviewers were baffled and confused by its obliquities of narration and its multiplicity of viewpoints. (These features may have influenced Orson Welles's cinematic masterpiece, *Citizen Kane*, as well as fiction by William Faulkner.) A continuing debate concerns the latter part of the novel, set in Patusan: various critics claim that here the work becomes relatively conventional and lacks the searching complexity of the earlier *"Patna"* material. Nevertheless, the novel remains impressive in the vividness and virtuosity of its exploration of ethics, psychology, and politics— notably the politics of paternalistic imperialism. In Conrad's works, even the benevolent and well-meaning colonialist is usually doomed to failure. From factual materials (the abandoning of the stricken pilgrim ship *Jeddah* by its English captain and officers in 1880, and the life of James Brooke, the first "White Rajah" of Sarawak), Conrad had created an exuberantly kaleidoscopic vision. The romantic outlook is both relished and criticized, and Marlow's concluding account of Jim's death is a virtuosic feat of narrative ambiguity.

Conrad's *Nostromo* (1904) can be seen as a counterpart (though more radical and modernistic) to Tolstoy's *War and Peace*: epic in scale and scope, intensely imagined, superbly coordinated. It remained durably wise—even prophetic—in its depiction of international economic imperialism and the evolution of a modern state. Cunninghame Graham, the Hispanophile who had traveled widely in South and Central America, contributed to it, as did a vast range of writings that included G. F. Masterman's *Seven Eventful Years in Paraguay*, E. B. Eastwick's *Venezuela*, and Ramón Páez's *Wild Scenes in South America*. Swift's *Gulliver's Travels* may have added leverage to its perspectival shifts. There were detailed borrowings from several works by Anatole France. Enrico Clerici, a pugnacious bartender and admirer of Garibaldi who had been encountered by Cunninghame Graham in Paraguay, was transmuted into Giorgio Viola, while Dominique Cervoni can be discerned in Nostromo himself. Conrad, who possessed a remarkably retentive memory, was acquisitive and resourceful; but what emerged was no patchwork but a finely integrated creation of a credible historical, geographical, and diversely populated region, vast, four-dimensional, and explorable. Edward Garnett and Cunninghame Graham did, however, feel that the final emphasis on Nostromo himself was reductive; the book, said Graham, should have been entitled *"Costaguana."*

In *The Secret Agent* (1907), that novel of anarchism, espionage, political duplicity, and urban sleaziness, Conrad undertook an experiment in sustained irony: "Even the purely artistic purpose, that of applying an ironic method to a subject of that kind, was formulated with deliberation and in the earnest belief that ironic treatment alone would enable me to say all I felt I would have to say in scorn as well as in pity."[53] Prompted by the 1894 bomb explosion in Greenwich Park, and influenced by Dickens's *Bleak House* and Ibsen's *The Wild Duck*, this novel emerged as utterly distinctive and modern, even modernistic, in its creation of a dank, gloomy city of isolated, uncomprehending and uncomprehended denizens. If the forces of law and order seem to prevail, they do so for tarnished reasons, while the innocent suffer along with the guilty. The anarchists are depicted as parasitic and slothful grotesques, like illustrations from Cesare Lombroso's textbooks on congenital criminality and degeneracy, while the narrator surveys the whole with the sardonic relish of a pedantic connoisseur of corruption. (Lombroso's theories were both exploited and satirized by Conrad.[54]) As "a sustained effort in ironical treatment of a melodramatic subject,"[55] *The Secret Agent* would exert considerable influence, notably on the works of Graham Greene and John le Carré.

During the period from 1898 to 1909, Conrad collaborated with Ford Madox Hueffer, originally Ford Hermann Hueffer, who, after courageous service in the Great War, would change his name again, to Ford Madox Ford. The collaboration resulted in some disappointing work: two novels and a tale: *The Inheritors* (1901), *Romance* (1903) and "The Nature of a Crime" (1909). Seeking (in vain) a popular readership, *The Inheritors* combined science fiction with a political *roman à clef*, while *Romance* owed some debt to Stevenson and would influence Graham Greene's first novel, *The Man Within*. "The Nature of a Crime" was published under the name of "Baron Ignatz von Aschendrof," in which the last four letters spell "Ford" backward, while the last ten letters include those of "Conrad"; and Anton Aschendorff was a Fordian ancestor. The collaboration (which ended acrimoniously in 1909) was initially friendly, as Ford greatly admired Conrad, and his fluency in composition often helped to overcome the work blockages that regularly beset his partner. He also cooperated with Conrad in producing the autobiographical volume, *The Mirror of the Sea*: indeed, parts of it were probably written by Ford, who received a substantial share of the payments. Eventually Ford, whose *English Review* featured work by an admirable range of writers (including Cunninghame Graham, D. H. Lawrence, Ezra Pound, and T. S. Eliot), would gain renown with *The Good Soldier* (1915), and would commemorate the collaboration in lively though unreliable volumes of reminiscence.

Notable nonfictional work in this period includes Conrad's letters to Cunninghame Graham, a sequence in which he expresses, often with fine rhetorical panache, his most pessimistic views of human nature and the human situation. In a letter of 1898, for instance, he invokes the Second Law of Thermodynamics, the law of entropy: "The mysteries of a universe made of drops of fire and clods of mud to not concern us in the least. The fate of a humanity condemned ultimately to perish from cold is not worth troubling about. If you take it to heart it becomes an unendurable tragedy. If you believe in improvement you must weep [...]. Life knows us not and we do not know life—we don't even know our own thoughts."[56] In contrast, a letter to the *New York Times*, published in 1901, provides a positive gloss on the theme of *homo duplex*: "The only legitimate basis of creative work lies in the courageous recognition of all the irreconcilable antagonisms that make our life so enigmatic, so burdensome, so fascinating, so dangerous—so full of hope!"[57] At their frequent best, Conrad's letters are characterized by sustained intelligence, logical lucidity, and rolling rhetoric. His essays vary between the slight and the impressive. An important essay is "Autocracy and War" (1905), in which Conrad predicts not only the Great War (as, accurately enough, an outcome of aggressive Prussian militarism) but also the Russian Revolution. The latter, he astutely says, will result only in a new and long-lasting tyranny. He also expresses the view that democracy will be dominated by commercialism and will be obliged to fight the battles of "material interests" (mainly capitalism): a view that he had already depicted in *Nostromo*.

Conrad always sought to maintain a gentlemanly and hospitable lifestyle, and his debts continued to accumulate during this period. Bouts of illness further impeded his writing. He was helped by loans from friends (notably John Galsworthy and William Rothenstein) and by charitable donations: from the Royal Literary Fund (£300 in 1902, £200 in 1908) and from the Royal Bounty Special Service Fund (£500 in 1904); and, in 1910, he was awarded a Civil List pension (provided by British taxpayers) of £100 per annum. Above all, James Brand Pinker, his literary agent from 1900 onward, advanced huge sums in the hope that the author would one day be financially prosperous. Indeed, Pinker became virtually the general financial manager of Conrad's household, clearing debts to tradesmen, paying unexpected bills, and even supplying pens when Conrad lost his. Pinker took huge risks to sustain Conrad's literary career. As Conrad was bad at meeting deadlines, there was a predictable quarrel in 1910; this combined catastrophically with the break with Ford and the stress of writing *Under Western Eyes*. Later, however, the friendship was restored; eventually the two men collaborated on the scenario of *Gaspar the Strong Man* (for a silent film that was never made), and spent a holiday on Corsica together.

By 1909, Conrad's debts totalled £2,250, at a time when the average annual earnings of a doctor were about £400. Not surprisingly, his letters are often jeremiads. He complains about his physical ailments, his mental state, and the daily struggle to produce literary work. "I had to work like a coalminer in his pit quarrying all my English sentences out of a black night," he told Garnett.[58] The completion of *Under Western Eyes* was marked by a breakdown during which, his wife recalled, for days he lay in bed conversing with the imaginary characters.

In *Under Western Eyes* (serialized 1910–11, published as a book in 1911), Conrad dared to challenge Dostoyevsky's *Crime and Punishment*. Conrad's novel certainly derives numerous features (large and small) from *Crime and Punishment*, notably a plot in which an intelligent Russian student rationalizes a treacherous and lethal deed but is subsequently led, mainly by love for a young woman, to confession and atonement. Yet, in comparison with *Crime and Punishment*, Conrad's novel is a lucid, concise, and politically more searching analysis of the young man's embroilment. The theme of haunting is exploited in various ways: in this novel haunted by Dostoyevsky, Razumov is haunted by the spirit of Haldin, the betrayed revolutionary, and the narrative is haunted by its ostensible narrator, a language teacher who cynically claims that words are "the great foes of reality."[59] In an "Author's Note" written in 1920, three years after the Russian Revolution, Conrad claimed that the political skepticism of *Under Western Eyes* had been vindicated by historical events: in Russia, tyranny had merely assumed a new name, for "the tiger cannot change his stripes nor the leopard his spots."[60]

Conrad's career then entered a transitional phase that extended from 1912 to 1919. It was transitional in at least two senses. First, while some novels and tales of this period are impressive, others indicate a decline in his powers. Second, sales of his work increased sufficiently to clear his debts and ensure his prosperity.

The main publications of this phase are: *A Personal Record* (originally *Some Reminiscences*), a volume of autobiographical reflections; *'Twixt Land and Sea* (which gathered three previously published tales, including "The Secret Sharer"); *Chance*; *Victory*; *Within the Tides* (a collection of four previously published tales); and *The Shadow-Line*. The short stories are markedly uneven in quality: while "The Inn of the Two Witches" is a trivial thriller, "The Secret Sharer" is vivid, complex, and searchingly ambiguous. Of the novels, *The Shadow-Line* is one of Conrad's finest maritime works, memorable in its depiction of the stresses on a young captain during a voyage that seems accursed.

Conrad's access to a larger public was greatly helped by *Chance*. It was serialized in 1912 in the *New York Herald*, which ran a publicity campaign emphasizing that Conrad was now writing with women in mind (an astute emphasis, given that women dominated the fiction-buying public). In an interview article, Conrad was quoted thus: "It gives me the keenest pleasure when I find womankind appreciates my work."[61] Alfred Knopf also zealously marketed the novel, which sold well: remarkably well, in view of its technical intricacy, which caused even Henry James, noted purveyor of prolixity, to complain of its long-winded deviousness. The book appeared in January 1914, and within two years there were numerous reprints. One explanation of the success of *Chance* is that feminist matters were then highly topical. Although Marlow, the main narrator of the work, makes various misogynistic comments, modes of male chauvinism are sardonically depicted, and centrality is given to a young woman's struggle through oppression to maturity. The book's pictorial dust wrapper gave prominence to the heroine. The novel endorsed romantic values, instead of treating them with irony as an earlier Conradian work might have done. The author had rewritten the ending to make it more positive, and he had told Pinker: "It's the sort of stuff that *may* have a chance with the public. All of it about a girl and with a steady run of references to women in general all along, some sarcastic, others sentimental, it ought to go down."[62] If women helped *Chance* to prosper, there was an element of justice, given Conrad's support for female suffrage.

In course of time, the name of Conrad had been advertised not only by the book publishers and reviewers but also by numerous magazines in Britain and abroad. Various essays by Conrad, and his two volumes of reminiscences, *The Mirror of the Sea* and

A Personal Record, had offered an effectively mythologized self. In these volumes we hear nothing of the Conrad who would rage at mealtimes and flick bread pellets at his guests, or mistakenly threaten his mother-in-law with a shotgun, or repeatedly haggle with creditors for further payments. Instead, we are shown the author as exiled Pole, experienced seafarer, and dedicated writer committed to such traditional values as truth, fidelity, and honor. Compared with the largely desk-bound and unadventurous lives of most authors, Conrad offered a romantic, exotic, and nobly memorable image, reinforced by the drawings and photographs of himself (neatly bearded, dignified, meditative: a handsome weathered sage) which increasingly appeared in the press. He had transmuted the man of anguished complexities into the much-traveled noble seer.

In 1914, he took his family on a visit to Poland, where he met a range of friends, relatives, writers, and intellectuals; in the essay "Poland Revisited" he would recall his emotions there. The timing was unfortunate: the Great War began, Conrad was in danger of being interned by the Austrian authorities, and with difficulty the Conrads returned via Vienna, Milan, and Genoa (Italy being still neutral then), reaching England in a Dutch steamer. During the Great War, although he was too old for military service, Conrad kept in touch with martial activities. In 1916, he joined the minesweeper *Brigadier* for one of her patrols, made a flight in a biplane from the Royal Naval Air Station at Yarmouth, sailed during stormy weather in a ship mending torpedo-net defences, and joined the "Q" ship *H. M. S. Ready* (a military vessel disguised as a merchantman) in its search for enemies. As he told Pinker: "Been practice-firing in sight of the coast. Weather improved. Health good. Hopes of bagging Fritz high."[63] Though he was often ill, depressed, and anxious, Conrad possessed large reserves of courage.

Meanwhile, Conrad's career was prospering. The success of *Chance* had not lacked harbingers. *'Twixt Land and Sea* had emerged quite successfully in 1912. This was the uneven volume comprising "A Smile of Fortune," "The Secret Sharer," and "Freya of the Seven Isles": two of his finest works followed by a disappointing melodramatic yarn. The first English edition numbered

3,600 copies, and the reviewers' praise was not adulterated by the once-customary warnings about Conrad's gloom and difficulty. In the month of *Chance*'s appearance, January 1914, *Lord Jim* was reissued in a large popular edition: 15,000 copies at a shilling each. Conrad was at last gaining general recognition. In the publishing world, success breeds success: now publishers rapidly reprinted almost all his earlier works, and the author could command large advances. For *Victory*, Pinker obtained £1,000 for the serial rights (in *Munsey's Magazine*) and £850 for the book. Even a short essay, "Tradition," earned £250 in 1918 when published in Lord North-cliffe's *Daily Mail*. (Ironically, Northcliffe had appeared in *The Inheritors* as Fox, one of the villains.) Meanwhile, Conrad was able to sell numerous manuscripts to the collectors John Quinn and T. J. Wise. Quinn, whose collection would prove highly profitable, paid £80 for the manuscript of *The Nigger*, for instance.

Respect for Conrad grew as his powers declined. The decline was uneven: to the last he could write passages of great beauty and eloquence. (Indeed, Conrad's ability to generate beauty—beauty of prose, of vista, and of concept—has not yet gained full recognition.) The volume *Within the Tides* (1915) contained some of his weakest tales, but was generally well received. The novel *Victory*, which appeared later in the same year, further extended his general popularity; and it still has its critical advocates, though its ironic sophistication is ill matched with stagey characterizations and dialogue. Whereas some critics, such as F. R. Leavis and Frederick R. Karl, have deemed *Victory* a major work, others (e.g., Douglas Hewitt and Albert Guerard) have found it flawed by melodrama both in the characterization of the villains and at times in the quality of its prose. Its narrative of a gentleman who "lives in sin" with an attractive young woman on a tropical island may well have helped to gain Conrad a wider readership. Further-more, its exotic settings and exciting situations (seductive heroine living with gallant rescuer, invasion by three murderous despera-does, attempted rape, spectacular conflagration) clearly appealed to Hollywood. Conrad had initially been dismissive of movies, but the cinema industry paid handsomely for the film rights to a range of his novels. In 1919 the rights to four of Conrad's works (*Lord Jim, Romance, Chance,* and *Victory*) brought $20,000—more than

£3,000, at a time when a pleasant four-bedroom house in London might cost £1,000. (Oddly, though the other novels in that group were filmed, *Chance* was not.) Conrad had renounced his annual Civil List pension in June 1917, and now the huge debt to Pinker could at last be cleared. The agent had thoroughly deserved his 10 percent of Conrad's earnings. With pardonable exaggeration, Conrad declared: "[T]hese books [of mine] owe their existence to Mr Pinker as much as to me."[64]

In the closing years of Conrad's life, collected editions of the works were issued by Doubleday in New York, by Heinemann, Gresham and Dent in London, and by Grant in Edinburgh. Conrad's main publications in this phase were *The Arrow of Gold* (1919), *The Rescue* (1920), *Notes on Life and Letters* (1921), and *The Rover* (1923). (Posthumously published volumes include the incomplete *Suspense*, *Tales of Hearsay*, *Last Essays*, and the fragmentary *The Sisters*. Parts of the correspondence would appear in G. Jean-Aubry's *Joseph Conrad: Life and Letters*.) A new friend during the later years was Bertrand Russell, the eminent skeptical philosopher, who found that Conrad's political wisdom concerning China and communism transcended his own.[65] In 1919, as a sign of burgeoning prosperity, Conrad moved into Oswalds, a large and elegant Georgian house at Bishopsbourne, near Canterbury, employing numerous servants and auxiliaries. In 1923 he visited the United States to lecture and give readings, and was treated as a great celebrity. On his return, he learned that his son Borys had clandestinely married: Conrad and Jessie had to "make the best" of this embarrassing situation; but the birth of a grandson helped the course of reconciliation. Borys had served in the army during the Great War, and had been gassed and shell-shocked. In 1927, he would be jailed for embezzlement.[66] Eventually, he would serve as first president of the Joseph Conrad Society, U. K. The Conrads' only other child, John Alexander, spent much of 1923 and 1924 at a boarding school, and would later make a successful career as an architect.

Joseph Conrad had hoped to emulate a previous Polish novelist, Henryk Sienkiewicz (author of *Quo Vadis?*), by winning the Nobel Prize for Literature, but failed to do so. Having declined numerous university doctorates, in 1924 Conrad courteously declined a knighthood offered by Britain's first Labour Prime Minister, Ramsay MacDonald. His health deteriorated: "I begin to feel like a cornered rat," he remarked;[67] and, on 3 August 1924, he died of a heart attack at his home.

After a service in Canterbury at the Roman Catholic church, St. Thomas's, Joseph Conrad was buried in the public cemetery on Westgate Court Avenue. The mourners included various old friends, notably Edward Garnett and R. B. Cunninghame Graham. Subsequently Graham published an obituary tribute to Conrad, "Inveni Portum" ("I Have Found Harbour"), which includes the following fine descriptive passage:

> His nose was aquiline, his eyes most luminous and full. It seemed his very soul looked out of them, piercing the thoughts of those whom he addressed [...]. His feet were small and delicately shaped and his fine, nervous hands, never at rest a minute in his life, attracted you at once. They supplemented his incisive speech by indefinable slight movements, not gestures in the Latin sense [...]. Something there was about him, both of the Court and of the quarter-deck, an air of courtesy and of high breeding, and yet with something of command. His mind, as often is the case with men of genius—and first and foremost what most struck one was his genius—seemed a strange compact of the conflicting qualities, compounded in an extraordinary degree, of a deep subtlety and analytic power and great simplicity.[68]

Around the time of his death, adulation of Conrad was at its height. Whether in the United States or in continental Europe, his prestige was great among writers and critics. There followed, in the 1930s, some decline in his reputation. He could sometimes seem an old-fashioned romantic when placed alongside the radical experimentalism of T. S. Eliot, Virginia Woolf, Ezra Pound, and James Joyce, or the urbanities of W. H. Auden, or the sophistication of Aldous Huxley. In the 1940s and 1950s, however, Conrad's works gained new topicality from a range of events: global warfare, political atrocities, the arrival of nuclear weaponry, the Cold War, and increasing awareness of the machinations of politicians. His general skepticism and his keen insights into political machiavellianism, the international scope of his works, his ironic vision and disenchanted view of human possibilities, and his complex moral stance (which included austere stoicism), all gave him increasing topical relevance. Repeatedly, in his technical ingenuity and thematic resourcefulness, he had anticipated (often critically) aspects of literary theory that became modish in the second half of the twentieth century. Conrad's fame and reputation have burgeoned, and have naturally been revitalized by controversies about imputed racism, sexism, and imperialism. He has influenced numerous writers in different continents. By way of the cinema, videos, television, the stage, picture books, and the electronic Web, he has reached vast international audiences. Marlow's claim, "We live, as we dream—alone,"[69] was already ironic in 1899; today the irony is global. Physically, Conrad died in 1924; culturally, he is now, it appears, more vital than ever. He remains a hero for our times, and his works continue to provide rich moral, intellectual, and imaginative sustenance to countless people around the world.

NOTES

I am very grateful to Owen Knowles and Zdzisław Najder for their constructive comments on drafts of this chapter.

1. Roland Barthes, "La Mort de l'auteur," *Mantéia* 5 (1968); published as "The Death of the Author," in *Image Music Text*, trans. Stephen Heath (New York: Hill and Wang, 1977), 142–48. The notion that the author should be disregarded had been propagated by Oscar Wilde, T. S. Eliot, W. H. Auden, and the so-called "New Critics," notably R. C. Ransom and Cleanth Brooks.

2. Jacques Derrida, *L'Ecriture et la différance* (1967), translated by Alan Bass as *Writing and Difference* (London: Routledge & Kegan Paul, 1978), 292. The nostalgia identified by Derrida renders readers deaf to irony.

3. J. C. Carlier, "Roland Barthes's Resurrection of the Author and Redemption of Biography," *Cambridge Quarterly* 29, no. 4 (2000): 386–93; reprinted in *Roland Barthes*, ed. Mike and Nicholas Gane, vol. 3 (London: Sage, 2004), 115–22. Because Barthes's essay, if taken literally, says that the reader constructs the meaning of a work, Carlier's construction (or, more precisely, construing) of the satiric meaning of Barthes's work can never be invalidated by the literalists. Carlier's case is logically irrefutable.

4. Quoted in Zdzisław Najder, *Joseph Conrad: A Life* (Rochester, N.Y.: Camden House / Boydell and Brewer, 2007), 13. Here and elsewhere, my editorial emendations are inserted within square brackets.

5. Ibid., 29. The Latin phrase *"memento mori"* means "reminder of death."

6. Ibid., 22.

7. Ibid., 42.

8. As Najder (36–37) points out, Bobrowski veiled the fact that his own relatives included the feckless and the insurrectionary.

9. Commenting on gun running by A. G. Spilsbury, Conrad remarked to Cunninghame Graham in 1898: "I've done better in my time but then I didn't act for a syndicate." The phrasing suggests that he is recalling the Colombian venture rather than the Mediterranean. But see the letters (4 February 1898 and 7 April [?] 1898) and editorial commentary in *Joseph Conrad's Letters to R. B. Cunninghame Graham*, ed. C. T. Watts (London: Cambridge University Press, 1969), 75–77, 81–82; quotation, 81.

10. Tadeusz Bobrowski to Stefan Buszczynski, 12 or 24 March 1879, in *Conrad's Polish Background: Letters to and from Polish Friends*, ed. Zdzisław Najder (London: Oxford University Press, 1964), 177.

11. Ibid., 177–78.

12. Letter dated 4 February 1898, in *Joseph Conrad's Letters to R.B. Cunninghame Graham*, 75.

13. Letter dated 24 May or 5 June 1883, in *Conrad's Polish Background*, 88.

14. Conrad to Aniela Zagórska, 25 December 1899, in *The Collected Letters of Joseph Conrad*, ed. Laurence Davies et al. (9 vols.; Cambridge: Cambridge University Press, 1986–2007), 2: 230.

15. Owen Knowles, "Conrad's Life," in *The Cambridge Companion to Joseph Conrad*, ed. J. H. Stape (Cambridge: Cambridge University Press, 1996), 8.

16. Quoted in Ugo Mursia, *Scritti Conradiani* (Milano: Mursia, 1983), 30.

17. Ibid., 32.

18. Alice Meynell's essay entitled "Decivilised" appeared in the *National Observer* (24 January 1891) and was reprinted in her book *The Rhythm of Life* (London: John Lane, 1893). The essay is reprinted as an appendix in *Almayer's Folly*, ed. Owen Knowles (London: Everyman Dent Orion, 1995), 190–92.

19. "Author's Note" to *Almayer's Folly*, ed. Knowles, 3–4.

20. See Cedric Watts, *The Deceptive Text: An Introduction to Covert Plots* (Brighton: Harvester, 1984), 52–53.

21. "Delayed decoding" (a term coined by Ian Watt) occurs when there is a marked delay between the textual presentation of a strange or problematic feature and its explanation. Often the sequence has this form: enigma; false decoding; true decoding. (Tellingly, the very first words of *Almayer's Folly*, "Kaspar! Makan!," initiate delayed decoding. Conrad begins his literary career by presenting the reader with an enigma to be resolved.) On a large scale, delayed decoding becomes covert plotting. As indicated above, covert plotting occurs when a plot sequence is presented so subtly, obliquely. or elliptically by the author that, though parts of it may be obvious, the reader may not perceive the sequence as a coherent whole until a second or subsequent reading of the text, if at all. (In *Almayer's Folly*, that scheme by Abdulla to destroy Almayer was so "covert" a plot that more than seventy years elapsed before critics identified it.) An intermediate example, an extended piece of delayed decoding that is resolved as a plot sequence within *Almayer's Folly*, concerns the apparent death of Dain in the river: a sequence in which, for a while, the Dutch authorities, Almayer, and the reader are fooled into thinking that the mutilated corpse of a boatman is that of Dain himself. See Cedric Watts, *The Deceptive Text*.

22. Letter dated 14 December 1897, in *Joseph Conrad's Letters to R. B. Cunninghame Graham*, 54.

23. *Almayer's Folly*, ed. Knowles, 135.

24. First noted by Yves Hervouet in "Conrad and the French Language," cited in *Almayer's Folly*, ed. Knowles, 186.

25. Conrad, "A Familiar Preface," in *A Personal Record*, ed. Zdzisław Najder (Oxford: Oxford University Press, 1988), xix.

26. Letter dated 31 January 1898, in *Joseph Conrad's Letters to R. B. Cunninghame Graham*, 71.

27. See Ian Watt, *Conrad in the Nineteenth Century* (London: Chatto & Windus, 1980), 51.

28. *Weekly Sun*, 9 June 1895, 1–2; *Spectator*, 19 October 1895, 530.

29. *Hysteron proteron* is a rhetorical term meaning "latter former" or "last put first." Conrad exploits this technique on a vast scale when, in three novels, he presents the story of Lingard in reversed chronological order. This is also an instance of transtextual narration, since the life of Lingard (like that of Almayer, Abdulla, Marlow, and many other Conradian characters) extends over several works. Delayed decoding implies *hysteron proteron*, as the author describes an effect while delay-

ing or withholding the *cause* of that effect. Examples abound exuberantly in "Heart of Darkness," *Lord Jim, Nostromo,* and *The Secret Agent.*

30. The original full text has been reprinted in *An Outcast of the Islands,* ed. Cedric Watts (London: Everyman Dent Orion, 1996).

31. Jessie Conrad, *Joseph Conrad and His Circle* (London: Jarrolds, 1935), 16.

32. Ibid., 15. Incidentally, although Conrad told Ephraim Redmayne that Jessie worked "at type-writing in the City," J. H. Stape argues that the standard of her typing indicates that she was not a professional typist. See J. H. Stape, *The Several Lives of Joseph Conrad* (London: Heinemann, 2007), 78.

33. Quoted in Owen Knowles and Gene M. Moore, *Oxford Reader's Companion to Conrad* (Oxford: Oxford University Press, 2000), 74.

34. Joseph Conrad, "The Return," in *Tales of Unrest* (London: J. M. Dent & Sons, 1947), 185.

35. Conrad to Kazimierz Waliszewski, 5 December 1903, in *Collected Letters of Joseph Conrad,* 3: 89. To regard Conrad as janiform (looking in contrasting ways, like the Roman god Janus) can facilitate an approach to his complexity.

36. Letter dated 8 February 1899, in *Joseph Conrad's Letters to R. B. Cunninghame Graham,* 117 (*Collected Letters of Joseph Conrad,* 2: 159, 160, for translation of French).

37. Edward Garnett, "Introduction," in *Letters from Conrad 1895 to 1924,* ed. Edward Garnett (London: Nonesuch, 1928), vii.

38. Wait, ironically while racially abusing an Irishman as an "Irish beggar," remarks: "You wouldn't call me nigger if I weren't half dead." In 1898 Conrad praised Cunninghame Graham's essay " 'Bloody Niggers'," a satiric attack on racism (particularly the racist term "nigger") and imperialism. The essay was first published in the *Social-Democrat* 1, no. 4 (April 1897): 104–9, and is reprinted in *Selected Writings of Cunninghame Graham,* ed. Cedric Watts (London, Toronto, and New Brunswick: Associated University Presses, 1981). During recent decades, the word "nigger" has been used in numerous Hollywood films (e.g., Tarantino's *Reservoir Dogs* and *Jackie Brown* or Kubrick's *Full Metal Jacket*) and in many rap lyrics (notably Fifty Cent's "What Up Gangsta"), and therefore any present-day critic who objects to Conrad's reportage of that noun may appear hypocritical.

39. Joseph Conrad, "Preface" to *The Nigger of the "Narcissus,"* ed. Cedric Watts (London: Penguin, 1988), xlix.

40. W. E. Henley, *"Invictus"* (1875): entitled "Echoes: IV: I. M. R. T. Hamilton Bryce" in *Poems* (London: Nutt, 1898; rpt., 1906), 119.

41. *The Nigger of the "Narcissus,"* 39.

42. These matters are defined and discussed in *The Deceptive Text*. Literary janiformity occurs when a text appears to be centrally or importantly paradoxical or self-contradictory.

43. See *Conrad on Film*, ed. Gene M. Moore (Cambridge: Cambridge University Press, 1997), 245.

44. Chinua Achebe, "An Image of Africa" (lecture, 1975), *Massachusetts Review* 18, no. 4 (winter 1977): 790, 788. A revised version (in which the phrase "bloody racist" becomes "thorough-going racist") can be seen in Achebe's *Hopes and Impediments* (London: Heinemann, 1988). The novelist Julian Barnes has remarked: "What a curious vanity it is of the present to expect the past to suck up to it": *Flaubert's Parrot* (London: Cape, 1984), 130. J. W. Burrow adds: "To illustrate the racial prejudices of our ancestors [. . .] provides both an easy research strategy and a cheaply won moral superiority": *Times Literary Supplement*, 13 June 1986, 653.

45. Joseph Conrad, "Heart of Darkness," in *"Heart of Darkness" and Other Tales*, ed. Cedric Watts (Oxford: Oxford University Press, 2002), 107.

46. Quoted in W. R. Lewis and Jean Stengers, *E. D. Morel's History of the Congo Reform Movement* (London: Oxford University Press, 1968), 205. Morel also praised "Heart of Darkness" in his polemic *The Congo Slave State* (London: Sampson Low, Marston, 1903).

47. Conrad to Roger Casement, 21 December 1903, in *Collected Letters of Joseph Conrad*, 3: 97; *Morning Post*, 12 October 1904, 8.

48. Joseph Conrad, "Geography and Some Explorers," in *Last Essays* (London: J. M. Dent & Sons, 1926), 25.

49. Those feminists included Nina Pelikan Straus, Bette London, Johanna M. Smith and Elaine Showalter. See Straus's "The Exclusion of the Intended from the Secret Sharing in Conrad's *Heart of Darkness*," *Novel* 20, no. 2 (winter 1987): 123–37; London's *The Appropriated Voice: Narrative Authority in Conrad, Forster, and Woolf* (Ann Arbor: University of Michigan Press, 1990); Smith's " 'Too Beautiful Altogether': Ideologies of Gender and Empire in *Heart of Darkness*," in Joseph Conrad: *Heart of Darkness*, ed. Ross C. Murfin (2nd edn.; New York: Bedford Books, 1996), 169–84; and Showalter's *Sexual Anarchy* (London: Bloomsbury, 1991).

50. Conrad, "Heart of Darkness" in *"Heart of Darkness" and Other Tales*, ed. Cedric Watts, 113.

51. Joseph Conrad, *Chance* (London: J. M. Dent & Sons, 1949), 144.

52. *Times*, 15 June 1910, 7.

53. "Author's Note" to *The Secret Agent*, ed. Cedric Watts (London: Everyman Dent Orion, 1997), 235.

54. See: Cedric Watts, "Telling the Time for Crime," *Merope*, Year 8, no. 18 (May 1988): 91–111; and my annotations to *The Secret Agent*, ed. Watts.

55. Letter dated 7 October 1907, in *Joseph Conrad's Letters to R. B. Cunninghame Graham*, 169 (*Collected Letters of Joseph Conrad*, 3: 491).

56. Letter dated 14 January 1898, in *Joseph Conrad's Letters to R. B. Cunninghame Graham*, 65 (*Collected Letters of Joseph Conrad*, 2: 16–17).

57. Conrad to the *New York Times* "Saturday Review," 2 August 1901, in *Collected Letters of Joseph Conrad*, 2: 348–49.

58. Letter dated 28 August 1908, in *Collected Letters of Joseph Conrad*, 4: 112.

59. Joseph Conrad, *Under Western Eyes*, ed. Paul Kirschner (London: Penguin, 1996), l5.

60. "Author's Note" to *Under Western Eyes*, ed. Kirschner, lxxxv.

61. *New York Herald*, Magazine Section, 14 January 1912, 3.

62. Letter dated 7 April 1913, in *Collected Letters of Joseph Conrad*, 5: 208.

63. Letter dated 8 November 1916, in *Collected Letters of Joseph Conrad*, 5: 678.

64. Conrad to John Quinn, 15 July 1916, in *Collected Letters of Joseph Conrad*, 5: 619.

65. See Bertrand Russell, *The Autobiography of Bertrand Russell 1872–1914* (London: Allen and Unwin, 1967), 207–10.

66. Knowles and Moore, *Oxford Reader's Companion to Conrad*, 74.

67. Quoted in Cedric Watts, *A Preface to Conrad*, 2nd ed. (Harlow: Longman, Pearson Education, 1993), 38.

68. "An extract from 'Inveni Portam: Joseph Conrad' by Cunninghame Graham," in *Joseph Conrad's Letters to R. B. Cunninghame Graham*, 214–15; quotation, p. 214. Graham's essay was first published (as "Inveni Portam" [*sic*]) in the *Saturday Review*, 16 August 1924, 162–63.

69. Conrad, "Heart of Darkness," in *"Heart of Darkness" and Other Tales*, ed. Watts, 130.

Joseph Conrad
and the Maritime Tradition

Mark D. Larabee

In 1923, Conrad wrote to friend and fellow author Richard Curle of his hope of shaking off the "infernal tail of ships" that he felt had unjustly qualified his transition from the maritime to the literary world. Looking back over his careers as sailor and writer, Conrad condemned the public's "obsession" with his "sea life," which, in his words, had "about as much bearing on my literary existence, on my quality as a writer, as the enumeration of drawing-rooms which Thackeray frequented could have had on his gift as a great novelist." Just because seamen appear in some of his books did not make them "sea stories," and in any case, less than a tenth of his work might count as "sea stuff." He explained that the links between his ships and his writing were a purely "biographical" rather than "literary" matter, and he wanted to avoid being labeled a "spinner of sea-yarns," a "master-mariner," or a "seaman writer."[1] Attending to such connections distorted the relation between art and history in his work, he believed, and for an insufficiently discerning reader, the origins of his fiction could eclipse its literary qualities.

Nevertheless, the circumstances of Conrad's sea career, and how they shaped his writing, have continued to interest critics. Their work has usually focused on the biographical facts of Conrad's sea years and the historical conditions and psychological effects of life in a merchant sailing ship. The two most extensive studies along these lines are still Jerry Allen's *The Sea Years of Joseph Conrad* (1965) and Norman Sherry's *Conrad's Eastern World* (1966).[2] Allen examines the episodes and people of Conrad's nautical past as the raw material for his fiction, reconstructing his voyages and connecting fictional characters to their real-life sources. Sherry aims especially at the shore world of the East, whose stories and personal relationships filled so much of the spells of idleness between Conrad's voyages. Both Allen and Sherry sought to extend the relatively small space devoted to Conrad's sea years in the most substantial biographies then written: G. Jean-Aubry's *Joseph Conrad: Life and Letters* (1927) and Jocelyn Baines's *Joseph Conrad: A Critical Biography* (1959).[3] Allen and Sherry have remained so influential that even as Zdzisław Najder downplays the importance of sea life to Conrad in *Joseph Conrad: A Life* (2007), he nevertheless incorporates their evidence and engages their claims.[4]

Other scholars have looked more closely at the psychological dimensions of the seagoing profession, particularly in terms of solidarity and Conrad's often-quoted designation of the ship as "the moral symbol of our life."[5] C. F. Burgess, in *The Fellowship of the Craft: Conrad on Ships and Seamen and the Sea* (1976),[6] extracts from Conrad's fiction and nonfiction an interpretation of the author's values, although he does not use source documents to relate Conrad to the material conditions of his times. In several essays, Robert Foulke details work aboard sailing ships and evaluates Conrad's fiction in light of the principles of seamanship. He demonstrates, for instance, that Conrad was both a reliable chronicler of maritime life and a writer who incorporated the details of that life into a literary array of complex and subtle attitudes toward the maritime profession.[7] To these studies we may add the recent *Joseph Conrad: Master Mariner* (2006) by Peter Villiers, based on a manuscript by his father, Alan Villiers.[8] This last book complements Allen's, Sherry's, and Foulke's work by relating the flavor of seagoing life in Conrad's day and addressing his motivations for beginning and pursuing his nautical career.

As comprehensive as these studies are, an account of Conrad and the maritime tradition in the broadest sense would require examining the full range of material, economic, technical, and cultural influences that made the Merchant Service what it was in his time. Such an account would also, ideally, synthesize the array of those inherited and unwritten practices, customs, and values that ordered the social world in which Conrad the sailor became Conrad the author. Given the limitations of space here, it will serve to address the maritime tradition in three prominent respects: as a corollary of a commercial enterprise in which patterns of movement and profit created psychological imperatives for its participants, as a forum for the exercise of loyalty complicated by conflicting demands, and as a setting for craftsmanship whose moral dimension was highlighted by the transition from sail to steam. What follows situates Conrad within these aspects of his historical context by considering their relation to his fiction, illuminating the core artistic techniques and moral precepts acquired in those ships whose potentially reductive biographical associations Conrad wished his readers to avoid.

Trade

When one thinks of the maritime tradition in Conrad's fiction, what may first come to mind is the beginning of "Heart of Darkness" (1899), with the narrator's affectionate and respectful portrayal of "ages of good service" and "the great spirit of the past" animating Britain's seagoing heritage. The narrator casts Sir Francis Drake and Sir John Franklin, "great knights-errant of the sea," as the heroes of this tradition, sailing in the *Golden Hind*, the *Erebus*, and the *Terror* to carry "the dreams of men, the seed of commonwealths, [and] the germs of empires" to the corners of the world (*Y* 46–47). Given the lush and evocative character of Conrad's romanticizing descriptions here, it is jarring to read in comparison John Masefield's poem "Cargoes," published in 1902—the same year that "Heart of Darkness" appeared in book form. Masefield juxtaposes the exotic cargoes of quinquireme and galleon with those of a "dirty British coaster" (coal and pig-lead, wood and "cheap tin trays"), providing a reminder of the prosaically commercial backdrop before which Conrad stages his scenes, tinted by a sunset glow, of centuries of adventure and conquest.[9]

These contrasts indicate how much the British Empire had by Conrad's time become one of trade more than discovery and subjugation. Britain's Merchant Service had played a key role in global exploration, but that era was closing in 1902—also the year in which former merchant sailor Ernest Shackleton almost reached the South Pole to fill in one of the earth's last blank spaces. Furthermore, the exploitative trade in "Heart of Darkness" is conducted by foreigners. In the rest of Conrad's sea life and fiction, British commerce does not involve ivory gathered by shackled Africans, but banal materials like those Masefield illustrates: coal, potatoes, sugar, wool, jute, and resin. Passengers are European tourists, Chinese laborers going home, or Muslims bound for Mecca, not ivory-seeking "pilgrims" or the "Eldorado Exploring Expedition" to the Congo (*Y* 77, 87). In the fiction, cargoes are sometimes the source of narrative conflict: spilled money and rioting Chinese passengers in "Typhoon" (1902), burning coal in "Youth" (1898), or rotting potatoes in "A Smile of Fortune" (1911). Generally, however, Conrad's nautical characters move in an unidealized business world of ordinary trade goods and unremarkable ships. As Marlow puts it in *Chance* (1914), consequently, "sea-life . . . stamps [a sailor's] soul with the mark of a certain prosaic fitness—because a sailor is not an adventurer" (*C* 47). For so many of Conrad's speakers, the sailor's world is the working empire. To situate Conrad with respect to the maritime tradition, then, we might start by placing his fictional voyages in the context of historical routes and cargoes (see table 1).

During the years of Conrad's sea career (1874–94), the patterns of Britain's foreign trade underwent considerable growth and change. In the latter half of the nineteenth century, while the population of the United Kingdom did not quite double in size, the worth of its foreign trade expanded nearly fivefold, and the tonnage cleared at home ports increased by more than seven times. Meanwhile, the share of cargo cleared in Britain carried by British ships, in relation to ships of all countries, steadily increased through the late nineteenth century to reach a peak of seventy-three percent in 1890. Throughout this period, British

Table 1. British Maritime Trade in Conrad's Sea Fiction

Text	*Vessel* (propulsion); Route	Fictional Cargo / Principal Historical Cargoes on that Route
The Nigger of the "Narcissus"	*Narcissus* (sail); Bombay to London	[n.s.] / jute, rice, tea, wheat, cotton, silk, ores, coffee
"Youth"	*Judea* (sail); London to Bangkok	coal / coal, textiles, hardware, opium
"Heart of Darkness"	[n.s.] (steam); Congo River	ivory / rubber, ivory
Lord Jim	*Patna* (steam); Singapore to Jeddah	Muslim pilgrims / Muslim pilgrims
"Typhoon"	*Nan-Shan* (steam); South China Sea (unnamed port to Fuchau)	Chinese laborers / textiles, metals, opium
"The End of the Tether"	*Sofala* (steam); Straits of Malacca	general cargo / tin, general cargo
"The Brute"	*Apse Family* (sail); Sydney to London	[n.s.] / wool, wheat, cattle products, ores, metals, timber
"The Black Mate"	*Sapphire* (sail); London to Calcutta	[n.s.] / coal, iron, steel, machinery, cement, salt, textiles, manufactured goods
(ditto)	(ditto); Calcutta to Dunkirk to London	jute / jute, rice, tea, wheat, cotton, silk, ores, coffee
"The Secret Sharer"	[n.s.] (sail); Bangkok to Singapore (to England)	[n.s.] / rice, teak, fish, pepper
"A Smile of Fortune"	[n.s.] (sail); Mauritius to Melbourne	sugar, potatoes / sugar, rum, coconut oil, vanilla, aloe fiber
"The Partner"	*Sagamore* (sail); London to Port Elizabeth (Cape Colony)	[n.s.] / iron, steel, machinery, cement, coal, textiles, manufactured goods

(continued)

Table 1. continued

Text	Vessel (propulsion); Route	Fictional Cargo / Principal Historical Cargoes on that Route
"Freya of the Seven Isles"	*Bonito* (sail); Malay Archipelago	rice / foodstuffs, raw materials, textiles, manufactured goods
Chance	*Ferndale* (sail); London to Port Elizabeth	dynamite / iron, steel, machinery, cement, coal, textiles, manufactured goods
"Because of the Dollars"	*Sissie* (steam); Malay Archipelago	[n.s.] / foodstuffs, raw materials, textiles, manufactured goods
The Shadow-Line	[n.s.] (sail); Bangkok to Singapore	teak / rice, teak, fish, pepper

Note: [n.s.] = not specified.

Conrad's imaginative world encompasses many more references to trade, sea voyages, and sailors than can be included in this table, which is limited to the primary vessels in stories in which British trade voyages of the late nineteenth and early twentieth centuries play a significant role. For this reason, I have left out the sea narratives of *The Rover, Romance, The Rescue,* and *The Arrow of Gold,* for example. Also, I have omitted the cruise of the steamer *Borgmester Dahl* in "Falk" (1903), carrying pitch-pine deals from Germany to New Zealand, as it was a German ship with a German crew.

Sources: "Congo Free State," 1902 *Encyclopædia Britannica,* in Joseph Conrad, *Heart of Darkness* (New York: Norton, 2006); Alexander George Findlay, *A Directory for the Navigation of the Indian Archipelago, and the Coast of China,* 3rd ed. (London: Richard Holmes Laurie, 1889) and *A Directory for the Navigation of the Indian Ocean,* 4th ed. (London: Richard Holmes Laurie, 1882); Adam W. Kirkaldy, *British Shipping: Its History, Organisation and Importance* (London: Kegan Paul, Trench, Trübner, 1914); Basil Lubbock, *The Colonial Clippers,* 2nd ed. (Glasgow: James Brown & Son, 1921); Hans van Marle and Pierre Lefranc, "Ashore and Afloat: New Perspectives on Topography and Geography in *Lord Jim,*" in Joseph Conrad, *Lord Jim* (New York: Norton, 1996); A. J. Sargent, *Seaways of the Empire: Notes on the Geography of Transport* (London: A. & C. Black, 1918).

ships made up at least forty percent of the world's merchant fleets (by tonnage), and about twenty percent of British shipping capacity never or seldom touched the home shores. Combined, these figures indicate both the vast increase in consumer demand at home and the extent to which Britain dominated global seaborne commerce.[10]

During this time, furthermore, trade between Britain and Asia became increasingly significant relative to the total profits and volume of British commerce worldwide. In 1880, while Britain's most important trading partner was the United States, British India occupied second place; after France and Germany, Australia was fifth.[11] Continuing changes to patterns of consumer demand and resource production altered the importance of various routes to and from Great Britain, leading to dramatically increased trade of food, raw materials, and manufactured goods between England and the Far East and Australia.[12] The region that saw the greatest commercial increase was Australia and New Zealand, the area to which Conrad made half his cruises from England. The total value of trade between Britain and this region (principally in wool, skins, foodstuffs, and minerals) more than doubled during the time of Conrad's sea service.[13]

While Britain's trade with the East grew disproportionately in this period, the opening of the Suez Canal in 1869 altered the means of getting there. Only steamships could take this route, which reduced the distance between London and eastern ports by up to forty percent.[14] However, the Suez Canal did not immediately make either the sailing ship obsolete or the longer route around the Cape of Good Hope impractical. First, transiting the canal incurred a delay of fifty hours in 1883, or up to three days if a sunken or grounded ship blocked the channel (which happened, on average, roughly three times a week).[15] Additionally, transit fees made passing through the canal something of a luxury. A worldwide outcry in 1883 in response to a proposed fifty percent increase in tolls required the appointment of an international commission to settle the issue.[16] Other factors contributed to a situation keeping sailing ships and the cape route more economically competitive than one might imagine. In comparison with the passage around Africa, the canal route did offer numerous convenient coaling stations—a necessity for steamships of that time, which required frequent coaling and would have had scarcely any room for cargo had they carried enough coal for long voyages. While sailing ships could not transit the canal, steamers were not then suited for the heavy weather in the southern Atlantic and Indian oceans. At the same time, the strong prevailing westerly winds in the "Roaring Forties" of the southern latitudes gave sailing ships the free propulsive force to mitigate the distance disadvantage of the southern route.[17]

In sum, these factors reduced the overall superiority of the canal route to near parity with that around the Cape of Good Hope, for both steamships and sailing ships. While the proximity of India to Suez meant that the canal route soon dominated trade to and from the subcontinent, vessels traveling between home and Australia—even steamships—predominantly followed the cape route. In 1880, only about forty percent of total cargo tonnage to and from Australia, India, and the Far East (both sail and steam) passed through the canal. Just seventeen percent of cargo homeward bound from Australia used the Canal, and less than two percent of cargo destined for Australia was shipped via Suez. By 1887, the fraction of total Australian cargo traffic traveling both directions through the canal had risen to only thirty percent, and a similar distribution along cargo routes was in place as late as 1912.[18]

In 1883 and 1889—during this period of protracted transition in the use of the Suez Canal—Conrad twice returned from the East to England as a steamship passenger via Suez and saw the canal and its traffic firsthand.[19] In 1893, looking for seagoing work again, he considered a job as a Suez Canal pilot. He thought that it would not pay much, but that it was "light" work worth pursuing.[20] Any positive feelings he had about the canal from these experiences were not shared by his fictional narrators, however. That of *An Outcast of the Islands* (1896), for instance, complains that "the sea of the past was glorious in its smiles, irresistible in its anger, capricious, enticing, illogical, irresponsible; a thing to love, a thing to fear"—that is, until French engineering "produced a dismal but profitable ditch." "[A] great pall of smoke sent out by countless steamboats was spread over the restless mirror of the

Infinite," he continues; "The hand of the engineer tore down the veil of the terrible beauty in order that greedy and faithless land-lubbers might pocket dividends" (*OI* 12). Likewise, the narrator of "The End of the Tether" (1902) laments that "the piercing of the Isthmus of Suez, like the breaking of a dam, had let in upon the East a flood of new ships, new men, new methods of trade. It had changed the face of the Eastern seas and the very spirit of their life" (*Y* 168). For these speakers, the opening of the canal had rung the death knell of the age of trade under sail and the romance and mystery of the sea.

These characterizations (without more background knowl-edge of commercial geography) could lead readers to share read-ily such a nostalgic view of the maritime tradition, in light of which Conrad's fictional sailing ships serve primarily as anachro-nistic settings for elegiac appreciations of the sailor's daily life. *The Nigger of the "Narcissus"* (1897), Conrad's first extended treatment of the sea life and its traditions, does invite just such a reading—as when the narrator describes Singleton, the ancient helmsman, as "a lonely relic of a devoured and forgotten generation" (*NN* 24). The book's eulogistic conclusion sounds another nostalgic note, with the description of the entry of the *Narcissus* into the center of industrial London positioning her as an artifact of a purer and nobler time.

Yet the historical record indicates how changes to trade pat-terns wrought by the opening of the Suez Canal were not quite as abrupt and extensive as some of Conrad's narrators claim; consequently, voyages like that depicted in this novel were not archaic final episodes in the dying age of sail transport. Even as this story incorporates rich symbolic, mythic, and other psy-chological dimensions that assist any romanticization of the maritime tradition, *The Nigger of the "Narcissus"* also portrays a historically specific commercial transaction typical of those cen-tral to the maintenance of Britain's trading empire. Thus, on one hand, the route and cargo of the *Narcissus* (in both her historical and fictional guises) provided a material framework whose com-mercial significance had a bearing on her crew's actions and can expand our understanding of the novel. On the other hand, the very omission of this material framework from the explicit level of the story, one might argue, permits Conrad's focus on this ship, as on ships in general, for the expression of moral symbolism.

In examining the route and cargo of the *Narcissus*, we should take into account the routes and cargoes not only of this particular vessel, but also of all the ships that the *Narcissus* represents. As at least one critic has noted, Conrad's depiction of the *Narcissus* effectively conflates several ships. The historical *Narcissus* was carrying coal to India by the time of Conrad's service in her, and she would likely have been loaded with jute or another bulk cargo on the return for his single 1884 trip between Bombay and Dunkirk.[21] However, certain episodes in the novel also evoke his memories of voyages in the wool clippers *Duke of Sutherland, Loch Etive*, and *Torrens*.[22] Conrad had served in the first two ships for roundtrips between London and Australia in 1878 and 1881. The *Torrens* was built primarily for passengers but carried a quantity of cargo as well on the wool route from South Australia.[23] In 1891–93, Conrad sailed on two voyages to and from Adelaide in this ship, which was a favorite of his. He once remarked that the name James Wait belonged to a crewmember in the *Duke of Sutherland*, and what he had witnessed at the embarkation of that ship "inspired" the opening scene of *The Nigger of the "Narcissus."*[24] Thus, it is instructive to read the novel's portrayal of the maritime tradition as an account influenced by the trade that Conrad knew intimately through his voyages in the Australian wool fleet, a narrative therefore implicitly bearing the marks of the commercial-geographical conditions outlined above.

As we have seen, the relative advantages between steamers and sailing ships, and between the cape and Suez, were not clearcut for trade with the East. Consequently, the duration of a passage played a crucial role in the profitability of a cargo ship's run, and sailing ship captains prided themselves on one practice more than any other: carrying the most sail possible, which translated into the shortest possible voyage times.[25] Passage speed might seem important only when the cargo was something perishable, such as tea. In fact, it was the tea trade that led to a revolution in merchant ship design in the mid-1800s, as naval architects refined hull forms to achieve maximum hydrodynamic efficiency. Yet speed was essential in the wool trade as well, for even though this particular cargo was imperishable, the time it took for wool to arrive in England had a major effect on the seller's profit.

In the Australian wool trade, the ships with the record and reputation of being the fastest were loaded last, which conferred a substantial mark of distinction but nevertheless put the captain in a position of needing even more haste to stay ahead of ships sailing at nearly the same time. Captains raced their ships against each other in the homeward passage, not only to enhance their reputations, but also for the advantage of getting their cargo to the wool market first. Wool sales in London took place in the first three months of the year, and once enough ships had reported their arrival in the English Channel, the market would close the first lists of sales. Ships that had reported in by noon on the first day of the sales would be included for that sale period. Captains arriving later would have to warehouse their cargo for several months, paying storage and other fees and also probably taking a loss from lowered wool prices. Consequently, captains of fast (i.e., late-starting) ships were sometimes offered a sizable bonus for arriving in time to catch the sales.[26]

The *Torrens* was a special case, being known as one of the fastest and most financially successful ships of her kind. A popular passenger ship on the England to Adelaide run, she was one of several small ships owned by three firms competing on the South Australian wool route back to England. The masters of the *Torrens* and others of her class conducted an especially intense rivalry, taking advantage of the smaller size of their ships to carry proportionally more sails than would have been possible on larger vessels. In the words of chronicler Basil Lubbock in *The Colonial Clippers* (1921), these captains "put a high value on their reputations as desperate sail carriers," and it was said of their crews that they rarely wore a dry shirt, so much seawater consequently came over the sides. Speedy passages were such a point of pride and comparison that tables of voyage time records are a prominent feature of books such as Lubbock's, which includes with its description of the *Torrens* a list of her outward voyages and the number of days each took.[27]

Like the captains of the *Torrens* and her sister ships, Captain Allistoun of the fictional *Narcissus* places a premium on speed.

Because Conrad leaves the cargo of the *Narcissus* unspecified in the novel, though, one might accept at face value the narrator's interpretation that Allistoun "drove" his ship "unmercifully" simply because "his secret ambition was to make her accomplish some day a brilliantly quick passage which would be mentioned in nautical papers" (*NN* 30–31). Yet attributing Allistoun's behavior to mere vanity makes sense fully (and has its moral force) only if we read this story as one far removed from the profitable routes of Suez-transiting steamships, that alternate realm of "greedy and faithless landlubbers," in the words of the narrator in *An Outcast of the Islands*. According to such a reading, Allistoun's "secret ambition" can be understood not only as a private moral failure, but also as the futile gesture of an isolated and alienated seaman whose expertise the world has passed by. For him, the fleeting fame of a newspaper mention would help offset the progressive demise of an economic model upon which he had founded his livelihood. This conclusion would also have resonated with Conrad's contemporary readers, who would have thought first of the Suez Canal as the principal route to the east and of the steamship as the principal means of transport. (Ever since 1874, after all, this was the sole route adopted by the P&O Lines, the foremost passenger line to the Orient.)[28]

As if orchestrated in spatial opposition to a Suez Canal transit, the climax of *The Nigger of the "Narcissus"* takes place in a storm off the Cape of Good Hope. Gale winds push the vessel over onto her side, where she lies inert with her rigging partially submerged, in danger of sinking at any moment. The captain helped cause this event by leaving on too much sail in worsening weather; then he refuses to cut away the masts so the ship can right herself. Because of Captain Allistoun's decisions, this episode of physical crisis becomes a moral one as well. Allistoun is opposed by the mutinous sailor Donkin, who wants to cut the masts away. Soon afterward, the dying James Wait has to be rescued from his sickbed in a room on the open main deck. Allistoun's actions seem illogical on their surface, contradicting the advice given in standard seamanship manuals.[29] What he does makes more sense, however, if we relate his actions to the context of Australian cargo routes and the worth of a speedy passage. By keeping the ship's masts and rigging intact, he preserves the possibility of resuming the voyage quickly, despite the increased chance of sinking the ship in the gale.

This context sheds some light not only on Allistoun's calculated risk in refusing to cut away the masts in the storm, but also on the manner in which he orders his exasperated crew to trim the sails continually to the best advantage during a spell of variable light winds. When he contrives "to shove, and dodge, and manœuvre his smart ship through sixty miles in twenty-four hours" (*NN* 48), he exhibits attitudes and actions that would have been familiar to Conrad from his time in Australian wool clippers. Like the historical *Narcissus*, the fictional ship is not a wool clipper, and the Bombay to Dunkirk route does not put this vessel on the courses of the wool trade. Intriguingly, however, James Wait wears a "woollen nightcap," his hair is described as wool, and at one point he is "only a cold black skin loosely stuffed with soft cotton wool" (*NN* 34, 70, 71, 171). If we consider this ship a composite fictional counterpart of the historical *Narcissus*, the *Torrens*, and the wool clippers *Duke of Sutherland* and *Loch Etive*, moreover, we can see how Allistoun's behavior reflects the state of mind of a captain ultimately concerned with more than putting his name in the newspapers. While Allistoun's fictional sea career began in whalers and then moved to the East Indian trade, his actions also indicate the cultural influence of the wool trade that Conrad knew: a part of the maritime tradition in which speed was valued for explicit economic reasons (*NN* 30). In fair weather, as in foul, Allistoun simply drives his ship the way some of his historical counterparts did in a period of rising demand for Australian wool, transition from sail to steam, and increasing but not yet dominant use of the Suez Canal.

The prolongation of these transitions in technology and commerce made voyages such as those inspiring Conrad's novel still financially practical, even if fraught by a narrow and diminishing profit margin, and unfamiliar to Conrad's readership. When Conrad incorporates part of what he saw in this trade while omitting its larger context, he enables two narrative strategies while benefiting from his readers' unfamiliarity with the details of trade routes. He can draw on parts of the maritime tradition in order to construct compelling fictional characters from the raw materials of autobiographical elements. Additionally, he can pivot in his fiction from the material conditions of the commercial world to the moral conditions of the sailors populating it. Conrad can thereby productively frame Allistoun's behavior as motivated purely by "secret ambition" and vanity, pit a crewman against the captain in a contest of wills over a seemingly needless endangerment of the ship, and focus on Wait as the embodiment of conflicts over truth and loyalty in an isolated social microcosm.

Our knowledge of these interlocking strategies, first, qualifies any critical characterization of sailing ships in the late nineteenth century exclusively as antiquated nautical specimens, aboard which the hopelessness of competing with steamships created an atmosphere conducive primarily to elegiac encomia to a sailor's vanishing profession. Additionally, we can see how Conrad's selective abstraction of the *Narcissus* from her historical predecessors was essential for making the vessel an exemplary instance of the ship as "the moral symbol of our life." This is a symbol that could be imbued with associations to the traditions of the craft while being detached from commercial transactions and attention to the bottom line. The exemplary case of the *Narcissus* (treated at length above in order to illustrate this larger point) demonstrates how Conrad could draw from the maritime tradition while also shaping it for his readers.

Fidelity

When *The Nigger of the "Narcissus"* appeared near the beginning of Conrad's writing career, he set an enduring tone for a characterization of the maritime tradition in a work praised by Henry James in 1902 as "the very finest & strongest picture of the sea and sea-life that our language possesses—the masterpiece in a whole class."[30] Nearer the end of his life, and two decades after having left the sea, Conrad squarely addresses the maritime tradition and its relation to material conditions in his essay "Tradition" (1918). He wrote this piece for the *Daily Mail* in response to a perceived slight against the heritage of the Merchant Service and its role in the Great War.[31] He tells the story of a torpedoed merchant ship, whose captain cheerfully distributed life belts aboard the sinking vessel, remaining as the last man aboard and surviving the lethal downward suction. After regaining consciousness, the captain then sailed a lifeboat 150 miles to safety. The chief engineer described the captain's confidence, calmness, seamanship, and nonchalant attitude as if saving eighteen lives "was to him an everyday occurrence." Conrad cites this episode as "testimony to the continuity of the old tradition of the sea, which made by the work of men has in its turn created for them their simple ideal of conduct" (*NLL* 201). For Conrad, the ideal of a captain ready both to exercise authority over his crew and to sacrifice his life for them in the faithful discharge of his duties exemplifies the tradition of the Merchant Service in its purest form.

Work, ideals, and conduct are inextricably linked in this essay and others like it. "Work is the law," as Conrad quotes Leonardo da Vinci in the first words of "Tradition" (*NLL* 194); work creates the tradition, which then provides the exacting ideal that gives order and meaning to the calling of the sea. In "The Dover Patrol" (1921), his tribute to merchant sailors who helped keep the English Channel free of U-boats during the war, Conrad explicitly equates tradition with "a standard of conduct."[32] By their "plodding, dogged perseverance"[33] in the face of hostile action and losses, their "physical endurance, the inborn seamanship, the matter-of-fact, industrious, indefatigable enthusiasm,"[34] the men of the Dover Patrol "lived up to their old tradition and were found sufficient for the trust reposed in them."[35] Similarly, Conrad identifies "material conditions...the hard necessities besetting men's precarious lives" as the source of tradition in "Well Done" (1918), a piece for the *Daily Chronicle* similarly occasioned by Conrad's desire to commend the Merchant Service for their wartime efforts (*NLL* 183).

For Conrad, as these essays indicate, the state of war accentuated the qualities of meaningless chaos and violence already characterizing normal conditions of life at sea. The sea is an unfathomable "mystery," he writes in "Well Done"; it is "uncertain, arbitrary, featureless, and violent." The sea is the "greatest scene of potential terror, a devouring enigma of space" (*NLL* 184).

Thus, in the face of the existential destruction confronting any mariner during war or peace, such efforts as those of the torpedoed captain in "Tradition" epitomize an affirmation of the human interdependence that makes survival at sea possible at all. The idea of a community in which men rely on one another in a hostile environment may tempt readers to assume that the natural inclination of crews is to work together for mutual protection and benefit. But such a gloss on the seagoing social world neglects the considerable tensions and mutually exclusive loyalties that potentially divide its members, belie the unity of any "simple ideal of conduct," and necessitate the assertion of discipline to counteract the centrifugal impulses of human nature.

Differences between Conrad's nonfiction and fiction expose the nature of these conflicts and pivot on his use of the term "fidelity," one of the key concepts of Conrad's entire *oeuvre*. He accords this idea a preeminent place in his interpretation of all of life, declaring in the preface to *A Personal Record* (1912), "Those who read me know my conviction that the world, the temporal world, rests on a few very simple ideas; so simple that they must be as old as the hills. It rests notably, among others, on the idea of Fidelity" (*PR* xxiii). In *The Mirror of the Sea* (1906), "fidelity," "faith," "faithfulness," and related words appear no fewer than forty-five times, corroborating the extent to which this concept informs Conrad's thinking.

According to Conrad, the mariner's faithfulness has four principal objects: tradition, professional competence, shipmates, and the ship. In "Tradition," he identifies the "fidelity to right practice which makes great craftsmen" (*NLL* 194), as well as "fidelity to an exacting tradition" (*NLL* 197). Mariners also extend fidelity to one another as fellow workers in an enterprise whose hazards know no distinctions of rank. As Conrad explains in "Well Done," "The mysteriously born tradition of sea-craft commands unity in a body of workers engaged in an occupation in which men have to depend upon each other" (*NLL* 183). Consequently, the distinguishing characteristic of seamen is that they are "men whose material and moral existence is conditioned by their loyalty to each other and their faithful devotion to a ship" (*NLL* 192). This is another version of how the ship becomes "the moral symbol of our life" (*NLL* 188): it is the tangible object toward which men may direct a set of abstract, conflated fidelities.

For all the attractiveness that the notion of mutually reinforcing loyalties may have exerted for Conrad and his contemporaries, however, elsewhere in his writing we read how loyalties lead in different directions. For instance, sailors feel the contradictions of divided loyalties resulting from having been brought together at random, from a variety of backgrounds and motivations, to achieve a common goal. Although in *The Mirror of the Sea* Conrad praises the world of sail for the "fellowship" it engenders among crewmembers teaming together against the elements, his fiction tells a different story (*MS* 72). While Conrad claims in his preface to *The Nigger of the "Narcissus"* that the artist appeals "to the latent feeling of fellowship with all creation—and to the subtle but invincible conviction of solidarity . . . which binds together all humanity" (*NN* xii), and he describes the crew in that novel as "all akin with the brotherhood of the sea" (*NN* 30), the conflicts that erupt in the story put the notion of brotherhood to a severe test. As readers soon learn, the tale revolves around the tensions dividing the crew when "the unspoken loyalty that knits together a ship's company" (*NN* 11) is challenged by Donkin, whom the narrator describes in the same breath as a type of sailor who is ubiquitous and one who inevitably undermines the unity that the narrator has just enthusiastically proclaimed.

Conrad's own path to captain would have shown him firsthand the potential for conflicts of divided loyalty at various levels of rank. He began his nautical career as an apprentice in a French ship in 1874. In that position, for all practical purposes, he was an indentured employee junior to all others and with little scope for individual action. However, by the time he attained the rank of third mate, in the *Loch Etive* in 1880–81, he would have begun to see a more complex web of loyalties. This was his first job as an officer, and in the words of Charles Powell in *Chance*, "with us merchant sailors the first voyage as officer is the real start in life" (*C* 22). Not only was this billet a significant milestone on the way to captaincy, but also it was his initial acquaintance with the difficult position of being responsible for others and giving orders to more experienced men.

As third mate, Conrad assisted the first mate in his watch section and helped supervise the seaman at their daily labor.[36] Yet his relationship with the sailors he directed potentially compromised his ability to enforce his authority. In the Merchant Service, a third mate alternated between ordering the crew to perform their duties and sharing in their physical work. Such tasks included handling the sails while aloft on the yards, where the strenuous and life-threatening nature of this shared labor tended to level differences between ranks. Because of this ambiguous position, third mates found themselves in a position of divided loyalty. On one hand, they needed to distance themselves psychologically from the sailors to whom they issued orders that could potentially result in personal injury for the sake of safely navigating the ship. This circumstance would naturally lead third mates to identify primarily with the other officers in charge. On the other hand, taking part in the crew's physical work could lead to a familiarity, tending to reduce the psychological distance third mates were obliged to maintain.

Further promotion only complicated the web of conflicting loyalties, as Conrad would have seen in his position as second mate (in the *Palestine, Riversdale, Narcissus, Tilkhurst,* and *Falconhurst* in 1881–86; and the *Adowa* in 1893–94), first mate (also called "chief mate"; *Highland Forest* and *Vidar* in 1887–88 and *Torrens* in 1891–93), and master (called "captain" by courtesy; *Otago* in 1888–89) and acting master (in *Roi des Belges* in 1890). A second mate rated being addressed as "Mister" and lived in his own cabin, but like the third mate, he was an officer who went aloft and helped work the sails alongside the crew. Sailors even treated second mates with some derision, and in a sailor's expression then current, "being second mate doesn't get your hand out of the tar-pot."[37] Becoming first mate, and then captain, meant less direct association with the most junior members of the crew but an increased sense of responsibility for their lives, which amounted to loyalty of a different kind. Furthermore, the captain had to balance sometimes competing priorities of cargo, ship, and crew. In addition to being responsible for the lives of everyone aboard, he was also liable to the state for the safe navigation of his vessel and responsible to the owners for the ship's return and the speedy delivery of their merchandise. In such an environment, a host of different specific loyalties could appear and conflict with one another.

While life as a ship's officer meant facing the mutually exclusive directions in which a variety of competing loyalties led, Conrad's fictional characters tend to address these conflicts through reasserting discipline. Such reassertions occur at critical moments in Conrad's stories, turning the resolution of narrative tensions into the resolution of divided loyalties as well. *Chance*, for instance, incorporates these conflicts at defining moments for Powell, a newly minted second mate. In the conversation between Powell and Marlow that frames the narrative, Marlow explains, "The exacting life of the sea has this advantage over the life of the earth, that its claims are simple and cannot be evaded" (*C* 32). The story that follows portrays an exploration or test of this assertion, as Powell eventually faces those unavoidable claims and resolves their contradictions by exercising discipline.

At first, Powell feels an unalloyed and meaningful "secret emotion" accompanying his assumption of authority as he gives "his first order as a fully responsible officer" (*C* 285): getting hands topside to make sail. It is not long, however, before he finds himself drawn "to break the established rule of every ship's discipline" (*C* 294) by engaging the helmsman in conversation in order to find out more about the de Barrals. In speaking to the helmsman, he unintentionally encourages that familiarity with the crew symbolized by the "tar pot" of shared labor and loyalty. Powell wants merely to be "getting hold of some other human being" (*C* 294), but by doing so, he also demonstrates a "laxity" that the helmsman feels encouraged to exploit.

It is through Powell's attempt to correct disciplinary leniency that the novel's plot takes a crucial turn and he earns his moral reward. Only by bending down to pick up a coil of rope from the deck does Powell make the momentous discovery that he can see from the main deck down into the captain's cabin through a pane of clear glass in the skylight, thereby enabling him to witness de Barral poisoning Captain Anthony's drink. Powell's claim that he was motivated "by an impulse which had nothing mysterious in it" (*C* 410) might lead us to see this event as one more incident of mere happenstance in a larger world ruled by chance. Yet the coil of rope is in that position precisely because of "the oversight of the sweepers" (*C* 410)—a chance event nevertheless the result of a breakdown in discipline. For Powell to take no action would imply a tacit endorsement of the crew's unseamanlike inattention to detail. Consequently, Powell's stooping to correct this fault himself unites the reestablishment of shipboard discipline to both the novel's plot element of exposing the villain and the shift in Powell's balance of loyalty from the crew to the captain whose life he saves.

The additional existence of a remarkably similar set of circumstances in "The Secret Sharer" (1910) reiterates the significance to Conrad of the stakes of loyalty and discipline illuminated by Powell's action. The narrator of "The Secret Sharer" regrets dismissing the ship's officers from the night watch on deck, thereby having "prevented the anchor-watch being formally set and things properly attended to" (*TLS* 97). He goes on to wonder "whether it was wise ever to interfere with the established routine of duties" (*TLS* 97). Like Powell speaking to the helmsman, he inadvertently breaks the ship's discipline despite "the kindest of motives," and he projects an "informality" that leaves him "vexed" (*TLS* 97). He redeems himself, though, by hauling in a rope ladder the crew had left hanging over the side, an act he undertakes because, in his words, "exactitude in small matters is the very soul of discipline" (*TLS* 96–97). Again, as in *Chance*, the protagonist's own attention to detail signals to the crew the officer's intolerance of substandard performance and reestablishes the primacy of loyalty to the ship and the craft over feelings of community.

Certainly, because the rope ladder in "The Secret Sharer" has Leggatt at the other end, the narrator's action sets in motion a train of events resulting in the narrator's sense of possessing a riven self. The captain's anxious efforts to keep Leggatt hidden highlight the division of loyalty between a fellow seaman whose act of murder was at least partly accidental, on the one hand, and, on the other hand, a moral ideal calling the narrator to follow the law if he wants his own law aboard ship to be followed. At the end of this story, however, another act of asserting discipline—the narrator's directing his crew to sail the ship nearly onto the rocks of Koh-ring despite their fearful reactions—resolves those divisions and reestablishes order. In both "The Secret Sharer" and *Chance*, it is through such actions that one lives up to the "simple ideal of conduct" that Conrad praises as one of the foundations of the maritime tradition.

Craft

While for Conrad the highest calling of the maritime tradition involved the moral claims that the tradition laid on its heirs, material changes to the ships in which sailors exercised their fidelity undermined the influence of those claims. Contrasts between the work performed in sailing ships and in steamers began to alter the way contemporaries thought about labor. One chronicler notes how, by the turn of the century, deckhands had come to be seen as less important to the business of seamanship in the age of steam than they had been before—becoming little more than unskilled laborers.[38] Conrad pronounces a similar lament about longshoremen in *The Mirror of the Sea*. "Stevedoring, which had been a skilled labour," he writes, "is fast becoming a labour without the skill" (*MS* 47). Conrad was witnessing a dissociation of effort from craftsmanship, brought about by the less complex technical demands of work in and around steamships. In his writing, however, differences between the complicated labor of handling sails and the mere toil of shoveling coal into a firebox serve more than the expression of nostalgia for a dying art. Conrad draws parallels between the technical and moral demands of the sailor's craft in an attempted preservation of tradition in the face of historical change.

Marlow hints in *Lord Jim* (1900) that the "whole secret" of "the craft of the sea" can be "expressed in one short sentence" (*LJ* 44), although he never provides the expression. While Ian Watt surmises that the secret consists of a Nelsonian call to duty, C. F. Burgess points to the passage in *The Mirror of the Sea* (*MS* 67) where Conrad describes a mariner's sole mission as that of keeping his ship from running aground.[39] This more prosaic interpretation helps us once more differentiate between versions of the maritime tradition drawing on romanticized history and of the quotidian demands of the sailor's work. For while the frame narrator may hearken back to Drake and Franklin as "bearers of a spark from the sacred fire" in "Heart of Darkness" (*Y* 47), when Conrad claims in *The Mirror of the Sea* that what warmed him aboard the *Highland Forest* in an Amsterdam winter was the "sacred fire for the exercise of [his] craft," he is writing about loading cargo in a sailing vessel. As first mate and acting captain of an empty ship, he undertook a daily "expedition," "like an Arctic explorer setting off on a sledge journey towards the North Pole" (*MS* 50–51) (in his apparently unironic but telling formulation) that consisted of petitioning his charterers ashore to deliver their merchandise as soon as possible so he could superintend its stowage by stevedores. More importantly, this passage appears in a chapter of *The Mirror of the Sea* dedicated to the relation between moral and technical aspects of the ship's stowage.

The first mate was responsible for the stowage of the ship, whose trim (the relative draft at bow and stern) influenced its speed, and whose location of the center of gravity affected how it would respond to wind and sea. Conrad made a significant mistake in distributing the cargo while loading the *Highland Forest*. As he tells the story in *The Mirror of the Sea*, when the captain finally arrives, Conrad remarks that he hoped it was sufficient for one third of the cargo to be "above the beams"— or in that part of the ship above the cargo holds (which had transverse beams at their tops). The captain recognizes that for this particular ship, however, the proportion loaded above the beams was too little and the center of gravity consequently too low. In these conditions, the ship became "much too stable," meaning that it rolled more quickly and righted itself too forcefully (*MS* 52–53).[40] As a result, the *Highland Forest* made its crew miserable on the passage to Semarang; a number of spars were carried away, one hitting Conrad and sending him to a hospital for three months.

As this episode made clear to Conrad, proper stowage was a matter of life and death. Yet such a point becomes clear only in a sailing ship. "The modern steamship," he explains in contrast, "is not loaded within the sailorlike meaning of the word. She is filled up. Her cargo is not stowed in any sense; it is simply dumped into her through six hatchways, more or less." As long as the propeller stays underwater and something heavy or dirty does not ruin what lies underneath, "you have done about all in the way of duty" that haste permits (*MS* 47). The pejorative connotations of "simply dumping" cargo into a ship, accompanied by the carelessness of the qualifier "more or less" and contrasted with the "sailorlike meaning" attached to loading and the umbrella of "duty" under which these actions take place, indicate the extent to which life in a steamship represented for Conrad a condition of decline from moral accountability, whose calling he promotes through valuing technical proficiency.

Another example of Conrad's extrapolation from technical to moral claims appears in his treatment of navigation, without doubt one of the most highly technical subjects of nautical knowledge. To go from sighting stars with a sextant to drawing a set of lines marking the ship's position on a chart involves laborious calculations and an understanding of trigonometry and relative time and motion. In *The Mirror of the Sea*, however, Conrad stresses the ritualistic dimension of this process. He explains that a ship's Departure (his capitalization) is not the leaving of port but the leaving of the sight of land. A departure "is distinctly a ceremony of navigation," and the ship's "enterprise of a passage" does not begin until then. More to the point, departure has its primary significance not for the ship but for the crew. At this moment, "It is not the ship that takes her Departure; the seaman takes his Departure by means of cross-bearings which fix the place of the first tiny pencil-cross on the white expanse of the track-chart, where the ship's position at noon shall be marked by just such another tiny pencil-cross for every day of her passage" (*MS* 3–4). Through navigation, men's separation from the affairs of shore becomes ritually certified, and the religious overtones of a series of penciled crosses testify to the quasi-spiritual purchase of this trigonometric calculation.

Technical manuals furnished Conrad with additional starting points for moral commentary. To cite one instance, in his essay "Outside Literature" (1922), he praises "the honorable ideal...of perfect accuracy,"[41] regulating the writing and reading of Notices to Mariners (technical bulletins for updating navigational charts).

Another example appears in his likely transformation of a real seamanship guide into the fictional *Inquiry into some Points of Seamanship* in "Heart of Darkness." Marlow's "extraordinary find" in the hut below the Inner Station, this sixty-year-old nautical manual by "Towser," or "Towson...Master in his Majesty's Navy" (*Y* 99), could very well have been inspired by *Observations on Some Points of Seamanship* by Anselm Griffiths (1824). Not only are the titles of these fictional and real works nearly identical, but also Griffiths, like Towson, was a Royal Navy captain. Furthermore, the second (and final) edition of Griffiths's *Observations*, which varies little from its predecessor, was exactly sixty years old in 1888—the year Conrad began his only permanent command and reached the pinnacle of his sea career.

The differences between the seamanship guides by Griffiths and Towson, however, are even more instructive than their similarities. Marlow exclaims about Towson's *Inquiry* that it "looked dreary reading enough, with illustrative diagrams and repulsive tables of figures" (*Y* 99). However, Griffiths's *Observations* contains hardly any diagrams and tables at all—just a handful of simple instances in a book of more than 300 pages. Nor do Griffiths's entries, while encyclopedically formatted, provide a great many technical details; in his words, he merely intends to offer "a little summary or leading view of things," with the "principal object" to "induce a habit of thinking." He wants to provide the "why and wherefore," and he concedes that "to those who are scientific seamen, some of the articles may appear insignificant." In place of science, he appeals to values in a text graced by a conversational style and illustrative anecdotes. Griffiths begins by stressing a captain's necessary "sense of duty" in relation to the "King's instructions" and before providing his entries on chains and anchors, he explores such topics as the moral significance of the captain's official signature, the legal obligations of proper record keeping, and the need for vigilance against fraud.[42]

In reshaping Griffiths's *Observations* into Towson's *Inquiry* (if we accept that one was the source for the other), it would seem that Conrad turns a guide with a substantial moral emphasis into an exclusively technical manual. Yet Marlow describes Towson's

Inquiry as embodying "a singleness of intention, an honest concern for the right way of going to work, which made these humble pages, thought out so many years ago, luminous with another than a professional light" (*Y* 99). The essence of Conrad's art here consists of eschewing Griffiths's explicit discussion of morally correct thinking in favor of identifying technical competence aboard a sailing ship as the locus of "right practice." At the heart of this difference lies an explanation of Conrad's view of the maritime tradition. The source of honesty is professionalism, moral and technical exactitude are mutually reinforcing, and the ideals of craftsmanship expressed "so many years ago"—made appropriately metaphorical by describing Towson's *Inquiry* as a mariner's guiding light—still hold true.

Conclusion

Considering the use of Towson's *Inquiry* as an embodiment of the maritime tradition returns us full circle to the status of writing as a key link between Conrad's nautical and artistic worlds. In *A Personal Record*, he likens the vocation of writing to that of sailing, in the shared metaphysical universality of their appeals and ends. "I dare say I am compelled, unconsciously compelled, now to write volume after volume," he explains, "as in past years I was compelled to go to sea, voyage after voyage. Leaves must follow upon each other as leagues used to follow in the days gone by, on and on to the appointed end, which, being Truth itself, is One—one for all men and for all occupations" (*PR* 18). Conrad's observations of human nature during his seagoing career had furnished him with more than raw material for his imaginative works. The conventions of nautical writing also gave him a sensitivity to written precision, which served in his fiction as fidelity to the truths of experience. The results of this lesson in writing from the maritime tradition, and the sense of duty to his reader that he acquired from writing at sea, we acknowledge today as among the hallmarks of his art.

We also recognize Conrad as the most deliberate artist to write in English about the nautical craft. He addresses the necessity of precise expression in *The Mirror of the Sea*, for example, where he criticizes the journalistic habit of describing a crew as having "cast" an anchor. The term "cast" has other particular uses, and as he explains, the proper formula is that the ship is "brought up to an anchor." The difference is crucial, in his view, because of the symbolic resonance of an anchor, which is an "honest" piece of nautical equipment, "forged and fashioned for faithfulness." Therefore, to write inaccurately of "casting" it overboard represents a symbolic (if inadvertent) jettisoning of fidelity. He adds that "to take a liberty with technical language is a crime against the clearness, precision, and beauty of perfected speech." Perhaps such a transgression would not be noticeable to a journalist, but according to Conrad, such lapses do not befit "the newspapers of the greatest maritime country in the world" (*MS* 13–15).

Furthermore, Conrad's use of the term "crime" hints at the importance of clarity and precision in the ship's official log, which carried the legal weight of evidence in court. The log was the official record of the ship's location and business; marriages, births, and deaths aboard; and other matters pertaining to the crew, such as wages, illnesses and injuries, and offences and punishments. Maritime law required that the log be signed by the master, contain accurate details, and be delivered to the superintendent of the Mercantile Marine Office at the end of a foreign voyage.[43] Consequently, logs had to be scrupulously correct, but alterations on the final version called into question their legal validity. Hence, several logs were prepared: a "scrap" log written in pencil, an ordinary log, and the official log—just as a series of drafts leads to the final version of a work of literary art.[44]

The necessarily dry precision of what Conrad designates in "Falk" (1903) as "log-book style" (*TOS* 185) infuses the letters home from Captain MacWhirr in "Typhoon," and it would seem from this latter work at least that Conrad indicts logbooks for their inadequacy as a means of fully recording experience. The unimaginative MacWhirr, "faithful to facts," records each "minute detail" (*TOS* 14) of the *Nan-Shan*'s voyages in epistles his wife barely reads (*TOS* 93–94). Yet Mrs. MacWhirr emerges from the tale as a less sympathetic figure than her husband, and the practice of writing the ship's log was uppermost in Conrad's mind

15. Ibid., 329; A. J. Sargent, *Seaways of the Empire: Notes on the Geography of Transport* (London: A. & C. Black, 1918), 49.

16. Kirkaldy, *British Shipping*, 328.

17. Sargent, *Seaways of the Empire*, 29.

18. Ibid., 10–11, 20–21, 51.

19. Najder, *Joseph Conrad*, 95, 133.

20. Ibid., 186; Conrad to Marguerite Poradowska, 18 December 1893, and Conrad to Marguerite Poradowska, 20 December 1893, in *Collected Letters of Joseph Conrad*, 1: 134–35, 136–37.

21. Gerald Morgan, "The Book of the Ship *Narcissus*," in *The Nigger of the "Narcissus,"* ed. Robert Kimbrough (New York: W. W. Norton, 1979), 203.

22. Ibid., 209.

23. Basil Lubbock, *The Colonial Clippers*, 2nd ed. (Glasgow: James Brown & Son, 1921), 157–62; Najder, *Joseph Conrad*, 178.

24. G. Jean-Aubry, *Joseph Conrad: Life and Letters*, 1: 77. The sailor's name in the *Duke of Sutherland* was actually George White; see Jerry Allen, *The Sea Years of Joseph Conrad*, 166.

25. Basil Lubbock, *The Last of the Windjammers* (Glasgow: Brown, Son & Ferguson, 1927), 1: 42–43.

26. Lubbock, *The Colonial Clippers*, 123–24.

27. Ibid., 144–45, 162.

28. *Travellers P&O Pocket Book* (London: Nissen & Arnold, 1888), 39.

29. Seamanship advice given, for example, in A. H. Alston, *Seamanship, and Its Associated Duties in the Royal Navy*, 1st ed. (London: Routledge, Warne & Routledge, 1860), 199–200; see also Foulke, "Conrad and the Power of Seamanship," 18–19; Foulke, "Creed and Conduct in *The Nigger of the 'Narcissus,'*" *Conradiana* 12, no. 2 (summer 1980): 113–15.

30. Henry James to Edmund Gosse, in *A Portrait in Letters: Correspondence to and about Conrad*, ed. J. H. Stape and Owen Knowles (Amsterdam: Rodopi, 1996), 36.

31. The term "Merchant Service" became "Merchant Navy" by order of King George V in 1922, in recognition of the risks merchant sailors undertook along with their Royal Navy comrades during the war. See A. G. Course, *The Merchant Navy: A Social History* (London: Frederick Muller, 1963), 17.

32. Joseph Conrad, "The Dover Patrol," in *Last Essays* (Garden City, N.Y.: Doubleday, Page & Co., 1926), 58.

33. Ibid, 63.

34. Ibid, 61.

35. Ibid, 63.

36. R. J. Cornewall-Jones, *The British Merchant Service: Being a History of the British Mercantile Marine from the Earliest Times to the Present Day* (London: Sampson Low, Marston, 1898), 287.

37. Ibid., 286.

38. Clement Jones, *British Merchant Shipping* (London: Edward Arnold, 1922), 117, 129.

39. See Burgess, *The Fellowship of the Craft*, 82–83, and Ian Watt, *Conrad in the Nineteenth Century* (Berkeley: University of California Press, 1979), 312.

40. Jones, *British Merchant Shipping*, 108–9.

41. Conrad, *Last Essays*, 43.

42. Anselm John Griffiths, *Observations on Some Points of Seamanship; with Practical Hints on Naval Œconomy, &c., &c.*, 2nd ed. (Portsmouth: W. Harrison, 1828), iii–ix, 2.

43. Cornewall-Jones, *The British Merchant Service*, 291–94; John H. Malcolm, *The Merchant Shipping and Relative Acts: Classified for Ready Reference and Designed for the Use of H. M. Judges and Magistrates, Government Officials, Solicitors, Assessors, Shipowners, Shipmasters, Etc.* (Edinburgh: William Hodge, 1912), 203–6.

44. Jones, *British Merchant Shipping*, 126.

Conrad and the Literary Marketplace

Joyce Piell Wexler

A choice between literary quality and popularity would have been unthinkable for Joseph Conrad when he embarked on his writing career. The example of Victorian novelists whose work was praised and profitable made both goals seem attainable, but he discovered that the expansion of the literate audience had increased the distance between highbrow and middlebrow taste. High sales had become a sign of mediocrity, and publishers were more often portrayed as philistines than as patrons of serious literature. Nevertheless, the literary marketplace sustained Conrad's career materially and aesthetically. Commercial publishers made it possible for him to earn a living as an author, and their editorial advice helped him achieve his rhetorical aim of communicating with readers.

Although the income of popular authors was beyond his reach, Conrad rapidly grasped the rules of the literary market. Publishers were eager to buy manuscripts for all segments of the audience, though not at the same price. Seeing inferior work earn more money, serious writers were sometimes tempted to abandon their aesthetic principles and appeal to the broadest taste, but pleasing middlebrow readers was harder than they realized. As George Henry Lewes observed in 1898, a rhetorical match between author and reader was not entirely a matter of choice:

"This is not luck, but a certain fitness between the author's mind and the public needs."[1] When Conrad attempted to copy the formula of a popular novelist like Guy Bothby, he failed: "I can't get the secret of this fellow's manner. It's beyond me, how he does it!"[2] Conrad could not produce the qualities he knew popular novels needed—easy style, plenty of action, romantic atmosphere, a happy ending.[3] Adapting to the differences between the Victorian audience and his own, he learned how to use his reputation to increase sales.

Critics respected Conrad's desire for a large audience as long as sales were low. Commercial failure merely confirmed the poor taste of the majority audience. When *Chance* became a bestseller in 1914, however, some critics interpreted Conrad's newfound popular success as the sign of a sudden sellout. Despite critical suspicion of popularity, Richard Ohmann's study of canon formation shows that writers need commercial success as well as critical esteem to enter the historical canon.[4] Certainly, Conrad always wanted his books to sell, and his motives were never merely economic. He also wanted the "average man" to understand what he was striving for, and he shaped his fiction with his reader in mind. Conrad was as concerned with readers when writing *Lord Jim* and *Nostromo* as he was when writing *Chance*. The high sales of *Chance* consolidated the benefits of his reputation.

Conrad successfully negotiated the period's competing models of authorship. From his entry into the literary market in the 1890s to the publication of *Chance*, his letters stake out various positions. Some adopt the romantic image of the poet whose inner vision is inviolable. The weakness of this view of authorship, as Conrad realized, is that it too easily justifies a bohemian indifference to any audience. Other letters invoke Flaubert's model of the writer as professional. As Pierre Bourdieu argues, Flaubert invented the modern artist as the "full-time professional dedicated to his work, indifferent to the exigencies of politics as to the injunctions of morality, and recognizing no jurisdiction other than the specific norm of art."[5] The disadvantage of this model is that it addresses a coterie of other experts. Conrad portrayed himself both as the romantic creator, powerless before his imagination, and as a careful workman honing his skills. He struggled to express his ideas sincerely, but he made readers' responses the test of his sincerity. He admired the workmanship and consistency of the professional, but he refused to settle for a coterie audience.

Complicating interpretation of the letters, Conrad was often disingenuous.[6] He disparaged his work when he felt proud of it to avoid seeming boastful. He flattered his correspondents. He wished for money when he was poor, and he professed indifference to sales when he was rich. Early in his career, Conrad humbly said that he depended on inspiration to compensate for his ignorance of the public and his lack of craftsmanship, but as he gained experience, he considered erratic control of his work a sign of ineptitude. He modified his methods of achieving his aesthetic and rhetorical aims when his publishing experiences changed his conception of readers. Between the poles of helplessness and mastery hovered his ideal of the serious writer committed to mediating between inner vision and audience response.

The themes of fidelity and solidarity are as central to Conrad's vocation as they are to his fiction. Fidelity demanded a romantic sincerity, keeping faith with his own standards; solidarity required a connection to a community. He found that solidarity was the more elusive objective. As he wrote in 1892: "One quickly gets to know oneself. The difficulty comes in knowing others."[7] In addition to the difficulty of finding his audience, in 1895 Conrad expressed a deep rhetorical despair about communicating with any reader: "No man's light is good to any of his fellows. That's my creed—from beginning to end. Thats [sic] my view of life—a view that rejects all formulas dogmas and principles of other people's making. These are only a web of illusions. We are too varied. Another man's truth is only a dismal lie to me.... You can see now how little anything I may say is worth to anybody."[8] Although comparable skepticism led other writers to invent forms as idiosyncratic as their experiences, Conrad tried to express his vision as comprehensibly as possible.

Despite his awareness of the difficulty, if not the impossibility, of being understood, he did not relinquish this goal. In contrast to Victorian novelists' assumption of an intimate relationship with readers, his starting point was the fundamental isolation of the individual. No matter how faithfully he rendered his vision, no matter how scrupulously he tried to make the reader see as he did, Conrad doubted that sincerity alone would lead to solidarity. Beyond knowing oneself, Conrad was committed to conveying his knowledge to readers. As he wrote a friend while working on *The Nigger of the "Narcissus,"* "for one writes only half the book; the other half is with the reader."[9] Conrad tried to meet the reader halfway.

To know his audience better, Conrad turned to publishers for advice. His first submission, *Almayer's Folly*, led him to Edward Garnett, then a reader for T. Fisher Unwin. Unwin's nephew described the typical path of an unsolicited manuscript through readers to his uncle: "The 'discoveries' were Edward Garnett's and W. H. Chesson's, but to T. Fisher Unwin must be given the credit both for employing them and acting upon their advice. . . . T. F. U. always believed that if a book had quality it would make its way, whether the author was known or not."[10] Conrad's work impressed both readers, and Unwin confirmed their judgment with an offer. Conrad's report of his first meeting with Garnett portrays the publisher's reader as a middleman between art and money. Assuming a tone of mockery, Conrad wrote his aunt:

> "We are paying you very little," he told me, "but, remember, dear Sir, that you are unknown and your book will appeal to a very limited public. Then there is the question of taste. Will the public like it? We are risking something also. We are publishing you in a handsome volume at six shillings, and you know that whatever we bring out always receives serious critical attention in the literary journals. . . . Write something shorter—same type of thing—for our Pseudonym Library, and if it suits us, we shall be very happy to be able to give you a much better cheque."[11]

Despite the tone and the exaggeration (he never wrote for the Pseudonym Library market), Conrad explains the economics of publishing accurately. He realized that he had to accept low offers to enter the literary market. If his first books attracted critical attention, he would be able to use good reviews to raise his price.

Garnett's version of their meeting emphasizes Conrad's willingness to defer to the editor's professional opinion. Garnett recalled that when he read a draft of *Almayer's Folly*, he was "enthralled by the strange atmosphere and poetic vision," but he criticized the characterization of Willems.[12] Conrad welcomed his suggestions and revised several passages accordingly. Although Garnett represented the publisher, Conrad had to remind Garnett that sales were as important to him as art was. Garnett assured Conrad that it was a "necessity for a writer to follow his own path and disregard the public's taste." Conrad, however, disdained such idealism: "I *won't* live in an attic!"[13] This anecdote illustrates a sympathy for artists typical of editors and publishers. Garnett, though he represented the publisher's interests, idealized the independence the writer enjoyed, but Conrad, the artist, sought a secure place in society.

Garnett's support and advice were crucial to Conrad's literary development. Conrad's letters to him from 1895 to 1899 combine praise, gratitude, and dependence. Even discounting much of this as flattery, one feels Conrad's indebtedness. Mentor, critic, agent, conscience—Garnett was all these. In Garnett, Conrad found an ideal reader: "To be read—as you do me the honour to read me—is an ideal experience—and the experience of an ideal..."[14] Eager for Garnett's comments, Conrad besieged him for criticism and praise. When the former came, he chafed but usually followed Garnett's advice. When the latter arrived, Conrad waxed ecstatic and begged for reassurance that the compliments were sincere.

As Conrad's "ideal" reader, Garnett helped him learn how to reach the ordinary reader. Conrad asked him, "Am I mindful enough of Your teaching—of Your expoundings of the ways of the reader?"[15] Garnett never told Conrad what to write. His role was to provide feedback. He might identify passages that were unclear, inconsistent, unconvincing, or tedious, but only Conrad could rewrite them. Garnett also encouraged Conrad, assuring him that *Almayer's Folly* was both good and likely to be popular: "I think it will strike the Public too (the great gross Public that you accuse me of knowing!) as very interesting and very fresh."[16] Conrad sought Garnett's advice to advance his career, certainly, but he did not see his desire to reach an audience as a betrayal of his art. He respected Garnett's integrity too much to suspect him of serving the publisher's interest at the expense of the author's. Conrad revised his work in response to Garnett's literary and commercial advice because he felt that it would improve his books.

When Conrad could not please Garnett, however, he invoked romantic ideas of the spontaneous origin of art to justify himself. He protested that he could not rewrite the twenty-fourth chapter of *An Outcast of the Islands*, though he saw its faults: "Nothing can unmake my mistake. I shall try—but I shall try without faith, because all my work is produced unconsciously (so to speak) and I cannot meddle to any purpose with what is within myself—I am sure you understand what I mean.—It isn't in me to improve what has got itself written."[17] Although Conrad tried to mitigate Garnett's disapproval by attributing his work to an unconscious source, this was not Conrad's final word. His next paragraph begins, "Still with your help I may try. All the paragraphs marked by you to that effect shall be cut out."[18]

Working with Garnett, Conrad learned that sincere expression of sincere impressions did not necessarily produce a reciprocal response. Conrad struggled to cast his vision in a form that would produce the effect he sought on the reader. He described his dissatisfaction with the manuscript of *Outcast* in terms of his failure to achieve the rhetorical effect he intended: "I had some hazy idea that in the first part I would present to the reader the impression of the sea—the ship—the seamen. But I doubt having conveyed anything but the picture of my own folly—I doubt the sincerity of my own impressions."[19] Conrad respected the reader's response as the test of the writer's sincerity. Sincerity was to be measured by the rhetorical success of producing an impression of sincerity on the reader; the reader's judgment validated the writer's authenticity.

Flaubert's model of the author as professional also gave Conrad an argument to excuse delays and ask for more money. Like a lawyer billing for his time, he equated the value of his work with the amount of labor expended. Urging Unwin to get as much as possible for serial rights of the unfinished manuscript of "The Rescue," Conrad first defended the sincerity of the work and then asked to be compensated for the difficulty of producing it: "Bad or good I cannot be ashamed of what is produced in perfect single mindedness—I cannot be ashamed of those things that are like fragments of my innermost being produced for the public gaze." Then he switched to another argument: "But I must live. I don't care much where I appear since the acceptance of such stories is not based upon their artistic worth.... And if you knew the wear and tear of my writing you would understand my desire for some return."[20] Buttressing romantic self-exposure with Flaubertian wear and tear, this plea must be set against his cynical estimate only a year later of another writer's attempt to use it: "But it comes to this, if his point of view is accepted, that having suffered is sufficient excuse for the production of rubbish. Well! It may be true too. I may yet make my profit of that argument."[21] These inconsistent arguments reflect competing ideologies of authorship at the time.

While Garnett embodied Conrad's sense of his audience in the years of his apprenticeship, a turning point came when Conrad was writing *The Nigger of the "Narcissus."*[22] Still confessing his doubts to Garnett, Conrad introduced a new tone of intransigence, which he reinforced by gradually sending Garnett less copy. At the end of 1896, he wrote his editor: "It is as if I had broken with my conscience, quarreled with the inward voice."[23] He followed this apology with an assertion of confidence in his new work: "Of course nothing can alter the course of the "Nigger." Let it be unpopularity if it *must* be. But it seems to me that the thing—precious as it is to me—is trivial enough on the surface to have some charms for the man in the street. As to lack of incident, well—it's life."[24] Still concerned with the "man in the street," he nevertheless defended his own judgment.

Conrad asked twice as much for *The Nigger of the "Narcissus"* as he had been paid before. Having published Conrad's previous books at a loss, Unwin balked. Booksellers bought all 1100 copies of the first edition of *Almayer's Folly*, but despite favorable reviews, the books sold slowly. Nevertheless, Unwin continued to back his judgment with money. He published Conrad's next book, *An Outcast of the Islands*, and wanted to buy *The Nigger of the "Narcissus"* as well. Conrad, however, decided to respond to an inquiry he had received from Smith, Elder & Co., though their offer was no better than that of Unwin. Garnett urged Conrad to seek another publisher or an agent. Conrad submitted the new book to William Heinemann & Co. Here Garnett acted as Conrad's friend and agent rather than as Unwin's employee. Garnett edited the manuscript of *The Nigger of the "Narcissus"* and persuaded Sidney Pawling to accept it for Heinemann. Garnett also persuaded William Blackwood to publish it serially in *Blackwood's Magazine*. Gratefully, Conrad wrote Garnett: "You sent me to Pawling—You sent me to Blackwoods—when are You going to send me to heaven?"[25] In addition to offering better terms than Unwin for *The Nigger of the "Narcissus,"* Pawling sold the serial rights to *The Rescue* in Great Britain and the United States for the respectable sum of £250, and Conrad expected another £100 for the still-unfinished book.[26]

Unwin was still planning to publish *Tales of Unrest* to capitalize on the success of *The Nigger of the "Narcissus,"* but Conrad was outraged that Unwin might injure Heinemann's sales. If Unwin had published both books, no conflict would have occurred, yet Conrad called Unwin a "scoundrel": "The man is unsafe and I am a fool when dealing with such a type for I can't understand it."[27] He asked Unwin to delay publication, and Unwin agreed to wait. Despite losses on earlier books, Conrad's defection to Heinemann, and the burden of trying to sell short stories instead of a novel, Unwin complied with Conrad's requests. His reward was Conrad's self-righteous indignation at the publisher's materialism. From Unwin's point of view, his investment in Conrad's early, unprofitable books was lost when Conrad decided to leave him at the first sign of a better offer. Seeing the early promise in *Almayer's Folly* and *An Outcast of the Islands*, Unwin had both commercial and aesthetic reasons to continue to support Conrad, though not as lavishly as Conrad demanded.

Conrad was aware of the contradictions of the literary marketplace, and he was professional enough to assess his prospects accurately. He understood that the fragmentation of the reading public created several markets. Analyzing his position in 1898, after the publication of *The Nigger of the "Narcissus,"* he distinguished his own viable public from both a wide audience and a coterie:

I have some—literary—reputation but the future is anything
but certain, for I am not a popular author and probably I never
shall be. That does not sadden me at all, for I have never had
the ambition to write for the all-powerful masses. I haven't the
taste for democracy—and democracy hasn't the taste for me.
I have gained the appreciation of a few select spirits and I do
not doubt I shall be able to create a public for myself, limited
it is true, but one which will permit me to earn my bread. I do
not dream of fortune; besides, one does not find it in an ink-
well. But I confess to you I dream of peace, a little reputation,
and the rest of my life devoted to the service of Art and free
from material worries.[28]

He establishes his serious aesthetic aspirations by disavowing
sales in favor of critical esteem. Nevertheless, his dream of success embraces both art and money.

Despite his clear-sighted description of the literary market,
Conrad yearned for the fame and fortune his predecessors had
achieved: "Now, note the inconsequence of the human animal:
I want to rush into print whereby my sentimentalism, my incorrect attitude to life—all I wish to hide in the wilds of Essex—shall
be disclosed to the public gaze! Do I do it for money? Chi lo sà! Perhaps. Or no!—it would be too indecent. I am in a bad way. Now if
I could only attain to become (is that English?) to become a minor
Thackeray decency would be preserved and shekels gathered at
the same time."[29] Although Thackeray could gather shekels without compromising his standards, Conrad increasingly felt that he
had to choose between them. Assessing the relationship between
popularity and literary value in 1898, Conrad dismissed writers
who were merely popular: "Grant Allen's *Woman Who Did* . . . had
a kind of success, of curiosity mostly and that only among the
philistines—the sort of people who read Marie Corelli and Hall
Caine. Neither of these writers belongs to literature. All three
are very popular with the public—and they are also puffed in the
press. There are no lasting qualities in their work. The thought
is commonplace and the style (?) without any distinction. They
are popular because they express the common thought, and the
common man is delighted to find himself in accord with people

he supposes distinguished."[30] Conrad proceeded to contrast such writers with those he admired: Rudyard Kipling, J. M. Barrie, George Meredith, Turgenev, George Moore, T. Watts-Dunton, and H. G. Wells—authors who were both critically acclaimed and economically successful. Although Conrad was contemptuous of the broad popular audience, he also dreaded writing for a coterie. He believed that if his writing had "lasting qualities," it would earn him both critical recognition and a livelihood.

Conrad aspired to the consistent productivity of the professional. He did not regard writing as inevitably unreliable. He usually blamed himself for his writing blocks, seeing them as character defects. He knew the value of skill and steadiness—traits esteemed by his period but rarely associated with genius. In 1905 he distanced himself from the romantic image of the artist: "I own to a, not I hope very peculiar, dislike of falling, even by the remotest appearance, into the class of those disorderly talents whose bohemianism, irregularity and general irresponsibility of conduct are neither in my tradition and my training nor in my character."[31] Regarding work as an expression of character, Conrad tried to approach writing in a workmanlike way.

Conrad attracted a discriminating public, but he sought payment on a scale only popular novelists attained. The profitable market for romance, mystery, adventure, and escape novels made so many inferior writers rich that Conrad and others with artistic aspirations felt underpaid. Although highbrow writers defined their art in opposition to popular fiction, they nevertheless resented the fact that less skilful writers earned more than they did. As much as he disdained this equation of aesthetic worth and market value, he did not consider esteem alone adequate recompense. It was hard to be content with the income that the literate minority audience provided. Instead of writing only for the elite minority audience and accepting the income it provided, Conrad tried to expand his audience.

In addition to the professional question of craftsmanship and the practical question of earning a living, an audience was essential to Conrad's art. In the 1897 preface to *The Nigger of the "Narcissus"* he announced: "My task which I am trying to achieve is, by the power of the written word to make you hear, to make you feel—it is, before all, to make you *see*."[32] His editor persuaded him to delete an even more emphatic statement of his desire to communicate with his reader: "And, after all, everyone desires to be understood."[33] Conrad connected this rhetorical aim to the romantic value of sincerity: "In a single-minded attempt of that kind, if one be deserving and fortunate, one may perchance attain to such clearness of sincerity that at last the presented vision of regret or pity, of terror or mirth, shall awaken in the hearts of the beholders that feeling of unavoidable solidarity...which binds men to each other and all mankind to the visible world."[34] Conrad stipulates a practical test of sincerity—producing a response of solidarity in the reader. The alternative view that the writer's sincerity alone guaranteed the quality of his work too easily justified the kind of writing that Conrad's pride in his craft made him disdain.

When strong critical acclaim for *The Nigger of the "Narcissus"* failed to generate commensurate sales, Conrad's confidence in the public's judgment faltered. Telling a friend about the reviews, he described his rhetorical dilemma at the end of 1897: "When writing one thinks of half-a-dozen (at least I do) men or so—and if these are satisfied and take the trouble to say it in so many words then no writer deserves a more splendid recompense. On the other hand there is the problem of the daily bread which can not be solved by praise—public or private."[35] Painfully aware of a dearth of readers, Conrad made two important rhetorical decisions. He narrowed his target audience to a particular group embodied in the readership of *Blackwood's Magazine* (or "Maga"), and in 1898 he introduced Marlow as a narrator in "Youth." After buying the serial rights to *The Nigger of the "Narcissus,"* William Blackwood replaced Garnett as Conrad's practical and ideal reader, and "Maga" gave Conrad an audience he understood. As he recalled in 1911, "One was in decent company there and had a good sort of public. There isn't a single club and messroom and man-of-war in the British Seas and Dominions which hasn't its copy of Maga—not to speak of all the Scots in all parts of the world."[36] Imagining particular readers, Conrad was able to expand his audience. Ian Watt links Conrad's familiarity with "Maga" to the creation of Marlow: "The first Marlow story, 'Youth,' was also the first story which Conrad ever wrote with a particular group of readers—that of *Blackwood's*—in mind. This defined audience may have given Conrad the initial psychological impetus towards dramatising a fictional situation in which a narrator rather like Conrad addresses an audience rather like that of *Blackwood's*."[37] Marlow helped Conrad control the relationship between narrator and reader that was fundamental to Flaubert's model of the art novel. In addition to Marlow's formal value, the use of an embedded narrator served a rhetorical purpose for Conrad.[38] Just as Conrad found that he had to conceive of his audience narrowly, so Marlow specifies his audience in the text. While Conrad's actual readership has always been far broader than the audience Marlow stipulates, imagining particular narrators and readers helped Conrad make rhetorical decisions.

In the preface to *The Nigger of the "Narcissus"* Conrad states that his goal was to write honestly about what he knew intimately, yet he was so concerned with rhetorical effect that he was willing to alter his ideas, even distort them, to make them seem true to the reader. As he wrote Garnett in 1901, "Every truth requires some pretence to make it live."[39] Discussing technique with John Galsworthy, he observed, "And conviction is found (for others—not for the author) only in certain contradictions and irrelevancies to the general conception of character (or characters) and of the subject."[40] In 1900 he explained to Blackwood that he shaped the ending of *Lord Jim* with an idea of the reader's comprehension in mind: "It is my opinion that in the working out of the catastrophe psychologic disquisition should have no place. The reader ought to know enough by that time."[41] Comparing *Lord Jim* to "Youth" and "Heart of Darkness," Conrad again linked his rhetorical and aesthetic intentions:

> The structure of it is a little loose—this however need not detract from its interest—from the "general reader" point of view. The question of *art* is so endless, so involved and so obscure that one is tempted to turn one's face resolutely away from it. I've certainly an idea—apart from the idea and the subject of the story—which guides me in my writing, but I would be hard put to it if requested to give it out in the shape of a

fixed formula. After all in this as in every other human endeav-our one is answerable only to one's conscience.[42]

Pulled in two directions, Conrad asserted his interest in the "general reader" yet also insisted that he wrote for his own conscience. Conrad wanted the income of popular novelists to buy time to write the kind of complex work that appealed to a minority audience, but he dared not hope for commercial success from *Lord Jim*: "One decent success with a book would give me a chance to breathe freely. But will it ever come? I fear that from this ... vol. I must not expect relief."[43]

David Meldrum, who was Blackwood's literary adviser, believed that Conrad would be worth supporting. Meldrum's report on *Lord Jim* stated: "commercially speaking, it is good, I think..."[44] Sales justified Meldrum's opinion. The first edition of 2100 copies sold out, and two months later a second impression of 1050 copies was ordered.[45] Meldrum assured Blackwood that "Conrad is a man whose coming into his own may take very long but is bound to result one day..."[46] A few weeks later he added: "I wish I could believe that he would ever be 'popular' in the popular sense, but he is too good for that. On the other hand, it would seem that over 'Lord Jim' he is coming into his own quicker than so 'unfashionable' and clever an author his [has] any right to expect in these days..."[47] Meldrum's assessment recognizes that Conrad was successful with a discriminating minority audience, smaller than a popular audience but larger than a coterie.

Lord Jim received the kind of critical acclaim Conrad was beginning to expect: "If Jim has any selling success (which I doubt) I would have a clear road to run after the end of the *Rescue*. Otherwise I can see I shall have a difficult existence before me."[48] The novel's appeal to a discriminating audience was not the least of its attractions. An unsigned notice in *The Manchester Guardian* began:

> Mr. Joseph Conrad's work has long been known to novel readers who search for their literature, and to them the publication of *Lord Jim* may rank as a memorable event. It is not to be accepted easily, it cannot be read in a half dose, and by the

great public which multiplies editions it may remain neglected or unknown. Yet it is of such remarkable originality and merit that one may look for an emphasis of critical opinion which, as in the case of Mr. Meredith, can force a great reputation in the face of popular apathy or distaste.[49]

The reviewer pays tribute to serious fiction's ability to command a durable audience, if not a popular one. Writing in 1900, the reviewer expresses the period's dichotomy between a "great public" and a discriminating audience. Critical acclaim had economic value too. Such praise was enough to convince Blackwood to continue to lend Conrad money.

Conrad learned to use his reputation to increase his price. In 1902 he wrote to George Blackwood: "I am read for my quality and cannot regard anything else. My quality is my truth. The rest may go."[50] Writing to a businessman, Conrad adopts a professional tone, stressing his ability to maintain the quality of his art as if it were a product. When pressed to deliver his manuscript, however, Conrad looked for excuses. He protested that the example of Victorian novelists placed an unfair burden on him. Comparing himself to great Victorians, he defended his length and complexity, yet he pleaded for time by calling himself a modern:

> I am long in my development. What of that? Is not Thackeray's penny worth of mediocre fact drowned in an ocean of twaddle? And yet he lives. And Sir Walter, himself, was not the writer of concise anecdotes I fancy. And G. Elliot [*sic*]—is she as swift as the present public (incapable of fixing its attention for five consecutive minutes) requires us to be at the cost of all honesty, of all truth, and even the most elementary conception of art? But these are great names. I don't compare myself with them. I am *modern*, and I would rather recall Wagner the musician and Rodin the Sculptor who both had to starve a little in their day—and Whistler the painter who made Ruskin the critic foam at the mouth with scorn and indignation. They too have arrived. They had to suffer for being "new."[51]

Driven to contradiction, Conrad demanded as much time as the Victorians had, yet he aligned himself with the moderns who sacrifice popularity for art. He admitted that contemporary readers lacked the Victorians' patience, yet he invoked the romantic model of the artist as martyr whose poverty and suffering were the penalty for being original. He also asserted that as a professional author he was confident that the quality of his work would ultimately win an audience large enough to justify the publisher's concessions.

Conrad's assertion proved true. Six months later Meldrum confirmed the lasting value of Conrad's work in a letter to Blackwood: "I am especially glad about 'Youth.' But I knew Conrad was good—in fact 'Youth' I hold to be the most notable book we have published since George Eliot, and so do other judges. 'Lord Jim' and 'Youth' will go on selling for twenty years, I have no doubt; and it will become a question soon whether they ought not to be put in more popular—say 3/6d—form, like 'Ships.' That appears to be the recognised method with the works of men of his high, tho' not popular, repute."[52] If not bestsellers, his novels justified themselves commercially as steady sellers.

Conrad's career stabilized in 1899 when he put his work in the hands of the literary agent J. B. Pinker. Agents were a recent addition to the literary marketplace. They helped authors deal with the ideological dichotomy between art and money by negotiating frankly with publishers. Overcoming their initial reluctance to pay the percentage that agents charged, authors soon saw the benefit of having an advocate who was not embarrassed to discuss payment. Publishers initially opposed agents for the same reason, but as major writers increasingly employed intermediaries, publishers not only accepted agents but began to rely on their recommendations. The bond between agent and author replaced the personal relationship between publisher and author. Pinker took charge of Conrad's finances to free him to write. To support him until there was a completed manuscript to sell, Pinker paid him per 1000 words submitted each week. Permitting Pinker to sell everything as he thought best, Conrad gained a measure of freedom from financial worry. He continued to promise Pinker salable work but still could not control its length or complexity. At the same time that he was assuring Pinker that he would meet completion dates with commercial novels, in letters to his friends he expressed doubts about finishing or selling current work. His characteristic pattern was to develop an idea for a short story, promising Pinker that there would soon be something simple to sell. Inevitably, the idea would seize him, complicate itself, and require thousands of words to work out. However differently they are judged, *The Secret Agent* and *Under Western Eyes* developed the same way that *Lord Jim* was written. As Conrad said in 1907, "I am long because my thought is always multiple..."[53] Despite the pressure of debt, Conrad could not stop elaborating. Finishing quickly was in his financial interest, yet length was also an asset because novels brought in more money than stories.

Frustrated that there was no direct correlation between talent and income, Conrad periodically complained that he was unable to realize either his aesthetic or his rhetorical intentions. Of his forthcoming volumes of stories, one for Blackwood, one for Heinemann, he said in 1902: "I don't believe either in their popularity or in their merit."[54] Seeking refuge in the model of the writer as suffering artist, he wrote that "one writes for oneself even when one writes to live and in the hope of being read by an immortal multitude"; the author's "solitary thought cannot be imparted to a public."[55] Yet two years later he chided H. G. Wells (of all people) for deliberately limiting his public:

> Why should you say that you write only for people who think this or that: Who feel this or the other thing? And if you even think so—and so intend—there is no necessity to *say* so. That's what I mean by saying that such a declaration serves your sincerity at the expense of the truth—which is in you to expand and propagate. After all, why should you preach to people already convinced? That sort of thing leads only to a sort of high priesthood in a clique and it should be left to people who seek simply the satisfaction of their vanity. It is just to the unbelievers that you should preach; and believe me that no one is so benighted (emotionally or rationally) not to be spoken to with some effect by *him* who can speak.[56]

Conrad contrasts sincerity (what the author feels) with truth (what the reader can be made to feel). Instead of addressing a coterie of acolytes, he embraced the rhetorical goal of changing readers.

Publishers sustained Conrad in his most prolific period. Frederick R. Karl characterizes Pawling's sale of the still-unfinished
manuscript of *The Rescue* as "a sudden boost" when Conrad
was working on *Lord Jim* and "Heart of Darkness."[57] Conrad
received £250 for serial rights to *Lord Jim* and expected another
£100 for the book.[58] From 1898 to 1899 he wrote "Youth" and
"Heart of Darkness." *Lord Jim* was finished in 1900, and *Nostromo* was published in 1904. Less than a decade after publishing
his first book, *Almayer's Folly*, in 1895, Conrad was widely recognized as a great writer. In 1904 Sir Hugh Clifford wrote in the
North American Review, "Mr. Conrad's books, I say it without
fear of contradiction, have no counterparts in the entire range
of English literature. . . . His is a notable achievement, a tremen-
dous success."[59] Similarly, in 1908, John Galsworthy wrote in
Fortnightly Review, "The writing of these ten books is probably
the only writing of the last twelve years that will enrich the
English language to any great extent."[60] In 1912 James Huneker
proclaimed that Conrad was "the only man in England to-day
who belongs to the immortal company of Meredith, Hardy,
and Henry James."[61] Conrad's rapid rise indicates how quickly
he mastered the literary marketplace to achieve financial and
critical success.

Critical acclaim and publishers' support did not end Conrad's difficulties. As he became more confident, he demanded
more money and more time. In contrast to Victorian writers
who earned literary independence through sales, Conrad had
more acrimonious relationships with publishers after receiving
critical recognition. He complained that he could not write fast
enough to support himself: "my inability to work fast enough to
get my living. It is ridiculous and sad and wearisome, and that it
is true does not make it any less offensive."[62] Conrad wrote rapidly enough to produce a book a year, more than most popular
writers, but he wanted more money than this pace could generate. Karl justly observes, "The money that came in was certainly
not commensurate with Conrad's worth as an artist, but on the
other hand, it could have been sufficient with more careful attention to outlay."[63] In short, his work appealed to a large enough
public to support him. He reached a viable public, if not a mass

audience, and publishers were willing to subsidize him because they expected his work to sell in the future.

Despite publishers' support, Conrad lost control of his work by living on advances. When publishers granted his requests for money, Conrad felt pressure as well as gratitude. Loans burdened him with the obligation to produce copy quickly. Mounting debts and expenses caused him to agree to deadlines he could not meet. Working under financial pressure, Conrad considered his later work inferior. He felt that he was succumbing to the "Grub Street" aspect of publishing. Depressed and unsure of himself, he wrote Garnett in 1902: "My expression has become utterly worthless: it is time for the money to come rolling in."[64] The book he was writing at the time, however, was *Nostromo*. Similarly, apologizing for the faults of *Under Western Eyes*, he told John Galsworthy that "good work takes time; ... This I could not afford to do. I went on the obvious lines and on these lines I developed my narrative to give it some sort of verisimilitude. In other words I offered to sell my soul for half a crown—and now I have neither the soul nor the coin—for the novel is not finished yet. A fool's bargain ..."[65] Later Conrad blamed his dissatisfaction with the progress of *Victory* on his need for money, telling Bertrand Russell: "seduced by the tempter's gold, I allowed myself to be drawn into 'fixing' a date for delivery of an unfinished novel—for the first time in my life."[66] Although it was hardly the first time, Conrad used the dichotomy of art and money to excuse work he feared would fail. Conrad assumed that others would understand that financial need caused him to compromise the quality of his work.

Saying that he wrote for money was an excuse, but saying that he wrote for readers was part of Conrad's aesthetic. Describing the writer's relationship to society in 1905, he insisted on the writer's obligation to readers. The novelist's task, he wrote, was to mediate between his imagination and his audience's experience: "In truth every novelist must begin by creating for himself a world, great or little, in which he can honestly believe. This world cannot be made otherwise than in his own image: it is fated to remain individual and a little mysterious, and yet it must resemble something already familiar to the experience, the thoughts and the sensations of his readers."[67] His rationale appears in advice to another writer as he argues that his suggestions are justified by the public's needs: "You may not like a full close—but the ordinary reader expects it. And the ordinary reader also wants the nail hit on the head before his eyes very simply in order that he should *see* the nail. Later on you will realize the inconceivable stupidity of the common reader—the man who forks out the half-crown."[68] This advice was not simply a concession to increase sales; it also reflected his continuing effort to communicate with his audience. Throughout his career Conrad believed what he told Garnett in 1911: "control of the public's (audience, readers) attention is in a sense the beginning and end of artistic method."[69] Conrad inveighed against the public, but he could not renounce it. He wrote John Galsworthy in 1910:

> A public is not to be found in a class, caste, clique or type. The public is (or are?) individuals. Le *public introuvable* is only *introuvable* simply because it is all humanity. And no artist can give it what it wants because humanity doesn't know what it wants. But it will swallow everything. It will swallow Hall Caine and John Galsworthy, Victor Hugo and Martin Tupper. It is an ostrich, a clown, a giant, a bottomless sack. It is sublime. It has apparently no eyes and no entrails, like a slug, and yet it can weep and suffer. It has swallowed Christianity, Buddhism, Mahomedanism, and the Gospel of Mrs. Eddy. And it is perfectly capable, from the height of its secular stability, of looking down upon the artist as a mere windlestraw![70]

The indifference of the marketplace was far more frustrating than its preferences. It would buy anything. To reach a wide public, he tried to simplify his work, yet this strategy did not necessarily produce simpler novels. Conrad vilified the kind of writing that was merely popular but never disdained popularity itself.

Suffering great ambivalence while writing *Chance*, Conrad was contradictory in his letters. He alternated defensive warnings with promises that it would be salable, if not popular:

> *Chance* itself will be altogether different in tone and treatment [from *The Secret Agent*] of course, but it will be salable I believe. By the end of September you will have a really considerable lot

of it to show. Of course it will not be on popular lines. Nothing of mine can be, I fear. But even Meredith ended by getting his sales. Now, I haven't Meredith's delicacy, and that's a point in my favour. I reckon I may make certain of the support of the Press for the next few years. The young men who are coming in to write criticisms are in my favour so far. At least all of whom I've heard are. I don't get in the way of established reputations.... There is nothing in me but a turn of mind, which, whether valuable or worthless, cannot be imitated.[71]

The last sentence accurately describes the range of possibilities open to most authors. Aiming for a wider audience than his earlier work had reached, Conrad tried to adopt popular strategies, such as an appealing title, a young girl as subject, and an agreeable ending. He admitted changing the ending to make it "nicer": "I am thinking of the public."[72] Garnett cynically remarked that despite eulogistic notices, probably the "figure of the lady on the 'jacket' of *Chance* (1914) did more to bring the novel into popular favor than the long review by Sir Sidney Colvin in the *Observer*."[73] Conrad also disparaged the book. After it appeared, he dismissed a friend's praise, "I am glad you find Chance tolerable. I don't."[74] Although Conrad felt that his deliberate efforts to make the novel popular diminished its aesthetic value, reviewers praised its attention to form and narrative technique. It was judged one of his most modern, and C. E. Montague wrote that in *Chance* Conrad carried his narrative technique "further than ever."[75] Conrad believed that he had copied popular models, but reviewers discerned aesthetic complexity.

   Chance rewarded Conrad's publisher and agent for their confidence in him. The English edition sold 13,000 copies in two years. Conrad was proud of the fourfold increase in his usual sales figures: "Seven editions of *Chance*=12000 copies (to date)—which for England is very good and for me something absolutely fabulous."[76] *Chance* won immediate critical acclaim as well as high sales, yet Conrad wrote Galsworthy: "How I would have felt about it ten or eight years ago I can't say. Now I can't even pretend I am elated. If I had *Nostromo*, *The Nigger* or *Lord Jim* in my desk or only in my head I would feel differently no doubt. As to the commercial side: Methuen made a ridiculous advertising splash (which was jeered at in the provincial press) and in the sixth week stopped advertising. They confess to 12,500 copies printed...but how much of that is sold I don't know."[77] He regretted that the financial benefits of reputation were not retroactive. Judging his earlier books superior, he felt cheated of his proper remuneration, which would have made both his domestic and artistic life easier. Despite his regret, he was able to use his aesthetic reputation to raise his price. Negotiating the price for serializing *Chance*, Conrad told the new editor of the *English Review* that in 1899: "B'wood's Maga: accepted my *Lord Jim* a much closer knit and more complicated work with a remote psychology—sailors, Malays, and so on—whereas *Chance* is English in personages and locality, much easier to follow and understand. It was a very new form then; and yet old Maga had the audacity to take it up when we all were much less advanced than we are now and Conrad was a practically unknow[n] writer."[78] The superior tone, the guarantee of propriety, the confidence in the value of his work were all elements of his attitude to his audience. Here Conrad separated each book and attempted to put a price on it according to its merits, but his bargaining indicates that he knew his works acquired a cumulative value greater than any single work possessed. The reason he was able to earn so much for his later work was that his earlier work was so highly acclaimed.

As Conrad's audience increased, he invoked the myth of the artist's indifference to the public more tendentiously. Such romanticized pronouncements became more frequent as he tailored his work to suit "average" readers. In contrast to his initial unwillingness to "live in an attic," he glorified suffering now that he was out of danger: "Suffering is an attribute[,] almost a condition of greatness, of devotion, of an altogether self-forgetful sacrifice to that remorseless fidelity to the truth of his own sensations at whatever [*sic*] cost of pain or contumely which for me is the whole credo of the artist."[79] Similarly, in contrast to his frank concern with money while struggling with *The Nigger of the "Narcissus," Lord Jim,* and *Nostromo,* in 1907 while working on *Chance* and deliberately writing for a wide audience, Conrad claimed that he was not thinking of money: "While I am writing

I am not thinking of money. I couldn't if I would. The thing once written I admit that I want to see it bring in as much money as possible and to have as much *effect* as possible."[80] Aware of the dichotomy between popularity and quality, he insisted that his desire for sales did not require any compromise of artistic integrity.

Conrad's 1920 preface to a new edition of *Chance* reaffirmed his rhetorical intentions, despite his increased awareness of the difficulty of achieving them. Echoing his preface to *The Nigger of the "Narcissus,"* he demonstrated the constancy of his desire to communicate with readers. By 1920, however, popular success made him defensive about this strong rhetorical aim. He correctly anticipated that popularity would make readers think that he had compromised his aesthetic standards for sales. The 1920 preface expresses his unswerving commitment to a constant rhetorical goal, but he adds a more vehement defense of solidarity against the ideology of the artist as professional: "what I always feared most was drifting unconsciously into the position of a writer for a limited coterie; a position which would have been odious to me as throwing a doubt on the soundness of my belief in the solidarity of all mankind in simple ideas and in sincere emotions."[81] Unwilling to accept the limited audience that initially appreciated his vision, he reaffirmed his belief in the solidarity of all mankind and implicitly defended the need to make his work more accessible to reach a wide public.

Conrad's desire for sales was an artistic compulsion as much as a financial necessity. The rhetorical circuit of author, publisher, and reader was as important to the development of his fiction as psychological factors were. Despite anxiety along the way, Conrad attained canonical status and financial security in a relatively short time. The quality of his writing was recognized immediately. Editors and publishers offered advice that helped him realize his aesthetic intentions and build an audience. He was included among the "immortals" of his generation, and his critical reputation brought financial rewards. Thanks to his mastery of the literary marketplace, Conrad's writing career validated the ideals that his fiction embodies: fidelity and solidarity, being true to oneself and true to others.

NOTES

1. George Henry Lewes, *The Principles of Success in Literature* (London and Felling-on-Tyne: Walter Scott Publishing, 1898), 9.

2. Edward Garnett, ed., *Letters from Joseph Conrad, 1895 to 1924* (New York: Bobbs-Merrill, 1928), 25.

3. Frederick R. Karl, *Joseph Conrad: The Three Lives* (New York: Farrar, Straus and Giroux, 1979), 525.

4. Richard Ohmann, "The Shaping of a Canon: U.S. Fiction, 1960–1975," *Critical Inquiry* 10, no.1 (September 1983): 199–223.

5. Pierre Bourdieu, "Flaubert's Point of View," trans. Priscilla Parkhurst Ferguson, *Critical Inquiry* 14, no. 3 (spring 1988): 551.

6. Edward Garnett cautions that Conrad's letters cannot always be taken literally: "I must add a word here about Conrad's play of irony. He was so perfect an artist in the expression of his moods and feelings that it needed a fine ear to seize the blended shades of friendly derision, flattery, self-depreciation, sardonic criticism and affection in his tone" (*Letters from Joseph Conrad*, 20). Specifically, "When Conrad was particularly pleased with his work he pooh-poohed it in his letters—'This is the sort of rot I am writing now,' he says for example about *Heart of Darkness* . . ." (ibid., 27).

7. Conrad to Marguerite Poradowska, 19 October 1892, in *The Collected Letters of Joseph Conrad*, ed. Laurence Davies et al., 9 vols. (Cambridge: Cambridge University Press, 1983–2007), 1: 119.

8. Conrad to Edward Noble, 2 November 1895, in *Collected Letters of Joseph Conrad*, 1: 253.

9. Conrad to Cunninghame Graham, 5 August 1897, in *Collected Letters of Joseph Conrad*, 1: 370.

10. Sir Stanley Unwin, *The Truth about a Publisher* (London: George Allen and Unwin, 1960), 80.

11. Conrad to Poradowska, London, 10 October 1894, in *Collected Letters of Joseph Conrad*, 1: 180.

12. Garnett, *Letters from Joseph Conrad*, 8.

13. Ibid., 9.

14. Conrad to Garnett, 15 March 1895, in *Collected Letters of Joseph Conrad*, 1: 205.

15. Letter dated 13 April 1896, in *Collected Letters of Joseph Conrad*, 1: 273.

16. Garnett, *Letters from Joseph Conrad*, 19.

17. Letter dated 24 September 1895, in *Collected Letters of Joseph Conrad,* 1: 246–47.

18. Ibid., 1: 247.

19. Conrad to Garnett, 10 June 1896, in *Collected Letters of Joseph Conrad,* 1: 287.

20. Letter dated 22 July 1896, in *Collected Letters of Joseph Conrad,* 1: 293.

21. Conrad to Garnett, 11 October 1897, in *Collected Letters of Joseph Conrad,* 1: 395.

22. See also Peter D. McDonald, *British Literary Culture and Publishing Practice, 1880–1914* (Cambridge: Cambridge University Press, 1997), 67. McDonald argues that Conrad pitched the novel to W. E. Henley's circle: "By writing the *Nigger* with an eye on Henley and the *New Review,* Conrad did all he could to safeguard his place in the field, and, when the gamble paid off, he entered his major phase" (67).

23. Letter dated 29 November 1896, in *Collected Letters of Joseph Conrad,* 1: 321.

24. Ibid.

25. Letter dated 28 August 1897, in *Collected Letters of Joseph Conrad,* 1: 378.

26. See Conrad to Spiridion Kliszczewski, 12 April 1898, in *Collected Letters of Joseph Conrad,* 2: 54.

27. Conrad to John Galsworthy, January 1898, in *Collected Letters of Joseph Conrad,* 2: 11.

28. Conrad to the Baroness Janina de Brunnow, 2 October 1897, in *Collected Letters of Joseph Conrad,* 1: 390.

29. Conrad to E. L. Sanderson, 26 March 1897, in *Collected Letters of Joseph Conrad,* 1: 347.

30. Conrad to Aniela Zagórska, 25 December 1898, in *Collected Letters of Joseph Conrad,* 2: 137.

31. Conrad to Edmund Gosse, 19 May 1905, in *Collected Letters of Joseph Conrad,* 3: 248–49.

32. Joseph Conrad, *The Nigger of the "Narcissus"* (New York: Doubleday & Co., 1914), xiv.

33. Conrad to Garnett, 28 August 1897, in *Collected Letters of Joseph Conrad,* 1: 377 n. 2.

34. Conrad, *The Nigger of the "Narcissus,"* xiv.

35. Conrad to Sanderson, 26 December 1897, in *Collected Letters of Joseph Conrad*, 1: 434.

36. Conrad to J. B. Pinker, 12 or 19 November 1911, in *Collected Letters of Joseph Conrad*, 4: 506.

37. Ian Watt, *Conrad in the Nineteenth Century* (Berkeley: University of California Press, 1979), 212.

38. See Fredric Jameson, *The Political Unconscious* (Ithaca, N.Y.: Cornell University Press, 1981), 219–20. Jameson also sees Marlow performing this function but considers it reactionary: "The representational fiction of a storytelling situation organized around Marlow marks the vain attempt to conjure back the older unity of the literary institution" before it was disrupted by "market relations" (219–20).

39. Letter dated 7 August 1901, in *Collected Letters of Joseph Conrad*, 2: 352.

40. Letter dated 11 November 1901, in *Collected Letters of Joseph Conrad*, 2: 359.

41. Letter dated 19 July 1900, in *Collected Letters of Joseph Conrad*, 2: 283.

42. Conrad to William Blackwood, 22 August 1899, in *Collected Letters of Joseph Conrad*, 2: 193–94.

43. Conrad to David S. Meldrum, 3 March 1900, in *Collected Letters of Joseph Conrad*, 2: 254.

44. Meldrum to William Blackwood, 19 July 1900, in *Joseph Conrad: Letters to William Blackwood and David S. Meldrum*, ed. William Blackburn (Durham, N.C.: Duke University Press, 1958), 107.

45. *Joseph Conrad: Letters to William Blackwood and David S. Meldrum*, 116 n. 1.

46. Meldrum to William Blackwood, 3 December 1900, in *Joseph Conrad: Letters to William Blackwood and David S. Meldrum*, 116.

47. Meldrum to William Blackwood, 19 December 1900, in *Joseph Conrad: Letters to William Blackwood and David S. Meldrum*, 122.

48. Conrad to Meldrum, 1 September 1900, in *Collected Letters of Joseph Conrad*, 2: 289.

49. Karl, *Joseph Conrad: The Three Lives*, 509.

50. Letter dated 20 May 1902, in *Collected Letters of Joseph Conrad*, 2: 413.

51. Conrad to William Blackwood, 31 May 1902, in *Collected Letters of Joseph Conrad*, 2: 418.

52. Meldrum to William Blackwood, 19 December 1902, in *Joseph Conrad: Letters to William Blackwood and David S. Meldrum*, 172–73.

53. Conrad to Garnett, 8 October 1907, in *Collected Letters of Joseph Conrad*, 3: 492.

54. Conrad to Garnett, 10 June 1902, in *Collected Letters of Joseph Conrad*, 2: 424.

55. Conrad to H. B. Marriott Watson, 28 January 1903, in *Collected Letters of Joseph Conrad*, 3: 13.

56. Letter dated 19 September 1903, in *Collected Letters of Joseph Conrad*, 3: 63.

57. Karl, *Joseph Conrad: The Three Lives*, 423. Nevertheless, Karl separates Conrad's rhetorical intentions from his aesthetic achievements: "What we are suggesting for Conrad in this period is such an intense immersion in the powers of his own imagination that he left behind all conscious intentions, all statements of motivation, all planned theories of art and his position within it" (451).

58. Conrad to Siridion Kliszczewski, 12 April 1898, in *Collected Letters of Joseph Conrad*, 2: 54.

59. Hugh Clifford, "The Genius of Mr. Joseph Conrad," *North American Review* 571 (June 1904): 843, 852.

60. John Galsworthy, "Joseph Conrad: A Disquisition," *Fortnightly Review* n.s. 83 (April 1908): 630.

61. James Huneker, "A Visit to Joseph Conrad, The Mirror of the Sea" *New York Times Magazine* (17 November 1912): 4.

62. Conrad to Helen Sanderson, 26 September 1899, in *Collected Letters of Joseph Conrad*, 2: 173.

63. Karl, *Joseph Conrad: The Three Lives,* 547.

64. Letter dated 10 June 1902, in *Collected Letters of Joseph Conrad*, 2: 424.

65. Letter dated 30 November 1908, in *Collected Letters of Joseph Conrad*, 4: 155.

66. Letter dated 14 February 1914, in *Collected Letters of Joseph Conrad*, 5: 345.

67. Joseph Conrad, "Books" in *Notes on Life and Letters* (Edinburgh and London: John Grant, 1925), 6.

68. Conrad to Norman Douglas, 29 February 1908, in *Collected Letters of Joseph Conrad*, 4: 52.

69. Letter dated 7 March 1911, in *Collected Letters of Joseph Conrad*, 4: 422.

70. Letter dated 1 November 1910, in *Collected Letters of Joseph Conrad*, 4: 385.

71. Conrad to Pinker, 30 July 1907, in *Collected Letters of Joseph Conrad*, 3: 460.

72. Conrad to Pinker, April 1912, in *Collected Letters of Joseph Conrad*, 5: 49.

73. Garnett, *Letters from Joseph Conrad, 1895 to 1924*, 15.

74. Conrad to Cunninghame Graham, 30 January 1914, in *Collected Letters of Joseph Conrad*, 5: 336.

75. Karl, *Joseph Conrad: The Three Lives*, 743.

76. Conrad to Warrington Dawson, 17 February 1914, in *Collected Letters of Joseph Conrad*, 5: 351.

77. Letter dated 19 March 1914, in *Collected Letters of Joseph Conrad*, 5: 365.

78. Conrad to Austin Harrison, 28 March 1912, in *Collected Letters of Joseph Conrad*, 5: 45.

79. Conrad to Dawson, 20 June 1913, in *Collected Letters of Joseph Conrad*, 5: 239.

80. Conrad to Pinker, 27 September 1907, in *Collected Letters of Joseph Conrad*, 3: 481.

81. Joseph Conrad, *Chance* (Edinburgh and London: John Grant, 1925), viii–ix.

Conrad and Politics

Allan H. Simmons

 Polish Inheritance

Józef Teodor Konrad Korzeniowski was born on 3 December 1857 at Berdichev in Podolia, a part of the Polish Commonwealth that had been appropriated into the Russian Ukraine in 1793. Hence his inheritance was a Poland of the heart rather than a political reality: the Polish Republic would only be restored in 1918 after the First World War. He was the only child of Apollo and Ewelina (Ewa) Korzeniowski, members of the *szlachta* or landowning nobility, whose Nałęcz coat of arms displays a knotted handkerchief to symbolize, as myth has it, the field-dressed wound of a patriotic ancestor.

Both of Conrad's parents were ardent nationalists, and, in October 1861, shortly before Conrad's fourth birthday, Apollo's clandestine political activities led to his arrest by the Russian authorities and imprisonment in the Warsaw Citadel, described by Apollo as "the city's ever-ready machine of destruction, and at the same time an immense dungeon where tzardom buries Polish patriotism,"[1] while Conrad recalled: "in the courtyard of this Citadel—characteristically for our nation—my childhood memories begin."[2] Photographs of Ewa depict her wearing black, emblematic of the state of national mourning. In a letter to Apollo in 1861 she writes: "Everyone is in black here, *even the children*; our little one has been constantly asking to go into mourning."[3] In 1862 the family was exiled to Vologda, 300 miles northeast of Moscow. Ewa, who was sentenced in her own right for conspiring against the state, died in exile, while Apollo Korzeniowski followed her within two years of his release in 1867, leaving the eleven-year-old Conrad an orphan. His father's gravestone bears the inscription: "victim of Muscovite tyranny."

The orphaned Conrad, following his father's coffin through the streets of Cracow, would later remember how the funeral procession provided a focus for patriotic sentiment: "What I saw with my own eyes was the public funeral, the cleared streets, the hushed crowds; but I understood perfectly well that this was a manifestation of the national spirit seizing a worthy occasion. That bareheaded mass of work people, youths of the University, women at the windows, school-boys on the pavement, could have known nothing positive about him except the fame of his fidelity to the one guiding emotion in their hearts" (*PR* x). Unsurprisingly, Conrad inherited what Cedric Watts calls "his father's defiant love of Poland."[4] His only story to deal directly with a Polish subject, "Prince Roman," is based on the true story of Prince Roman Sanguszko, centering on the exploits of a heroic and self-sacrificing aristocrat committed to the struggle for the independence of Poland, "That country which demands to be loved as no other country has ever been loved" (*TH* 51).

Nineteenth-Century Europe

The nineteenth century was the age of the nation-state, when emerging national identities, driven by the belief fostered by the French Revolution that inherited power could be overthrown, found political expression. This expression can be heard, for example, in the music of Smetana and Dvořák in Bohemia (later Czechoslovakia), or Erkel and Bartók in Hungary, where national identity is proclaimed by unlocking and giving voice to the folk heritage that had been long suppressed under, in this case, the Hapsburg Empire, whose authorities spoke only in German. Poland's struggle for independence from Russia, a country Conrad contemptuously described as "Slavo-Tartar Byzantine barbarism,"[5] is thus but one manifestation of the gathering reaction to the established order across Europe. In the face of territorially voracious neighbors, Austria, Prussia, and Russia, through the Partitions of 1772, 1793, and 1795, Poland disappeared as a nation-state—and from the map of Europe—until 11 November 1918, when the reborn independent Poland was proclaimed, with Józef Piłsudski as head of state.

In *A Personal Record* Conrad unreservedly links his family's unhappy fortunes to those of the Polish nation through an account of his maternal great-uncle, Mikołaj Bobrowski. Like many of his compatriots, the idealist Bobrowski enlisted as a wild goose in Napoleon's *Grande Armée*. In a six-year career, that lasted until the emperor's defeat and exile in 1814, he rose to the rank of captain and received the title *chevalier* in the Légion d'honneur, thereby automatically earning Poland's highest military award, the Order Virtuti Militari.[6] Conrad's focus, however, is the disastrous retreat from Moscow in the winter of 1812, during which Bobrowski and his fellow stragglers were reduced to dining on a meal of Lithuanian dog in order to survive. In Conrad's treatment, the anecdote doubles as family inheritance and national parable.

While the Congress of Vienna in 1815 reestablished the old order, the connection forged between national identity and political power proved to be an irresistible driving force behind the nineteenth century's revolutionary movements. For example, in 1848, the year that also saw the publication of Friedrich Engels and Karl Marx's *Communist Manifesto*, revolutions shook Europe. Sparked by rebellions in Palermo and Paris, popular nationalist insurrection spread from Poland in the East to Ireland in the West, as the tremors of political upheaval were felt in Germany, Austria, Belgium, and Switzerland. Although few of these revolutions lasted beyond the end of the year, and, as seen in Prague, retribution could be bloody, it did have important political consequences. Metternich, chancellor of the Austrian Empire fell, as did the "July monarchy" of France's Louis-Philippe.

A map of Europe at mid-century shows how the vast Russian and Austrian empires had swallowed many eastern European "nations," with Germany and Italy divided into numerous petty states dominated by Austria. It was in 1871 that Otto von Bismarck fashioned the nation-state of Germany out of some 300 local political units, some dating from the Holy Roman Empire. Among European countries, only Italy had awaited unity for a comparably long time. If the revolutionary movements of 1848 soon petered out, the impact of both the *Risorgimento* for Italy's unification and the nationalist movement in Germany would be felt long afterwards.

But while the century's revolutionary movements, inspired by newly awakened nationalism, were to lead to a Europe of nation-states, Poland's case was different: hers was a struggle to *reemerge* as a state having been historically subject to foreign rule. In many ways the proverbial Sick Man of Europe, this historic nation failed to win autonomy or independence despite being a persistent thorn in the Russian Empire's side: Poles staged a series of unsuccessful insurrections against foreign domination across the nineteenth century—in 1830–31, 1846, 1848, and in the January uprising of 1863–65. In the light of Conrad's subsequent espousal of British nationality, it is intriguing to find the English Chartist poet, Ernest Jones, in his "March of Freedom" (1848), likening the Whig prime minister, Lord John Russell, to Tsar Nicholas and describing Ireland as "The Poland of the West."[7]

Russia

Conrad's familial and national background left him with a lifelong detestation of Russia and things Russian. In "Autocracy and War," an essay occasioned by the Russo-Japanese War of 1904–5, Russia is "a yawning chasm open between East and West; a bottomless abyss that has swallowed up every hope of mercy, every aspiration towards personal dignity, towards freedom, towards knowledge, every ennobling desire of the heart, every redeeming whisper of conscience" (*NLL* 100). Unsurprisingly, Conrad is often vehement about Poland's separate and distinctively Western traditions. In a late letter to Charles Chassé, one of a number of critics to refer to

Conrad's "Slavonism," Conrad wrote: "it would have been more just to charge me at most with 'Polonism.' Polish temperament, at any rate, is far removed from Byzantine and Asiatic associations." Rather, he continues, "Poland has absorbed Western ideas, adopted Western culture, sympathized with Western ideals and tendencies as much as possible," the country's main task being "the struggle for life against Asiatic despotism at its door."[8]

In time, Conrad's anti-Russian stance would strain his relationship with the Garnetts, who were among his earliest English friends: "Straight from the sea into your arms, as it were," is how he described his relationship with Edward Garnett.[9] Constance Garnett was, and remains, noted for her translations of the major Russian writers, including Turgenev's *A Desperate Character* (1899), which she dedicated to Conrad. For his part, upon receiving a copy of her translation of *The Brothers Karamazov* (1912), Conrad claimed that Dostoyevsky "is too Russian for me. It sounds to me like some fierce mouthings from prehistoric ages" and that his art "does not deserve this good fortune."[10] That said, critics have noted sufficient correspondences between *Crime and Punishment* (1866) and *Under Western Eyes* (1911) to conclude that Conrad's familiarity with Dostoyevsky's novel was such that his own work serves as a kind of corrective to it. Thus, as André Gide recalled, the mere mention of the Russian author's name was sufficient to make Conrad shudder, but as Kirschner puts it, "Conrad's antipathy to Dostoyevsky, like many antipathies, carries a strong suggestion of secret kinship."[11]

Russia comes in for obvious condemnation in Conrad's fiction. In "Heart of Darkness," Kurtz's hopelessly misguided apologist is the Russian harlequin; in *The Secret Agent*, the sinister mastermind behind the plot to blow up the Greenwich Observatory is Mr. Vladimir, a Russian diplomat. But such critiques coexist with Conrad's evenhandedness towards Russians elsewhere. "The Warrior's Soul," for instance, is unexpectedly sympathetic in its treatment of tsarist officers, describing their pity towards Napoleon's exhausted troops. Of *Under Western Eyes*, the most autobiographical of his political novels, he confessed: "I had never been called before to a greater effort of detachment: detachment from all passions, prejudices and even from personal memories"

(*UWE* viii). This did not prevent the ever-sensitive author from rounding on Garnett for his review of the novel:[12] "You are so russianised my dear that you don't know the truth when you see it—unless it smells of cabbage-soup when it at once secures your profoundest respect. I suppose one must make allowances for your position of Russian Embassador [*sic*] to the Republic of Letters."[13] Garnett's memory of this incident is recorded in an essay written a quarter of a century afterward: "I unjustly charged Conrad with putting hatred into the book and after re-reading the story twenty-five years later, I own I was wrong."[14]

Conrad is at his most fiercely denunciatory—and at his most prescient—about things Russian in his nonfiction. In his "Author's Note" to *Under Western Eyes*, for instance, written in 1920 for the "Collected Edition" of his works and in the wake of the Bolshevik Revolution of 1917, he concluded: "The oppressors and the oppressed are all Russians together; and the world is brought once more face to face with the truth of the saying that the tiger cannot change his stripes nor the leopard his spots" (*UWE* x). In "Autocracy and War" (1905) he had prophesied: "In whatever form of upheaval Autocratic Russia is to find her end, it can never be a revolution fruitful of moral consequences to mankind. It cannot be anything else but a rising of slaves," seeing in coming events "nothing more impressive than the convulsions of a colossal body" (*NLL* 102).

Conrad and British Politics

In October 1874, and not quite seventeen years old, Conrad made what he would later call "a, so to speak, standing jump out of his racial surroundings and associations,"[15] traveling to Marseilles and shortly afterward beginning his sea life. The story is well known: after three voyages to the Caribbean in the employ of Delestang et Fils he jumped ship, so to speak, and joined the British Merchant Service in 1878, beginning a career that would span the next decade and a half, during which, "a Polish nobleman, cased in British tar" in his own definition, he would work his way up through the ranks to become "a British master mariner beyond a doubt" (*PR* 120) in 1886, the same year in which he became a naturalized

British subject. Exchanging the French merchant marine for the British had a political dimension: as one of the tsar's subjects Conrad was liable to be called up for military service.

Conrad reveals his earliest political allegiances as Conservative in the letters written to Kliszczewski in late 1885.[16] Among Conrad's earliest writings in English, these date from his service as second mate in the *Tilkhurst* and are written from Singapore and Calcutta. The first, dated 13 October, reveals that he had read the (Conservative) *Daily Telegraph* sent to him by Kliszczewski and was "expecting great things"[17] in the wake of the Liberal government's defeat by a Conservative budget amendment in June 1885. Two months later, on 19 December, he comments on the election of November that year, that yielded a Conservative victory, but with a minority government: "I and the rest of the 'right thinking' have been grievously disappointed by the result of the General Election. The newly enfranchised idiots have satisfied the yearnings of Mr Chamberlain's herd by cooking the national goose according to his recipe....Joy reigns in St Petersburg, no doubt, and profound disgust in Berlin."[18] Looked at pragmatically, it would be surprising if Conrad's political allegiances were not Conservative. As a member of the British Merchant Service, he was part of the great web of communication that assimilated remote areas of the world into the British economy. The empire, the great fact of British life, thus provided him with a living, with security, and with a sense of communal recognition and belonging. And the Conservatives were perceived to be the party of empire. In his "Author's Note" to *Youth*, Conrad describes himself "the spoiled adopted child of Great Britain and even of the Empire" (*Y* x).

William Gladstone's decision to espouse the cause of Home Rule for Ireland split the Liberal Party in 1886 and ushered in, after decades of alternating Liberal and Conservative governments, twenty years of virtually uninterrupted Conservative rule sustained by an anti-Gladstone, anti–Home Rule alliance. At a moment when the empire was the currency of political debate, Gladstonian Liberalism was perceived as anti-imperial. Contemporaneously, the popular press censured the Gladstone government for its failure to save General Charles George Gordon, whose death at Khartoum in 1885 convulsed British society, representing both the death of a popular hero and an example of the failure of the British Empire. In effect, the campaign to avenge Gordon, by destroying the Mahdist revolution, lasted thirteen years, culminating in the Battle of Omdurman in 1898, where an army of some 50,000 desert tribesmen foundered in the face of the professionally trained forces of the greatest empire the world had seen, equipped with the Maxim gun. In a letter to W. E. Henley, of 3 January 1893, Rudyard Kipling noted with mock annoyance that his daughter, Josephine, had been born on 29 December, Gladstone's birthday, adding that if she had been a boy, he would have disposed of her "lest she also should disgrace the Empire."[19] By contrast, Benjamin Disraeli's purchase of shares in the Suez Canal, gaining a controlling interest for Britain, in 1875, and proclaiming Queen Victoria "Empress of India" the following year identified the Conservatives with the empire in the popular imagination.

As Eric Hobsbawm points out, the word "imperialism" first became part of the political and journalistic vocabulary at this point "in the course of arguments about colonial conquest": "Emperors and empires were old, but imperialism was quite new. The word (which does not occur in the writings of Karl Marx, who died in 1883) first entered politics in Britain in the 1870s, and was still regarded as a neologism at the end of that decade. It exploded into general use in the 1890s."[20] The economic and military supremacy that had yielded colonial empires was now systematically translated into formal conquest, annexation, and administration. As the Liberal J. A. Hobson, himself a critic of what he called "immoral" imperialism, put it, by 1900 the word was "on everybody's lips...and used to denote the most powerful movement in the current politics of the western world."[21] Nonetheless, Conrad's own family history complicates his political allegiance to a British Empire composed of territories whose boundaries took little account of tribal origins.

Certainly colored by an immigrant complex, and probably skewed by either the addressee or a perspective located on a merchant ship, Conrad's letter to Kliszczewski expressing disappointment over the election results is striking for its concatenation of ideas. First, Conservatism and tradition are under threat from socialist forces of avarice and decay: "the International Socialist Association are triumphant, and every disreputable ragamuffin in Europe feels that the day of universal brotherhood, despoliation and disorder is coming apace, and nurses day-dreams of well-polished pockets amongst the ruin of all that is respectable, venerable and holy"; and, second, the empire, viewed as the last bulwark against socialism, has been breached by "infernal" forces: "The great British Empire went over the edge, and yet on to the inclined plane of social progress and radical reform . . . the sun is set and the last barrier removed. England was the only barrier to the pressure of infernal doctrines born in continental back-slums. Now, there is nothing!" There follows this dire prediction: "The destiny of this nation and of all nations is to be accomplished in darkness amidst much weeping and gnashing of teeth, to pass through robbery, equality, anarchy and misery under the iron rule of a militarism [*sic*] despotism!"[22] Whether "born in Continental back-slums" or not, the "rush of social-democratic ideas" to which Conrad refers was gaining. Gladstone's Reform Bills in 1884 and 1885 extended the vote, preparing the way for the enlarged franchise guaranteed by the Act of 1918—up to which point only about sixty percent of adult males had the parliamentary vote. British political life mirrored the changing configurations and realignments of national identity. Its leanings toward socialism were evident in the founding of the Fabian Society in 1884, whose members included Sidney and Beatrice Webb, George Bernard Shaw, and H. G. Wells. In 1886, unemployed East Enders rioted in Trafalgar Square and looted shops on Oxford Street; in the two years that followed, strikes by East End match-girls and dockworkers launched the new and formidably powerful unionism. The need for an increasingly unionized working class to be represented in the House of Commons led to the formation in Bradford in 1893 of the Independent Labour Party, founded by Keir Hardie. (Hardie, an Ayrshire coal miner, had helped to form the Scottish Parliamentary Labour Party in 1888.) Membership of the trade union movement increased steadily: it doubled in the Edwardian years from two million in 1901 to over four million in 1913.[23]

Conrad thus entered into British society at a moment when its political landscape was being radically redrawn. In 1900, the Trades Union Congress supported the founding of the Labour Representation Committee, forerunner of the Labour Party. On all fronts there were challenges to the inherited social and political order: if the dock strike of 1889, the rail strike of 1911, and the coal strike the following year seemed to raise the specter of "mob rule" a century after the French Revolution, the increasing militancy of the suffragettes interrogated the assumptions of patriarchal society. Coordinated through such organizations as Mrs Fawcett's National Union of Women's Suffrage Societies in 1897 and the Pankhursts' Women's Social and Political Union in 1903, the campaign for women's votes politicized gender in the pursuit of a revised concept of British "citizenship." The term "feminism" came into use in the 1890s. Conrad added his name to a petition addressed to Prime Minister Asquith supporting a bill extending suffrage to women in *The Times*.[24] Conrad thus engages with British public life at a moment when the country is adapting itself to the idea of mass participation in national politics.

To these transformations within public life we can add the fact that, in 1892, the British elected their first Indian member of parliament. In 1902, Arthur Griffiths formed Sinn Fein ("ourselves alone") to promote the cause of Irish independence. More subtly, social revolution was ensured by the establishment of an increasingly literate population, the result of successive education acts between 1870 and 1893. Furthermore, the era of popular mass culture had begun: widespread circulation newspapers, tea-drinking, fish and chips, football and cricket, music hall, and, later, the cinema all have their origins in this period. The first public showing of film, by the brothers Lumière, was in 1895.

Published in 1897, the year of Queen Victoria's Diamond Jubilee, *The Nigger of the "Narcissus"* engages with the demand for workers' rights through the figure of Donkin, whose nickname, "Whitechapel," derives from a working-class district in east London. However unsympathetic is his presentation in the text, his boast, "I stood up for my rights like a good 'un. I am an Englishman, I am" (*NN* 11–12), has contemporary social relevance—not least when linked to his claim that the crew led a "dorg's loife for two poun' ten a month" (*NN* 100). In its valediction, this key text in Conrad's presentation of himself as an English author juxtaposes the different generations of seamen thus: "Singleton has no doubt taken with him the long record of his faithful work into the peaceful depths of an hospitable sea. And Donkin, who never did a decent day's work in his life, no doubt earns his living by discoursing with filthy eloquence upon the right of labour to live. So be it! Let the earth and the sea each have its own" (*NN* 172). The ostensibly easy contrast, fashioned in terms of conflicting sea and land values, is troubled however by such claims about Singleton's "inarticulate and indispensable" generation as that they lived "without knowing the sweetness of affections or the refuge of home" (*NN* 25). "Home," as this novella demonstrates, was becoming an increasingly politicized space.

At the end of the voyage of the *Narcissus*, Donkin declares to Captain Allistoun that he is "goin' ter 'ave a job ashore....No more bloomin' sea fur me" (*NN* 169). Within the broad division between sea and land values in the novella, this sentiment removes Donkin from the romanticized sphere where, however anachronistically, Singleton remains the presiding genius. But there is more to it. Vocally, Donkin's speeches are intentionally resonant: in the narrative's speech representation, the artist's ear is more attuned to and concentrates more upon reproducing Donkin's speech habits—not least those of labor agitation: this is not a call to "mutiny" but to "strike, boys, strike!" (*NN* 121). In other words, the register in which tradition is subverted is unmistakeably contemporary and unmistakeably demotic.

There is, too, in Conrad's comments to Kliszczewski a certain hauteur from the sailor who, when leaving at least two ships in which he had served, signed himself "de Korzeniowski." But Conrad, who would later admit, "Class for me is by definition a hateful thing,"[25] was responding to the irresistible momentum of social change that had been steadily gathering across nineteenth-century Europe. In Britain as elsewhere, the transformation of a predominantly rural workforce at the beginning of the century into an overwhelmingly urban one by its close inevitably acquired a political shape and, in so doing, threatened the domestic status quo. In a letter to Edward Garnett, Conrad described "The

Return," one of his earliest short stories, as portraying "the gospel of the beastly bourgeois."[26]

As an officer in the British Merchant Service, Conrad could hardly have been unaware of the increasing politicization of the seas through unionization and strikes. For example, he had firsthand experience of this when, on 7 August 1888, the *Otago*, his one and only command, narrowly managed to leave Sydney during labor problems, caused by the breakdown of negotiations between the Federated Seamen's Union of Australasia and the Steamship Owners' Association that threatened to erupt into violence. Recalling the incident in a letter to David Bone of 28 September 1920, Conrad declared the unionized seamen "Asses."[27] Similarly, his arrival in Sydney in early 1892, as first mate in the *Torrens*, was in the aftermath of the Marine Officers strike of August 1890.

Even as Conrad declared in his letter of 13 October 1885 to Kliszczewski, a fellow refugee from Poland, "When speaking, writing or thinking in English the word Home always means for me the hospitable shores of Great Britain,"[28] there was already a public clamor to restrict immigration into Britain. In a letter to *The Times* of 31 May 1904, the young Liberal Winston Churchill defended "the old tolerant and generous practice of free entry and asylum to which the country has so long adhered and from which it has so often greatly gained,"[29] but the Conservative government's "Aliens Act" of 1905 restricted immigration into Britain for the first time.

Further illustration of Conrad's early political views is provided by his letter of February 1896 to Ephraim Brownlow Redmayne, who had traveled as a passenger on the *Torrens* in October 1892. At this moment, Conrad declares, "The national Life seems to me to run haphazard, amongst pitfal[l]s."[30] These anxieties about his adopted homeland can be traced to the contemporary international predicament, where Britain's imperial interests in both southern Africa and South America were threatened. For instance, on 7 December 1895, the Marquess of Salisbury rejected American claims to an interest in the dispute over the border between Venezuela and British Guiana. Conrad's verdict on the times is bleak—"I have met, lately, many men who claim to direct the public opinion of this country; and I am almost appalled by the stupidity of some, the selfishness of others, the unscrupulosity of many"—and yet he finds consolation in the fact that "the heart of the nation is in the right place."[31]

This division between the "heart of the nation" and those who "direct the public opinion" recalls the views of another outsider, with whom Conrad often found himself compared in his early career, Rudyard Kipling. Stereotypically categorized as the "Poet of Empire," Kipling's complex attitudes toward democracy can be measured in his response to Queen Victoria's Diamond Jubilee of 1897: while apprehensive about the popular patriotism on display, he yet accepts that the future belongs to the common man: "The big smash is coming one of these days, sure enough, but I think we shall pull through not without credit. It will be the common people—the 3rd class carriages—that'll save us."[32]

Empire and Boer War

While Britain's domestic politics was dominated by class and social transformation, foreign politics remained those concerned with the business of the empire. But this empire, mainstay of the British economy, was subject to setback and, increasingly, challenge. The robust attitude towards her overseas possessions was signaled by Britain's new colonial secretary, Joseph Chamberlain. In 1895, in his first speech to the House of Commons in the administration of Prime Minister Salisbury, Chamberlain proclaimed his arch-imperial sentiments: "I believe in the British Empire, and I believe in the British race."[33] This rendered all the more poignant the failure of the Jameson Raid in early 1896. Led by Sir Leander Starr Jameson, and with clandestine support from Chamberlain, the raiders, supposedly "defending" the British minority in Johannesburg, would invade the city and, simultaneously, proclaim themselves the new government of the Boer Republic of Transvaal. In the event, the raid was easily repulsed by the Boers. This setback came in the year that saw the first major defeat of a white colonizing power when the Italians were defeated by the Abyssinians at Adowa.

This is not, of course, to suggest that the British Empire was crumbling. But public attitudes were changing, and where

Kipling in his "The English Flag" (1891) could inquire rhetorically, "what should they know of England who only England know?" G. K. Chesterton would respond only a decade and a half later with a question of his own: "What can they know of England who know only the world?"[34] Significantly Kipling's injunction in 1899 to "Take up the White Man's burden" was addressed to the United States rather than his own countrymen, suggesting that "responsibility" of imperialism had passed across the Atlantic. In a similar vein, his "Recessional" (1897), written for Queen Victoria's Diamond Jubilee, warns Britons against pride in their inevitably transient empire.

The Jameson Raid would have important consequences, not least because it served as the catalyst for German imperialism to declare its hand: on 3 January 1896, Kaiser Wilhelm II sent a telegram to President Paul Kruger congratulating him on successfully repulsing Jameson's invasion of the Transvaal. Indeed, Kipling remembered the Jameson Raid as "the first battle in the war of 14-18—a little before its time but necessary to clear the ground."[35] The Boer War of 1899–1902 offered an immediate indication of Germany's interest: used to fighting colonial wars against poorly armed natives, the British found the Boers well armed by Germany. Nonetheless, Britain's superior armaments ensured that, by 1900, the main Boer cities had been captured. Victory seemed certain—so much so, that Salisbury easily won the so-called Khaki election that year—but the Boers refused to surrender and resorted to guerrilla tactics. The British response was to burn Boer farmsteads and to herd the women and children into "concentration camps." It backfired when the high death toll in the camps led to public protests at home, ensuring that the victory, when it came, was a pyrrhic one.

Having left behind him a colonized Poland and written "Heart of Darkness," Conrad had yet, as Najder claims, "by his own choice...become a citizen of a country engaged in a war aimed primarily at enlarging the empire."[36] How he reconciled this contradiction is a moot point. He was, however, in no doubt about the dangers posed by the war, "the Krüger-Chamberlain combination" as he called it,[37] having correctly foreseen in October 1899 that "The victory—unless it is to be thrown away—shall have to be followed by ruthless repression. The situation will become repugnant to the nation. The *'reasonable English ideals'* (I am quoting Sir F. Milner's words) are not attained in that way."[38] To Conrad's lifelong friend of socialist commitment, R. B. Cunninghame Graham, the Boer War was nothing less than "a fight between two burglars."[39]

More practically, the fact of empire was demonstrably incommensurate with the means used to sustain it. To the pro-imperialists, the Boer War demonstrated the strength of empire: her white settler colonies sent troops to help—some 30,000 troops came from Canada, New Zealand, and Australia; to the anti-imperialists it demonstrated that the British Empire was overextended and undercoordinated. For example, the British government seemed unable to handle both the Boer War and the 1900 Boxer Rebellion simultaneously with any confidence. The national repercussions of the Boer War are summarized by H. C. G. Matthew and Kenneth O. Morgan in *The Oxford History of Britain*: "military ineffectiveness and the poor quality of recruits in the South African war led to a public cry among the propertied classes for a reappraisal of the economic, social, and even political arrangements of the nation as a whole."[40] But one damning contemporary statistic as to the state of the nation's health is Charles Booth's estimate, published in 1889 on the basis of an inquiry conducted the previous year, that 30.7 percent of Londoners lived in poverty.[41]

Early fiction

As a member of the British Merchant Service, the workhorse of the British Empire, Conrad saw the colonial world firsthand. When he turned his hand to writing, not only would the colonial world provide the context for many of his fictions, but his enduring fascination with what men do to form themselves into groups would also ensure that politics remain central to his work. Set in the Malay Archipelago, Conrad's earliest fiction offers a jaundiced image of Western imperialism, casting it as little more than crude commercialism. His "Author's Note" to *Almayer's Folly* (1895) engages with Alice Meynell's essay, "Decivilised" (1891), arguing instead that "there is a bond between us and that humanity so far away" (*AF* viii). This "bond" reduces in large part to what Nina Almayer perceives as mutual "sordid greed chasing the uncertain dollar in all its multifarious and vanishing shapes" (*AF* 43). Political parallels between East and West serve to reformulate cultural differences as essential similarities. For example, the machinations of Babalatchi, the one-eyed "statesman of Sambir" (*AF* 138), identify him with his frock-coated, nineteenth-century European counterparts. Not only this, but also, through Babalatchi, whose description may owe something to King Twala in H. Rider Haggard's *King Solomon's Mines* (1885), the myopia of political processes are exposed. In *An Outcast of the Islands* (1896), British and Dutch flags are expediently raised above trading stations on opposite sides of the river. Promising the protection of rival colonial powers, the result is often humor and national pastiche, as when the Chinese Jim-Eng refuses to take his hat off to the Dutch flag, claiming "he was an Englishman" (*OI* 182). It is left to Babalatchi to make the more serious observation about individual entrapment within the political process, noting in *Almayer's Folly* that "this emblem of Lakamba's power...was also the mark of his servitude" (*AF* 132).

Eschewing the easy them-and-us distinction that characterizes, and mars, so many late nineteenth-century "exotic" tales, Conrad's Malay fictions recognize an essential similarity between races, viewing them instead as puppets of historical and political processes. Set in the Malay Archipelago, these works are partly determined by the history of European influence in the region, revealing rival claims to this trading sphere. So, for instance, in *An Outcast of the Islands*, the Da Souzas are "degenerate descendants of Portuguese conquerors" (*OI* 4); Willems, from Rotterdam, arrived in the area in a Dutch East-Indiaman; while the "Rajah Laut—the King of the Sea" (*OI* 14), Tom Lingard, is English. But Conrad's strength is to articulate Occidental and Oriental influence, with economics used as a means to pass ironic comment upon colonialism. Significantly, Lingard's trading monopoly in Sambir destroyed by European underhandedness: it is his protégé, Willems, who betrays him. His rival, Syed Abdulla, is an Arab, and as an older, rueful Almayer observes in *Almayer's Folly*, "where they [the Arabs] traded they would be masters and suffer no rival" (*AF* 24). Economics provide not only the basis for aspirations and alliances, political and personal but also the expression of the larger forces of history and nationalism.

Political machinations among the islanders provide a parallel with Western influence in the archipelago. For example, at the beginning of *An Outcast of the Islands*, Rajah Patalolo presides in Sambir, under Lingard's protection; by the end of the novel, he has abdicated, and Lakamba is calling himself a sultan. What has occurred, in essence, is an economic coup: as Babalatchi and Lakamba realize, Lingard's power is a function of his trading monopoly; once this is removed, and Abdulla installed as the dominant trader, local politics can be reconfigured. Conrad's Eastern fictions quickly earned comparison with those of Kipling. The *Spectator* review of *Almayer's Folly*, for instance, concluded that "he might become the Kipling of the Malay Archipelago."[42] The political flavor of the age colors these early reviews, with both the *Daily News* and the *Critic*[43] claiming that Conrad's fiction had "annexed" the island of Borneo.

It was Conrad's African experiences in 1890 that brought home to him the full horror of colonial excesses. In the Congo Free State of King Leopold II of Belgium he witnessed what he later called in "Geography and Some Explorers," "the vilest scramble for loot that ever disfigured the history of human conscience and geographical exploration."[44] (*LE* 17). The Charter of the Congo State was granted by the Berlin Act of 1885 and subsequently endorsed by the Brussels Act of 1890. The Berlin Conference's decision to recognize King Leopold's sovereignty over the Congo was a compromise based on self-interest: none of the major colonial powers represented at the conference—among them, Britain, France, and Germany—was prepared to see an area of this size fall into the hands of a rival, and all saw the danger of becoming embroiled in a free-for-all in the Congo. Leopold, who in any event was acting individually rather than as representative of the Belgian parliament (which had little enthusiasm for his colonial schemes), was regarded as a neutral. Leopold's ownership of the Congo Free State, as it was called, lasted from 1885 to 1907.

Synonymous with the "Scramble for Africa," atrocities in Leopold's fiefdom led, ultimately, to international outrage, and the Belgian government voted to relieve their king of his African territory, annexing the Congo Free State in 1908. At the dawn of the motor car age, the equatorial forests of rubber trees in the Congo basin proved irresistible to European avarice, at the cost of untold Congolese lives. Conditions in country provided the impetus for the founding of the Congo Reform Association by Edmund Dene Morel in March 1904. In a letter to Arthur Conan Doyle, on 7 October 1909, Morel called "Heart of Darkness" simply "the most powerful thing ever written on the subject."[45] Conrad fictionalized his sojourn in the so-called Dark Continent in two stories, "An Outpost of Progress," which he called "the lightest part of the loot I carried off from Central Africa" (*TU* vii), and "Heart of Darkness." In both tales, colonialism is portrayed as "philanthropic pretence," naked greed masquerading as civilizing mission, and they share the theme of the gradual breakdown and dissolution of the European self, proved to be, like Kurtz, "hollow at the core" (*Y* 131).

The impetus behind European involvement in Africa, essentially economic imperialism, was described by Leonard Woolf in *Empire and Commerce in Africa* (1920): "It is true that the question whether Africans should be ruled by Frenchmen, Germans, Englishmen, Portuguese, Belgians, or Italians, has caused the most difficult and dangerous international situations, but the policy pursued in nearly all cases, and by all the States concerned, has been comparatively simple and direct. It is the policy of grab."[46] Between the early Malay fiction and the African tales, Conrad's work charts the inexorable development of European expansion: from the incidental and secluded trading post of Sambir in *Almayer's Folly* and *An Outcast of the Islands*, to the systematic exploitation of the jungle in "Heart of Darkness," where the industrial revolution is called into the service of avarice in the shape of river steamers and railways, and the succession of trading stations along the river charts the complete and intrusive nature of this "fantastic invasion" (*Y* 76).

The Major Phase

Conrad is generally viewed as a political skeptic. In his essay on Anatole France, of 1904, in which he dubs his celebrated contemporary "a great analyst of illusions," Conrad commends the French writer for perceiving that "political institutions, whether contrived by the wisdom of the few or the ignorance of the many, are incapable on securing the happiness of mankind" (*NLL* 33). Despite this, Conrad's fictions demonstrate his ongoing fascination with the political process, in particular, the manner in which it entraps the individual. Indeed, the entrapment of the individual within the nexus of political regulation and determination remains one of the persistent themes in his major fiction.

In an often-quoted image, described in an early letter to Cunninghame Graham, Conrad compared society to a knitting machine, which, however much we might want it to "embroider... goes right on knitting":

> You cannot by any special lubrication make embroidery with a knitting machine. And the most withering thought is that the infernal thing has made itself; made itself without thought, without conscience, without foresight, without eyes, without heart. It is a tragic accident—and it has happened. You can't interfere with it. The last drop of bitterness is in the suspicion that you can't even smash it. In virtue of that truth one and immortal which lurks in the force that made it spring into existence it is what it is—and it is indestructible!
>
> It knits us in and it knits us out. It has knitted time[,] space, pain, death, corruption, despair and all the illusions—and nothing matters. I'll admit however that to look at the remorseless process is sometimes amusing.[47]

Nor should the individual's powerlessness within "the system" be equated with detachment on Conrad's part. In a much later comment, in 1918, to H. G. Wells he defined the "fundamental" difference between them as follows: "You don't care for humanity but think they are to be improved. I love humanity but know they are not!"[48] Nowhere is the courage of this clear-eyed position better illustrated than in the trio of political novels—*Nostromo* (1904), *The Secret Agent* (1907), and *Under Western Eyes* (1911)—that, critics now generally agree, constitute his major achievement. Together they provide a stark counterpoint to the optimism and calm of the Edwardian period, the years between the death of Queen Victoria and the outbreak of the First World War. Between them, these three novels present the sophistication and the maturity of Conrad's political vision, while charting the transition in international politics from colonialism to imperialism, through the emergence of capitalism and *Weltpolitik*.

The audacious temporal scope of *Nostromo*, weaving together past, present, and future, makes of the fictional South American country of Costaguana both a realized and an allegorical place, with multiple resemblances to larger historical patterns. At the center of the novel, and the barometer of power in the country, is the San Tomé silver mine, ensuring that politics is inseparable from the shaping economic force defined simply as "material interests." Ultimately, it is the wealth from this silver that occasions and demands the succession of the Occidental Province from the rest of the country, while the geography of Sulaco, a natural harbor at the intersection of land and seaborne trade routes, might be said to thrust Costaguana into the way of colonial history.

The history of the mine is tied to the forces that shape the country's fortunes, commercial exploitation and foreign involvement. Initially worked by Indian slaves, it has been appropriated by the successive unscrupulous politicians, strong men, and rapacious army officers who litter Costaguana's history before being taken up by the Englishman, Charles Gould, whose tragic family history is linked with that of the country and whose forebears have owned the mine and been "robbed under the forms of legality and business" (*N* 56). In the present-tense action, Charles Gould has earned the nickname *El Rey de Sulaco* ("King of Sulaco"), and the mine, whose restoration has been underwritten by the American financier Holroyd, has become the dominant political force in the province. But while financing the government of Don Vincente Ribiera in Costaguana, the wealth of the mine has also attracted the avaricious attention of the Montero brothers, occasioning a revolution. While Giorgio Viola is one of the broadly sympathetic characters in *Nostromo*, his status as an outsider remains: "No native of Costaguana intruded" into "the Italian stronghold" (*N* 32) that is the Casa Viola.

The vertiginous historical sweep of the narrative finds its social expression in a political continuum, stretching from the anterior reference to "the time of Spanish rule" (*N* 3) in the opening sentence, supported by the high incidence of Spanish words in the text, to Holroyd's prophetic observation that "some day" the United States "shall run the world's business whether the world likes it or not. The world can't help it—and neither can we, I guess" (*N* 77). This evolution of colonial annexation into global capitalism is given an ironic twist when, in the novel's closing stages, the unidentified "hater of capitalists" at Nostromo's deathbed seeks further donations for the cause, claiming: "The rich must be fought with their own weapons" (*N* 562). Conrad's adroit manipulation of foreground and background in the novel ensures that individual experience is always related to broader political and historical circumstances. Indeed, the skeptical detachment of, say, Martin Decoud, or Nostromo himself, from the larger political designs in which they find themselves participating, serves to highlight the conflict between self-interest and collective governance. Thrust unwillingly and unwittingly into politics, these characters implicitly question the degree to which the individual can be made to carry collective significance. By extension, and in a gambit typical of literary modernism, *Nostromo* comes to interrogate the bourgeois form of the novel itself, as the force of collective experience is obscured by the focus upon individual experience.

This attention to the entrapment of the individual within the broader forces of politics, and thus with the problem of representing the sovereignty of collective action, would color Conrad's next political novel, *The Secret Agent*. Set in London, Conrad's great metropolitan novel takes as its starting point an actual historical event, the so-called Greenwich Bomb Outrage on 15 February 1894, when the anarchist Martial Bourdin accidentally blew himself up in Greenwich Park with a homemade bomb that he was, apparently, carrying towards the observatory. Late nineteenth-century London was stalked by fears of anarchist violence and had seen its share of bombings as Anarchists, Fenians, and other revolutionary groups tried to disrupt the social and economic order. A century after the French Revolution, social revolution was again in the air as the socialist movement, inspired by Karl Marx, and the International Anarchist Movement, founded by Mikhail Bakunin, led to partially successful revolts, like the Paris Commune of 1871 and the Russian uprising of 1905.

Unsurprisingly, the specter of the mad dynamiter, intent upon overthrowing the social order, haunted the late Victorian and Edwardian popular imagination, and at the heart of Conrad's novel is the Professor. Obsessed with developing the perfect detonator, he walks the streets of London, quite literally carrying a bomb in his pocket, a symbol of an inert society primed to explode. Commenting upon his theme of anarchism in the "Author's Note" to the novel, Conrad speaks of "a mankind always so tragically eager for self-destruction" (*SA* vii). Advocating the complete overthrow of the system, the Professor expresses his creed to Comrade Ossipon: "Nothing would please me more than to see Inspector Heat and his likes take to shooting us down in broad daylight with the approval of the public. Half our battle would be won then; the disintegration of the old morality would have set in its very temple. That is what you ought to aim at" (*SA* 73).

The action in *The Secret Agent* begins when Mr. Vladimir, ambassador at a foreign—presumably Russian—embassy, instructs the eponymous secret agent, Adolf Verloc, to commit an act of terrorism in order to undermine the country's "sentimental regard of individual liberty" (*SA* 29), which makes of it a haven for foreign revolutionaries fleeing repressive political regimes. In this, Vladimir is responding to historical fact. The list of political refugees who fled their own countries and sought sanctuary in Britain reads like a who's who of anarchists and revolutionary socialists and includes Bakunin, Kropotkin, and Marx, who wrote *Das Kapital* (1867) in the Reading Room of the British Museum. According to Vladimir, "England must be brought into line" (*SA* 29). Towards this, he proposes "an act of destructive ferocity so absurd as to be incomprehensible, inexplicable, almost unthinkable; in fact, mad" (*SA* 33). His preferred target is Greenwich Observatory. It is well chosen: instructing Verloc to "Go for the first meridian" (*SA* 37). Vladimir is symbolically advocating the destruction of temporal and spatial order.

The political gravity of the situation is obvious: from the neutrality of a foreign embassy, an ambassador incites an act of terrorism. National security is at stake. But this is not Conrad's target. Instead, while revealing not just the chain of self-serving dependence that links its various strata—double agent Verloc to Inspector Heat to the assistant commissioner to the secretary of state—*The Secret Agent* anatomizes British society, shifting the focus of political inquiry from foreign to domestic affairs, such as the distribution of wealth. As the assistant commissioner tells Secretary of State, Sir Ethelred, "From a certain point of view we are here in the presence of a domestic drama" (*SA* 222). Bringing the public and private spheres into correspondence not only ensures that Stevie's claim, "Bad world for poor people" (*SA* 171), is heard, but also allows the novel to question the social responsibility of government, not simply through the fortuitous means by which public security is preserved but more starkly through the graphic depiction of social inequalities. The ironic narrative tone is perfectly suited to the depiction of a world where anarchism serves as political expression and government has lost sight of its people.

The malign influence of the Russian state, felt way beyond its borders in *The Secret Agent*, also dominates *Under Western Eyes*, Conrad's "attempt to render not so much the political state as the psychology of Russia itself" (*UWE* vii). In light of his family history and the degree to which his novels are haunted by their origins, we may well believe him when he says: "My greatest anxiety was in being able to strike and sustain the note of scrupulous impartiality" (*UWE* viii). Set in St. Petersburg and Geneva, *Under Western Eyes* charts the development of a political consciousness, that of the university student Razumov, against the backdrop of the alienation between the Russian state and the liberal intelligentsia. Extending themes that have been developing in the previous two novels, Conrad explores the moral complexities of choice and betrayal in a historically and politically determined situation.

When the novel begins, the central character has his sights set on winning the silver medal for a philosophy essay and converting "the label Razumov into an honoured name" (*UWE* 14). Instead, the unexpected appearance in his rooms of a fellow student, Victor Haldin, shatters his private dreams by thrusting him into the world of Russian politics. For Haldin has turned to Razumov, whom he knows only slightly, for help escaping, having assassinated—"removed" (*UWE* 16) is his word—Mr. de P—, "the President of the notorious Repressive Commission" (*UWE* 7) whose aim seemed to be "the destruction of the very hope of liberty itself" (*UWE* 8). Without warning, the apolitical Razumov encounters a "crisis in his fate" (*UWE* 25) as he is trapped between the evident tyranny of a repressive tsarist regime and revolutionary fanaticism, which his reason resists—his name derives from the Russian word *razhum*, meaning "reason" or "mind."

In an attempt to stave off the collapse of his private world, Razumov betrays Haldin to the authorities, but his action is futile, and he quickly finds himself recruited as a tool of the state, part of its surveillance system, employed to spy upon revolutionary cells operating in exile, in neutral Switzerland. In effect, his private world has become state property, a point driven home to him when, in Geneva, he meets and falls in love with Haldin's sister, Nathalie. Events in Geneva, however, have a fated inevitability from the moment that Razumov comes under surveillance by the tsarist intelligence. Part One of the novel ends with Razumov preparing to leave the Secretariat at the end of his interview: "'Where to?' asked Councillor Mikulin softly" (*UWE* 99). This rhetorical question is all the more devastating because of its simplicity. At its most extreme, it addresses the plight of the twentieth-century man alienated from and yet enmeshed within the machinery of the state: there is nowhere for Razumov to go, no right to privacy, and no future.

Unwittingly thrust into politics, Razumov discovers that "his moral personality was at the mercy of these lawless forces," to the point where his very "existence . . . seemed no longer his own" (*UWE* 77–78). The sense of the individual at the mercy of the political system acquires contemporary, psychological inflection when, having first betrayed Haldin to the authorities, Razumov is then co-opted to repeat this betrayal as he infiltrates revolutionary circles abroad. Ultimately, though, this leads to a self-betrayal when, unable to endure his life of deception any longer, he confesses that he is a spy, with brutal consequences. If his love for Miss Haldin provides the catalyst for this self-betrayal, then the tension between the public and private selves it induces proves intolerable, leaving the individual unable to bear the schism. In Conrad's political vision, the pervasiveness of state influence is such as to corrode even the psychosexual self.

In *Under Western Eyes* Conrad engages with Russia and matters Russian on various levels. The death of Mr. de P—, for instance, draws upon incidents of the historical assassinations of Tsar Alexander II in 1881 and Minister of the Interior Vyacheslav Konstantinovich Plehve, in 1904, while the portrait of Councillor Mikulin owes a debt to Dostoyevsky's Grand Inquisitor in *The Brothers Karamazov* (1879–80). The arbitrariness of state power plumbs new depths in the fate of Councillor Mikulin, presented as a coda to the main action and revealing that Russian autocracy "does not limit its diet exclusively to the bodies of its enemies. It devours its friends and servants as well." In consequence of "one of those State trials which astonish and puzzle" the rest of the world, Mikulin "Went under, dignified, with only a calm, emphatic protest of his innocence—nothing more." But the vampiric nature of the Russian state is matched by its imperviousness: even while he is "turned... civilly into a corpse, and actually into something very much like a common convict," Mikulin offers "No disclosures damaging to a harassed autocracy, complete fidelity to the secrets of the miserable *arcana imperii* deposited in his patriotic breast" (*UWE* 305–6).

First World War

The First World War of 1914–18 provides the Modern era with its central historical moment. The cataclysmic effect of the conflict upon European society, culture, and politics would continue to be felt long after Conrad's death. An ill-considered visit to Austrian Poland in July 1914, a month after the assassination of Archduke Franz Ferdinand in Sarajevo, left the Conrads precariously cut off from England and witness to the mobilization for war before their anxious return home. Britain declared war on Germany on 4 August 1914, after the invasion of Belgium. The opening of *Victory* (1915) captures the period's sense of dislocation in its reference to "the age in which we are camped like bewildered travellers in a garish, unrestful hotel" (*V* 3). The Conrads' elder son, Borys, saw active service in France, where he was gassed and shell-shocked during the Second Army's advance into Flanders in mid-October 1918, a month before Armistice Day. In late August 1915, Conrad wrote to Ford Madox Ford, also gassed during the war: "Our world of 15 years ago is gone to pieces; what will come in its place God knows, but I imagine doesn't care."[49] Conrad pinned his faith on the nation rather than on its leaders, writing in January 1917 that "the national determination to see this thing through hardens as the cruel days go by. It's a pity better use is not made of it. But leaders of genius are rare."[50]

According to Lenin's treatise, "Imperialism, the Highest Stage of Capitalism" (1916), the war was the result of increasingly aggressive capitalist imperialism, with competition among the world powers for new markets and investment outlets leading inevitably to conflict. Alongside this economic rationale, one needs to set the complicated system of political alliances, resulting from concern over the balance of European power. For example, the Franco-Russian alliance was strategically founded on their mutual distrust of Germany and economically founded on French loans to Russia—(by 1914, nearly a third of all French overseas investment was in Russia, most of it in the form of state bonds).[51] Britain too was drawn into the system of expedient alliances and ententes. Thus, she entered into an alliance with Japan in 1902; then, when Japan became involved in a war with Russia in 1904, with France, so as to avoid having joint enemy of France and Russia; and then with Russia in 1907. Despite Foreign Secretary Sir Edward Grey's claim that "alliances, especially continental alliances are not in accordance with our traditions,"[52] as demonstrated by colonial events in North Africa—Germany's challenge to France at the Conference of Algeciras in 1906; or sending a gunboat to Agadir in 1911—Britain's days of isolation were over. By 1914, Germany was in an alliance with Austro-Hungary and Italy, diving Europe into two clear power blocs.

The old relationship between Britain and Germany had begun to show signs of strain. As early as 1895, German economist Max Weber had called for a new era of National Liberalism under the standard of *Weltpolitik*;[53] three years later, when Germany attempted to raise European support for Spain in the

Spanish-American War, Britain chose to support America; and in 1902, during the Venezuelan crisis, Britain joined with Germany and France in persuading Venezuela to repay her debts, only to side with America again as soon as Germany fired on Venezuelan ships. Conrad was often out of step with the government of his adopted homeland. For example, siding with Cunninghame Graham, he expressed sympathy for the Spanish in the Spanish-American War in 1898. Nonetheless, he concluded that it "would be *real fine*" to "set the States & Germany by the ears."[54] A letter of 25 December 1899 lays the cause of the Boer War at Germany's door: "This war is not so much a war against the Transvaal as a struggle against the doings of German influence. It is the Germans who have forced the issue. There can be no doubt about it."[55]

Conrad's fictional portrayal of Germans is mixed. In *Lord Jim*, for example, the *Patna* skipper's Bismarckian " 'blood-and-iron' air" (*LJ* 14) is more than balanced by the portrait of Stein. Despite this, German expansionism is wryly noted in "Heart of Darkness" when Marlow, looking at the map of Africa, comments: "and, on the East Coast, a purple patch, to show where the jolly pioneers of progress drink the jolly lager beer" (*Y* 55). The mood of the popular press towards Germany was jingoistic: in 1906, the *Daily Mail*'s serialized William Le Queux's *The Invasion of 1910*, depicting Germany's invasion of Britain; while, in December 1913, the schoolboy magazine, *Chums*, began a tale about a future Anglo-German war. Such populist fears inform Winnie Verloc's outburst about a story in a halfpenny revolutionary tract about "a German soldier officer tearing half-off the ear of a recruit, and nothing was done to him for it. The brute!... The story was enough to make one's blood boil. But what's the use of printing things like that? We aren't German slaves here, thank God" (*SA* 60).

The war also revived Conrad's interest in Polish affairs, and in June 1916 he drafted a memorandum to the Foreign Office, "A Note on the Polish Problem," describing Poland as an "advanced outpost of Western civilisation" (*NLL* 138) and Polonism as forever separate from either Germanism or Slavonism. While 1918 saw the political rebirth of Poland, antagonisms provoked by the redrawing of Europe's historical boundaries made Conrad uneasy. On Armistice Day, he wrote: "The great sacrifice is consummated—and what will come of it to the nations of the earth the future will show. I can not confess to an easy mind. Great and very blind forces are set free catastrophically all over the world."[56] Despite this, and while fearful about Poland's fate at the peace negotiations where he descried the fact that "The mangy Russian dog having gone mad is now being invited to sit at the Conference table, on British initiative!"—Conrad yet recognized that "The old order had got to die."[57]

Conclusion

In the last phase of his writing Conrad revived his interest in the Napoleonic period, already anticipated in such earlier tales as "The Duel" (1908) and "The Warrior's Soul" (1917). His last completed novel, *The Rover* (1923), is set during the French Revolution and the early years of the Napoleonic period and the unfinished *Suspense* (1925), published posthumously, against the backdrop of Napoleon's impending flight from Elba. One way of viewing his late preoccupation with Napoleon is as a return to European—and by extension Poland's—political history. The emperor had, after all, defeated the powers that had partitioned Poland, and both Conrad's paternal grandfather, Teodor Korzeniowski, and maternal great-uncle, Mikołaj Bobrowski, had served in Napoleon's army against Russia.

In "The Dover Patrol," written in July 1921 to celebrate the contribution of merchant seamen to the war effort, Conrad casts the First World War into historical relief, claiming "The opening years of the nineteenth century had their Great War, too."[58] The wars waged from 1803 to 1815 by Napoleon intimately involved England, which, hostile to Napoleon, faced invasion by France. To Conrad, "that war, like the one of our day, was waged against an attempt at universal domination," and he casts it as "a struggle of the old certitudes against a man embodying the new force of subversive beliefs."[59] Two years later Conrad called himself "a good European, not exactly in the superficial, cosmopolitan sense, but in the blood and bones as it were, and as the result of a long heredity,"[60] and it is a broader international vision, above all, that Conrad brought to bear upon British politics, and which led George Orwell to commend him for the maturity of his vision.[61]

Criticism of the political dimension of Conrad's works began with the first reviews, broadly appreciative of his engagement with difficult subject matter. To the *Morning Post*, of 19 September 1907, for example, *The Secret Agent* offers "a study of real value for the student of contemporary politics." Themes of the debate were set early: where Irving Howe (1957) detected antirevolutionary bias and was unsympathetic towards Conrad's conservatism, G. H. Bantock (1958) applauded the political novels' concern with order and social cohesion. The first full-length study of the "political imperative" in Conrad's fiction was Eloise Knapp Hay's *The Political Novels of Joseph Conrad* (1963) and was soon followed by Avrom Fleishman's admirable *Conrad's Politics: Community and Anarchy in the Fiction of Joseph Conrad* (1967), which examined the complicated nature of Conrad's commitment to the nation in his treatment of Europe and colonialism. More sophisticated—and intense—critiques would follow: as its title suggests, Frederic Jameson's analysis of Conrad in *The Political Unconscious: Narrative as Socially Symbolic Act* (1981) probes literary form itself (in *Lord Jim* and *Nostromo*) to expose its collusion in the imprisonment of history in ideology. Another ideologically driven response of the period, Benita Parry's *Conrad and Imperialism: Ideological Boundaries and Visionary Frontiers* (1983), interrogates the politics of representation in the colonial fictions.[62] Today, contextual studies of Conrad's political works persist alongside those responsive to theory-driven approaches such as post-colonialism or New Historicism. The continued attraction of these works is its-own testament to the relevance of Conrad's enduring vision of political man.

NOTES

1. Apollo Korzeniowski, "Poland and Muscovy," in Zdzisław Najder, ed. *Conrad under Familial Eyes*, trans. Halina Carroll-Najder (Cambridge: Cambridge University Press, 1983), 75.

2. Joseph Conrad to Wincenty Lutoslawski, 9 June 1897, in *The Collected Letters of Joseph Conrad*, ed. Laurence Davies et al., 9 vols. (Cambridge: Cambridge University Press, 1983–2007), I: 358.

3. Ewa Korzeniowska to Apollo Korzeniowski, 20 June or 2 July 1861, in *Conrad under Familial Eyes*, 51.

4. Cedric Watts, *A Preface to Conrad*, 2nd ed. (London: Longman, 1993), 51.

5. Conrad to George T. Keating, 14 December 1922, in *Collected Letters of Joseph Conrad*, 7: 615.

6. See J. H. Stape, *The Several Lives of Joseph Conrad* (London: Heinemann, 2007), 3–6.

7. A. N. Wilson, *The Victorians* (London: Hutchinson, 2002), 116.

8. Conrad to Charles Chassé, 31 January 1924, in *Collected Letters of Joseph Conrad*, 8: 291.

9. Conrad to Edward Garnett, 1 September 1923, in *Collected Letters of Joseph Conrad*, 8: 167.

10. Conrad to Garnett, 27 May 1912, in *Collected Letters of Joseph Conrad*, 5: 70–71.

11. Paul Kirschner, *Conrad: The Psychologist as Artist* (Edinburgh: Oliver & Boyd, 1968), 252.

12. [Edward Garnett], "Mr. Conrad's New Novel," *The Nation* (21 October 1911): 140–42.

13. Letter dated 20 October 1911, in *Collected Letters of Joseph Conrad*, 4: 488.

14. Edward Garnett, "Conrad's Place in English Literature" in *Conrad's Prefaces* (London: J. M. Dent & Sons, 1937), 26–27.

15. Conrad to Karol Zagórski, 22 May 1890, in *Collected Letters of Joseph Conrad*, 1: 52.

16. Kliszczewski is listed as Josef Spiridion in the 1881 census, suggesting that, like Conrad, his Anglicization included changing his name.

17. *Collected Letters of Joseph Conrad*, 1: 12.

18. Letter dated 19 December 1885, in *Collected Letters of Joseph Conrad*, 1: 15–16.

19. Andrew Lycett, *Rudyard Kipling* (London: Weidenfeld & Nicolson, 1999), 256.

20. Eric Hobsbawm, *The Age of Empire: 1875–1914* (London: Abacus, 2002), 60.

21. Ibid.

22. Letter dated 19 December 1885, in *Collected Letters of Joseph Conrad*, 1: 16.

23. H. C. G. Matthew and Kenneth O. Morgan, *The Oxford History of Britain: The Modern Age* (Oxford: Oxford University Press, 1992), 60.

24. *The Times* (15 June 1910): 7.

25. Conrad to Elbridge L. Adams, 20 November 1922, in *Collected Letters of Joseph Conrad*, 7: 595.

26. Letter dated 11 October 1897, in *Collected Letters of Joseph Conrad*, 1: 393.

27. *Collected Letters of Joseph Conrad*, 7: 183.

28. *Collected Letters of Joseph Conrad*, 1: 12.

29. Letter from Winston Churchill, *The Times* (31 May 1904): 10.

30. Letter dated 23 February 1896, in *Collected Letters of Joseph Conrad*, 9: 21.

31. Ibid., 22.

32. Kipling to J. W. Mackail, 21 July 1897, in Lycett, *Rudyard Kipling*, 300.

33. As quoted in Lycett, *Rudyard Kipling*, 276.

34. G. K. Chesterton, *Heretics* (London: John Lane, 1905), 42.

35. Kipling to Herbert Baker, 13 January 1934, in Lycett, *Rudyard Kipling*, 296–97.

36. Zdzisław Najder, *Joseph Conrad: A Life*, trans. Halina Najder (Rochester, N.Y.: Camden House, 2007), 300.

37. Conrad to John Galsworthy, 7 November 1900, in *Collected Letters of Joseph Conrad*, 2: 302.

38. Conrad to E. L. Sanderson, 26 October 1899, in *Collected Letters of Joseph Conrad*, 2: 211.

39. Cedric Watts and Laurence Davies, *Cunninghame Graham: A Critical Biography* (Cambridge: Cambridge University Press, 1979), 114.

40. Matthew and Morgan, *Oxford History of Britain*, 49.

41. Sir Robert Ensor, *England 1870–1914* (Oxford: The Clarendon Press, 1992), 301.

42. Norman Sherry, ed., *Conrad: The Critical Heritage* (London: Routledge & Kegan Paul, 1973), 61.

43. See ibid., 47, 50.

44. Joseph Conrad, *Last Essays* (Garden City, N.Y.: Doubleday, Page & Company, 1926): 17.

45. Edmund D. Morel, *History of the Congo Reform Movement*, ed. Roger Louis and Jean Stengers (Oxford: Clarendon Press, 1968), 205.

46. Leonard Woolf, *Empire and Commerce in Africa* (London: Labour Research Departmen and Allen and Unwin, 1920), 54–55.

47. Letter dated 20 December 1897, in *Collected Letters of Joseph Conrad*, 1: 425.

48. Rupert Hart-Davis, *Hugh Walpole: A Biography* (London: Macmillan, 1952), 168.

49. Letter dated 30 August 1915, in *Collected Letters of Joseph Conrad*, 5: 503.

50. Conrad to F. N. Doubleday, 22 January 1917, in *Collected Letters of Joseph Conrad*, 6: 14.

51. See Niall Ferguson, *The Pity of War* (London: Penguin, 1999), 44.

52. See Stephen J. Lee, *Aspects of British Political History 1815–1914* (London: Routledge, 1994), 263.

53. Ferguson, *Pity of War*, 19.

54. Letter dated 30 July 1898, in *Collected Letters of Joseph Conrad*, 2: 81.

55. Conrad to Aniela Zagórska, in *Collected Letters of Joseph Conrad*, 2: 230.

56. Conrad to Hugh Walpole, in *Collected Letters of Joseph Conrad*, 6: 302.

57. Conrad to Sir Hugh Clifford, 25 January 1919, in *Collected Letters of Joseph Conrad*, 6: 349–50.

58. Conrad, *Last Essays*, 58.

59. Ibid, 58–59.

60. Conrad to Ernst P. Bendz, 7 March 1923, in *Collected Letters of Joseph Conrad*, 8: 37.

61. George Orwell, *The Collected Journalism and Letters of George Orwell*, ed. Sonia Orwell and Ian Angus, 4 vols. (Harmondsworth: Penguin, 1970), 4: 505.

62. See Irving Howe, *Politics and the Novel* (New York: Horizon Press, 1957), 76–113; G. H. Bantock, "Conrad and Politics," *English Literary History* 25, no. 2 (June 1958): 122–36; Eloise Knapp Hay, *The Political Novels of Joseph Conrad: A Critical Study* (Chicago: University of Chicago Press, 1963); Avrom Fleishman, *Conrad's Politics: Community and Anarchy in the Fiction of Joseph Conrad* (Baltimore, Md.: Johns Hopkins University Press, 1967); Frederic Jameson, *The Political Unconscious: Narrative as a Socially Symbolic Act* (Ithaca, N.Y.: Cornell University Press, 1981); and Benita Parry, *Conrad and Imperialism: Ideological Boundaries and Visionary Frontiers* (London: Macmillan, 1983).

Joseph Conrad as Guide to Colonial History

Christopher GoGwilt

"Heart of Darkness" is not a factual report on the atrocities of Belgian exploitation in the Congo. *Lord Jim* is not a historical record of Britain's efforts to sustain its hegemony over global sea-trading routes in the Eastern Hemisphere. *Nostromo* is an entirely imaginary projection of the emergence of U.S. neo-colonial hegemony. *The Secret Agent* and *Under Western Eyes*, likewise, are not exposés documenting the bureaucracies for policing terrorism forged from the colonial rivalry between the British and Russian empires. Yet all these works capture something powerfully real about the various histories to which they refer. Conrad's fiction itself has become an indispensable guide to the history of colonialism, especially for the moment of the late nineteenth and early twentieth century, when European colonial nation-states, along with the United States, engaged in a planetary scramble for control over the earth's resources.

To gauge what sort of historical guide Conrad's fiction offers for understanding colonialism and imperialism we might consider three general contexts: the context in which Conrad himself wrote; the context within which successive writers, critics, and readers have situated Conrad's fiction; and the future context within which Conrad has yet to be read. Clearly the most immediately relevant and historically significant context is the one in which Conrad wrote, between the 1890s and the 1920s. This is the period of "high imperialism," distinguished by many of the events that make these years simultaneously the high tide mark of and a turning point against European imperialism: the partition of Africa in the 1880s; the Spanish-American War of 1898; the Boer War of 1899–1902; the Russo-Japanese war of 1904–5; the First World War of 1914–18; the Russian Revolution of 1917. With such memorable examples as the multicolored map of Africa in "Heart of Darkness," and the "Westerner's" partial glimpse of the map of the Baltic provinces in *Under Western Eyes*, Conrad provides the imagery by which readers continue to measure the colonial mapping of the world in what Eric Hobsbawm has called the Age of Empire.[1]

Conrad's work has also proved increasingly relevant for debates about what has happened since, during the period of decolonization that rescrambled the colonial map of the world to produce newly independent nations in Asia, Africa, and elsewhere in the Third World. These debates have, indeed, substantially shifted perceptions of colonial history—most notably by calling attention to perspectives that had been peripheral to the colonizers' vision. Following the lead of Third World writers and critics of Conrad—such as Chinua Achebe and V. S. Naipaul, to take two notably contrasting examples—Conrad's work has been read either as a measure of the colonial distortion of history or as a measure of the disruptive effects of decolonization itself. Either way, the images of Conrad's fiction—the titles "Heart of Darkness" and *Under Western Eyes* offer perhaps the most enduring, if also riddling images—have become common points of reference, debate, and contest, over the shape of colonial history in the wake of independence struggles. Itself a product of the changing world system at the height of Britain's overseas hegemony, Conrad's work remains a revealing guide to those reversals of global perspectives that accompanied the process of decolonization in the twentieth century, "moving the center" (in Ngũgĩ phrase) toward what once seemed marginal to world history.[2]

If Conrad's work is not a historical record of facts, it does stand in close proximity to the problem of recording such facts, and this makes it especially relevant to future historians of colonialism. The official archive of colonial history is notoriously biased. Catherine Elkins's study of colonial policies in Kenya, for example, calls attention to the systematic erasure of the record of British brutalities in suppressing the Mau Mau rebellions.[3] Explicitly drawing on Conrad's work, Adam Hochschild's study of the Belgian Congo unearths neglected and buried facts both about the atrocities perpetrated by colonial agents and about the struggles of those who fought against them.[4] Conrad's fiction stands in important relation to such studies precisely because of its marginal relation to the official records of the historical archives. As the Indonesian writer Pramoedya Ananta Toer said in 1995, discussing the significance of Conrad's fiction for Indonesian history, "In Conrad's works there are historical facts which have not been recorded elsewhere."[5] If the reception of Conrad's work has already played a part in recovering "facts" of colonial history overlooked, deliberately erased, or otherwise distorted, by the official records of Belgian, British, or Dutch colonial archives, future readings of Conrad may play a greater role still in guiding reevaluations of the processes of colonization and decolonization.

Conrad's Peripheral Vision

It is the peripheral vision of Conrad's grasp of colonialism that makes his fiction so enduring a guide to the changing historical moment in which he wrote. This peripheral vision is exemplified by the remote setting of the fictional "Sambir" of his first novel, *Almayer's Folly*, which foreshadows the multiplicity of ways in which the later work would register the changing geography of colonial experience in his time. The remoteness of setting is exaggerated still more in Conrad's later description, in *A Personal Record*, of the itinerary of his first novel's growth as a manuscript: set in a remote region of Borneo on the periphery of Dutch East Indies colonial control, the novel was begun in a London flat, traveled with him to the Congo and to the Ukraine, and witnessed his final maritime appointment on a ship that never left the French port of Rouen. These incongruous locations may at first appear to have little to do with the specific setting of *Almayer's Folly*, but the adventures Conrad ascribes to his first manuscript reveal in comic form the configuration of experiences from which Conrad forged his own identity as a writer, and his peripheral vision of the colonial realities of his time. Sambir—the Borneo setting of *Almayer's Folly*—is very different from the African setting of "Heart of Darkness," the European settings of *Under Western Eyes*, or the London setting of *The Secret Agent*. That difference is already inscribed as a problem of peripheral historical perspective into the narrative form of the novel, in its plotting, in its depiction of characters, and in its manipulation of language.

Anticipating the creation of an imaginary Latin American country, Costaguana, in *Nostromo*, Sambir constitutes a highly complex projection of historical "facts" about changing colonial social relations throughout Southeast Asia, including Conrad's own limited experience of the northeast Borneo region of Berau, his reading about other regions in the Malay Archipelago, and a fictional reconstruction of those readings and experiences into narrative form. The fictional Sambir, a settlement of mixed Bugis, Arab, and European inhabitants on coastal Borneo (present-day Kalimantan), provides as complex a realistic setting as one might expect for a nineteenth-century historical novel in the tradition of Maria Edgeworth and Walter Scott. The unusual location and Conrad's exoticized descriptions of tropical nature have led readers (such as Linda Dryden and Andrea White[6]) to classify Conrad's early fiction with imperial adventure romance rather than with the realist novel, but, as Ian Watt pointed out when he suggestively described it as a Flaubert novel set in the tropics,[7] it is the combination of exoticizing romance and banal realism that gives it imaginative shape. It is the gap between what readers expect from exotic romance and what readers expect from novelistic realism that allows Conrad to create the imagined community of Sambir.

Sambir offers a model for what economic historians have described as the colonial periphery. Like the remote region of northeast Borneo Conrad visited in 1887 during a series of trading trips to Borneo and Celebes as first mate of the steamship *Vidar*, the fictional Sambir is located, indeed, on the periphery of that colonial periphery—a remote settlement in only intermittent contact with steamship services from Singapore, the shipping nexus (or *entrepot*) for British trade in Southeast Asia, and with Batavia, the capital of Dutch colonial power throughout the East Indies. The economic significance of Sambir's peripheral relation to these nodal points of European colonial power (Singapore and Batavia) plays an important role in the plot of *Almayer's Folly*— and, indeed, in the projection of the first set of novels Conrad planned, the so-called Lingard trilogy of novels, not finished until toward the very end of his life. A considerable part of Almayer's "folly" hinges on the hopes he pins on having the British, rather than the Dutch, secure trading hegemony over Sambir. Almayer's misguided investment in British interests constitutes the last act in the sequence of Conrad's planned trilogy, which traces in reverse the history of an English Rajah's failed attempt to establish a material and political presence in the region. In this regard, Sambir provides a model for the ways in which Conrad's later novels will grasp, with varying shades of irony and critique, the economic facts of changing colonial relations from the late nineteenth to the early twentieth century.

There are of course striking differences between the economies of Conrad's different fictional locations—between, say, the ivory trade that fuels the slave labor and underdevelopment of central Africa in "Heart of Darkness," and the role of the silver mine that fuels the economic transformation and political turmoil of Costaguana in *Nostromo*. Each of these three notable fictions (the "Sambir" of *Almayer's Folly*, the central African setting of "Heart of Darkness," and the "Costaguana" of *Nostromo*) presents a rather different model of that emerging periphery to the world economy that would, later in the twentieth century, go by the name of the Third World. Costaguana, the fictional Latin American country brought into the global economic system through the development of the silver mine, represents the seemingly successful economic model of development—the success, however, only ensuring Costaguana's dependence on the economic and political forces tied to the "material interests" of the silver mine. The Congo of "Heart of Darkness," by contrast, emphasizes the failure of this same model of economic exploitation, revealing the logic of what has been called "underdevelopment," producing out of the very richness of the Congo's economic resources a region of violence, chaos, and inhuman suffering. These two celebrated cases offer contrasting models of the development—and under-development—of the colonial periphery in Conrad's time. The contrast is complicated, of course, both by the specific cultural and political geographies of their different Latin American and African settings and by the role Latin America and Central Africa have each played, since, in debates about colonialism, decoloniza-tion, and ongoing forms of economic exploitation. These works nonetheless offer revealing case studies for tracking the emer-gence of a peripheral Third World, necessary for, yet dependent on, the centers of the global economy.

As with the later fictional countries, Conrad's imaginative con-struction of the "model state of Sambir" (as it is ironically dubbed early in the novel) illuminates Conrad's close attention to the eco-nomic details of what contemporary figures sought to explain as the shift from "colonialism" to "imperialism" (as theorized by the English liberal economist J. A. Hobson in 1902[8]) or (as V. I. Lenin, following Hobson, put it in 1916[9]) from "industrial capitalism" to the ultra-imperialism of "finance capitalism." What precipitates the novel's ironic use of the term "model state" is the official rec-ognition that the British Borneo Company has "abandoned its claim to that part of the East Coast," leaving Sambir "under the nominal power of Holland."[10] The British Borneo Company rep-resents British interests in a form of colonial relation not directly tied to the state and in fact here distinguished from the form of sovereign state "power" associated with Holland, Britain's colonial rival in the region. As part of the ironic nuances attached to this phrase—"the model state of Sambir"—*Almayer's Folly* involves the reader in a complex process of evaluating the different claims to economic, political, and cultural prestige, locally, regionally, and globally. In *Nostromo* Britain's interests are engaged with the development of Sulaco and Costaguano through the agency of Captain Mitchell's Oceanic Steam Navigation Company. These interests involve other companies (notably the railway company), and in the end Captain Mitchell might be read as a sort of comic counterpart to Almayer, succeeding where Almayer fails, in the "folly" of banking on British investments in the region. What each has in common, however, is the precarious and contingent relation of the economic periphery, as an index of economic and political investment within a global economy of imperialism. The ironies, in each case, are inseparable from the wider implications of the plots—Captain Mitchell becomes the obtuse tour guide explaining Sulaco's history, presenting the parodic superficial "official" version of a historical process *Nostromo* imagines as infinitely more complex, tortured, and nightmarish; Almayer, as noted above, is blind to the plotting of politics and history around him. In *Nostromo*, Captain Mitchell's British interests come to serve a set of political alliances that undermine those British ideals. In *Almayer's Folly*, British trading interests come to serve the needs of Almayer's economic and political rival, the Arab trader Abdulla.

These national contradictions are embedded within the form of the chartered company, that transitional form of economic agency between colonialism and imperialism, or between "industrial capitalism" and "international finance capitalism." The most obvious example of the chartered company in Conrad's fiction is the Belgian company in "Heart of Darkness." With surreal or (following Ian Watt's reading) symbolist emphasis[11] it is simply called the "Company" ("a Company for trade"[12]) and provides a fictional counterpart to the chartered company "Société Anonyme Belge pour le Commerce du Haut-Congo" (Belgian Limited Company for Trade in the Upper Congo) that employed Conrad as second-in-command of the steamship *Roi des Belges*. Whether considered the transitional structure between colonialism and imperialism, corresponding to the "nucleus out of which Imperialism has grown,"[13] as Hobson saw it, or, as Lenin saw it, the point of contradiction between "the gigantic 'operations' (and gigantic profits) of finance capital and 'honest' trade in the free market,"[14] the position of chartered companies over the turn of the century was still crucial, especially within the orbit of British imperialism. Hobson calls attention to the significance of the British North Borneo Company, the Sierra Leone Company, the Royal Niger Company, the East Africa Company, the British South Africa Company,[15] all examples of chartered companies representing British economic, administrative, and military interests over the period in which Conrad was writing. Such companies, charged with negotiating treaties, equipped with occupying armies, and entrusted with administrative obligations, carried out the work of securing, partitioning, and administering colonial territories. In long historical perspective, these chartered companies look back to the first big European trading companies—the East India Company, above all—and forward to today's multinational corporations.

In each of the fictional cases described above—Costaguana of *Nostromo*, the Congo of "Heart of Darkness," and Sambir of *Almayer's Folly*—one can trace the role of the chartered companies in illuminating this transitional moment of "high imperialism." As Benita Parry's study of Conrad shows, *Nostromo* may be the most thoroughgoing fictional critique of that dynamic variously described by Hobson's liberal British and Lenin's revolutionary Russian critique of imperialism.[16] It is the combination of companies (the Oceanic Steam Navigation Company; the National Central Railroad company, financed by Holroyd's bank)—their consolidation into a cartel, or monopoly, following the interests of high finance capital—that shores up the "material interests" of the San Tomé mine, linking Costaguana to the economic world system. The chartered company that gives birth to the independent country (according to Hobson's model of economic development) or (according to Lenin's model) that makes the Latin American country in turn dependent (a "semi-colony") on the anarchic forces of international finance capital—this is the theme of *Nostromo* and it is played out on a scale larger than in Conrad's other works, although "Heart of Darkness" examines the grim features of racist labor exploitation, in what Hobson (and Lenin following him) recognized as the "classical instance": "the Congo Free State, where a 'militia' levy was made upon the population, nominally for defence, but really for the State and Chartered Company service in the 'rubber' and other industries."[17] Yet Conrad's "model state of Sambir" (held up as a "model" to set against the British Borneo Company) indicates the extent to which Conrad's experience of this contradictory moment of transition provides a powerful historical vision, albeit based on imaginative fictions rather than on the statistical facts cited by Hobson or Lenin.

Sambir constitutes a microcosm of the economic, social, and political relations and conflicts that characterize the shift from nineteenth- to twentieth-century forms of colonialism and imperialism—a shift in forms of global economic, social, and political control that J. A. Hobson defined simply as "imperialism"; that Lenin, following Hobson, characterized as the decisive shift from industrial to finance capitalism; and that recent writers have variously described as globalization, or the emergence of "Empire."[18] Sambir provides a microcosm for these changes by focusing on a specific cultural locality that is being defined by the alliances and antagonisms of a network of social forces from outside—Dutch colonial power, British and Arab trading interests, local Bugis settler interests, and Indies-wide anticolonial political movements. Yet if Conrad is able to invent a fictional microcosm corresponding to the social dynamic of colonial history over the turn of the century, the very invention of this location, geographically and historically, emerges through a form of narrative that complicates any description of social reality or "facts." Sambir itself is the stubbornly fictional name for a place that cannot be located on a map. It projects a contest of history, organized around the "folly" of the novel's title character, Almayer, who misrecognizes the social and political coordinates of the communities within which he imagines himself to be living.

Conrad in the Colonial Archive

Conrad's success in creating fictional models by which we can measure the real historical process of colonization rests, to a considerable degree, and paradoxically, on the success with which he elides, distorts, and displaces the real historical places, names, and experiences, on which his fiction is premised. As with the naming of Sambir itself—a name taken from a settlement ten miles from the historical "Berau" on which Sambir is based[19]—this involves a twofold process of first dislocating the fiction from historical fact with the effect, then, all the more powerfully of embedding those dislocated facts in a relation to history. If the invention of imaginary places such as Sambir names a fictional model of economic periphery, the difficulty of placing the name on the map and in history foregrounds the way in which these stubbornly fictional places also compel readers and critics to attempt to chart their relation to geographical reality and to historical facts. "Patusan" in *Lord Jim* presents an especially revealing example. Although the name appears on maps in books Conrad consulted, as the name of a settlement on the northwest coast of Borneo (Sarawak), the geographical coordinates of *Lord Jim*, according to recent critics (Hans van Marle and Pierre Lefranc[20]), situate Conrad's Patusan on the northwest coast of Sumatra. Patusan is exemplary of Conrad's practice of deliberately misnaming and misplacing the fictional coordinates of his colonial settings, a craft self-consciously adopted with the deliberately masked eastern setting of the end of "Youth," the first of the Marlow trilogy of tales (followed by "Heart of Darkness" and *Lord Jim*). Patusan—more clearly than Sambir—presents a fictional location that simultaneously insists on the symbolism of its utopian projection and links that fictional model to the historical record, and specifically the record of Henry Keppel's *Expedition to Borneo of H. M. S. Dido*, an account of Sir James Brooke's campaigns against piracy, which refers to the pirate settlement of Patusan (spelled Patusen). Keppel's (approving) description of the massacre of "pirate" villagers at Patusen (and elsewhere)[21] forms an important point of reference for Conrad's imaginative reconstruction of history in the Malay Archipelago—at times, as Robert Hampson notes, offering "an account of Brooke's 'war against pirates' from the victim's perspective."[22]

As the example of Patusan suggests, Conrad's peripheral vision emerges both from a fictional distancing and displacement of historical facts (relocating Patusan from the northeast coast of Borneo to the southwest coast of Sumatra) and from a sometimes surprising proximity to the historical archive (calling attention to gaps and biases in an authoritative historical record like Keppel's *Expedition*). A fundamental formative feature of Conrad's fiction is its reflection on the elisions, gaps, and biases inscribed in any authoritative record of history. The most vexed and contentious example of this is "Heart of Darkness," whose narrative embeds this double sense of relation to the textual authority of archives in the metaphor of marginal script. Kurtz's "valuable postscriptum"—"Exterminate all the brutes!"[23]—reveals a genocidal logic concealed beneath the rhetoric of missionary benevolence in Kurtz's official report for the (revealingly named) International Society for the Suppression of Savage Customs. The satirical reference here to what Conrad had already, in "An Outpost of Progress," parodied as the "high-flown language"[24] of speeches by King Leopold II on Belgian's "civilizing work" in the Congo, would have been clear to contemporary readers. Yet "Heart of Darkness" goes further than either "Youth" or *Lord Jim* in eliding all specific place-name references to the novella's Congo setting (the river is never identified as the Congo River); we learn of the Central Station and the Inner Station, but no specific place-names are mentioned following Marlow's reference to the Gran' Bassam and Little Popo in his account of the journey to Africa ("various places—trading places—with names like Gran' Bassam, Little Popo; names that seemed to belong to some sordid farce acted in front of a sinister back-cloth").[25] The deliberation of this elision has long been recognized as a part of the novella's aesthetic structure, whether in terms of what Ian Watt points to as the "symbolist" effect of eliding the definite article in the title's "Heart of Darkness" or in terms of the story's self-conscious manipulation of the trope of the "Dark Continent" (see, for example, Patrick Brantlinger[26]) governing European representations of Africa. This refusal to place and name the specific geographical location of "Heart of Darkness" sets the novella apart from historical records in a way that has made its relation to the historical record all the more insistent, whether for critics (such as Chinua Achebe) who point to the historical experiences obliterated by the story, for critics (such as Hochschild) who point to the historical facts registered by the story, or for critics (such as J. Hillis Miller[27]) who point out that it is a mistake to read the tale referentially at all.

This elision of reference has only increased the importance of "Heart of Darkness" as a point of reference for historical accounts of the Belgian atrocities in the Congo and, by extension, for the late nineteenth-century European "scramble" for colonial territories in Africa. Chinua Achebe's 1977 polemic against the critical canonization of the novella pinpoints one crucial reason for this when he argues that it projects a distorted "image of Africa" set up "as a foil to Europe." Achebe's polemic has itself become a canonical point of reference for debating the role of racism in evaluations of the work. In emphasizing the way the Congo setting reinforces an image of all Africa, however, Achebe calls attention to the critical difficulty in evading the elision of reference to the story's actual location. Achebe himself cannot escape such an elision and pays remarkably little attention to the facts of Belgian exploitation in the Congo, mostly because this, too, belongs to his polemical purpose to expose the normalizing force of an "English liberal tradition which required all Englishmen of decency to be deeply shocked by atrocities in Bulgaria or the Congo of King Leopold of the Belgians or wherever."[28]

Foregrounding the critical difficulty in explaining the relation between "Heart of Darkness" and the facts of colonial atrocities, Achebe's argument stands in revealing counterpoint to Hannah Arendt's pivotal use of the example of "Heart of Darkness" in the second part of her monumental 1951 three-part study, *The Origins of Totalitarianism*. Arendt's argument (a mid-twentieth-century recalibration of earlier liberal and revolutionary critiques of imperialism exemplified by Hobson and Lenin) is especially revealing in showing the extent to which the racism that Achebe identifies remains both the blindspot and the critical lens through which Conrad's text has repeatedly been made to perform a critique of imperialism. In her opening reference to "Heart of Darkness," she cites Marlow's description of the postscript to Kurtz's official report—"a flash of lightning in a serene sky: 'Exterminate all the brutes'"—to illustrate what she presents as the epitome of South African Boer racism and, by extension, the development of "race" as one of the two new "devices" (the other is "bureaucracy") for "political organization and rule over foreign peoples."[29] The slippage from the Belgian Congo to Boer South Africa is only one of the problematic features of Arendt's use of "Heart of Darkness." What justifies that slippage is the claim that the Boers and other "rootless" or "superfluous" European colonial adventurers like Kurtz embodied an experience of "race consciousness"—a racism—that became a "ruling device" that imperialism "exploited" as a "a major political idea."[30] The critique of racism here itself pivots on a racist claim for the equivalence of this "rootless" European "race consciousness" with that of the "black tribes" with whom they lived—a claim developed again from "Heart of Darkness," this time from Marlow's meditation on the feeling of "remote kinship" with "the prehistoric man" he sees in the Africans along the banks of the Congo River (almost precisely the passage Achebe, too, quotes at length).[31]

Arendt reproduces precisely the "image of Africa" for which Achebe critiques Conrad's novella. As Rob Nixon has pointed out, Arendt's conflation of disparate African histories in making Kurtz's scrawl—"Exterminate the brutes"—stand for a generalized colonial mentality contributes to an already-established tradition of travel writing, from André Gide up to V. S. Naipaul; a tradition that reproduces what Achebe dissects as the white racist "image of Africa" in its use of Conrad as a travel guide to the colonial history of Africa. In Nixon's terms, "in slipping from fiction to the literature of 'fact,' this trope ['heart of darkness'] and its constellation of phrases have accumulated a normative force, confining Africa to an invented consistency that militates against certain kinds of information, as well as historically and regionally more specific representations. The net effect is the image of a continent still debilitated by a measure of figurative arrest."[32]

This is not, however, simply to dismiss as racist Arendt's claim that Boer settlers, and other European adventurers like Kurtz, had regressed to the "prehistoric" conditions of African peoples. It is important to recognize the extent to which the entire argument about totalitarianism pivots around this blindspot. The wider axis on which her argument hinges is the contrast between the example of the Boers and that of the British. The former are associated with the "the worst elements in Western civilization," the latter with "the best, and sometimes even the most clear-sighted, strata of the European intelligentsia."[33] The Boers are credited with having introduced the device of "race as a principle of the body politic"; while the British are credited with having introduced "bureaucracy as a principle of foreign domination."[34] Arendt juxtaposes reputable and disreputable European examples in order to call attention to the *illusion* of respectability that results from the convergence of what is characterized as two forms (or "devices") of colonial exploitation, "race" and "bureaucracy." Both come together into what Arendt characterizes as the totalitarian logic of genocide—of "administrative massacres," as Arendt puts it, citing Carthill's assessment of British colonial policies in India. Arendt's crucial insight is that the rise of totalitarianism in Europe is to be related to the history of colonialism—that the forms of racism developed through Europe's "overseas imperialism" became an instrument in the administration of the concentration camps of Europe's "continental imperialism." Arendt's insight invites renewed archival attention to what links the practices of imperial policing "overseas" and on "continental" Europe. These links are already evident in the rivalry between British and Russian imperial police bureaucracies that underlies Conrad's *The Secret Agent* and *Under Western Eyes*. Both novels together might serve as a future guide in assessing the techniques of surveillance, torture, and "administrative massacre" that have recently been adopted, more or less self-consciously, in what might be called the administrative terrorism of today's so-called war on terror. But the deliberative use to which Arendt puts Conrad's troping of the "Dark Continent" to emphasize the colonial origins of Nazi and Soviet totalitarianism—implicitly transferring back to the continent of Europe the "darkness" imposed on Africa by Europe's "overseas" imperialism—all the more strikingly condenses and displaces the historical experiences of colonialism (not to mention the many forms of resistance against colonialism) throughout the African continent.

As multiple post-colonial readings of "Heart of Darkness" illustrate, however, Conrad's figurative play on the trope of the "Dark Continent" makes the language of historical "fact" difficult to disentangle from that of literary fiction. Its textual authority rests on the manner in which it inscribes itself ambivalently into an archive of untold ("unspeakable") historical facts. Naipaul's close identification with Conrad, according to Homi Bhabha, reveals an ambivalence in the very structure of colonial authority already at work in Conrad's text.[35] Following Naipaul, Bhabha's central example is the "extraordinary" discovery of the English book in Marlow's journey upriver.[36] The "Englishness" of this book on seamanship repeats a pattern of belatedness whereby the colonial authority of an English text is premised on a non-English reading: hence what fascinates Marlow about *An Inquiry into Some Points of Seamanship* is the Russian script in the margin rather than the English text itself.[37] In a slightly more basic political sense than Homi Bhabha discusses, the English text of "Heart of Darkness" itself is premised on a non-English experience: the francophone scene of the Belgian Congo means that Kurtz's report and much, if not all, of the dialogue would presumably be in French. Emphasizing the different kinds of European presence in the African colonial setting, this point has typically served to underscore the contrast between Marlow's sympathetic assessment of British colonialism and his antipathy toward other (notably French and Belgian) forms of colonial exploitation. As the example of Kurtz makes clear, however, English "sympathies"[38] are by no means unambiguously affirmed. The English that Kurtz and the Russian harlequin admire is, then (and in Homi Bhabha's sense), not quite English (Kurtz's "voice" speaks English, but it is not at all clear whether the Russian harlequin speaks English or French to Marlow); and this displaced linguistic and political register of English introduces a difference into the text of "Heart of Darkness" that Homi Bhabha diagnoses as "the *différance* of the colonial presence."[39] Conrad's own English, of course, is not quite "English" and that, arguably, is precisely what Naipaul admires in turn about the appearance of the "English book" in Africa—a point Sara Suleri makes noting how Naipaul deliberately fashions himself "as the Harlequin, the borderer on someone else's story,"[40] in his embrace of an English literary tradition exemplified by Conrad. Naipaul's reading underscores the extent to which the sharp and volatile differences over how to read the political "sympathies" of Conrad's "Heart of Darkness" that have characterized successive readings are already inscribed in the text's own ambivalent relation to the colonial archive.

Arendt's pivotal use of Conrad offers a striking example of how Conrad's work has become an important but ambivalent guide to colonial history. "Heart of Darkness" enables both Arendt's insight (into the colonial origins of European totalitarianism) and also her blindness (toward the specificity of African history). This combination of blindness and insight may be traced in Arendt's influence over Cold War liberal thinking; and it continues to shape recent debates about sovereignty and power, genocide and human rights (see, for example, Agamben, Butler and Spivak[41]). Each reading of "Heart of Darkness" becomes a scene of reading race, a parable about the legibility or illegibility of "race consciousness." Conrad's text will likely remain a touchstone for future debates about race and racism. It is a text that has engaged fiercely invested interpretative positions,[42] and indeed the multitude of different, proliferating readings of the text graphically demonstrate in what sense it is a split, hybrid text, in Homi Bhabha's sense, inscribing real differences over understanding the context of colonial history. As with the problem of locating Kurtz's English "sympathies" in "Heart of Darkness"—or, indeed, locating the geography of Conrad's imagined communities—the differences are there already in Conrad's text, determined by the volatile and changing responses to the experiences of colonialism and imperialism of Conrad's time. Successive readings may have drawn attention to those differences, but they have surely not resolved them. If it is difficult to imagine how future readings could resolve those differences, it is certainly likely that future readings will more fully measure how Conrad's texts relate to the archive of colonial history.

Conrad's English

In the 1919 "Author's Note" to *A Personal Record*, Conrad provided his own example of the ambivalence of colonial authority written into his use of English. Recalling his career-long friendship with Sir Hugh Clifford, the former administrator (and future governor) of Britain's Malay territories and then Governor of Nigeria, Conrad took the opportunity to issue "what in the diplomatic language is called [a] 'rectification'" of a statement Clifford had made about him in an article from 1898.[43] The dispute, couched in mock "diplomatic language," is clearly between friends; indeed part of its purpose is to foreground that friendship, suggesting a deliberate affiliation with British colonial authority. But the mock use of diplomatic language also introduces the possibility of a political difference (deliberately foregrounding the language of political negotiation of colonial administrators) that is then inextricably linked with the question of Conrad's use of English, "the fact of my not writing in my native language."[44]

The point of the dispute, or "rectification," is the claim that Conrad "exercised a choice" between English and French, a claim that Conrad denies, insisting that it was English that adopted him and not the other way around. The mere staging of this mock standoff between a non-native English speaker and "a man accustomed to speak unpalatable truths even to Oriental potentates"[45] performs a scene of contest with colonial authority that suggests the sort of "*différance* of the colonial presence" that Homi Bhabha finds as the constitutive ambivalence of authority in colonial texts. Even as Conrad signals his career-long close friendship with a high colonial official, he insists on marking a difference. This difference might be linked more clearly to the inherently double-sided function of the hegemonic use of English as a colonial language in light of the original claim Clifford made (in a 1904 article, not, as Conrad claims, in his 1898 anonymous review). Clifford there ascribes Conrad's choice of English to a specifically colonial sympathy with "men of British breed": "his sympathies were with the men of English race whom he had found scattered through the crannies of the world. Men of British breed, it seemed to him, would perhaps understand the things of which he had to tell as no other men could do. In the end, therefore, he decided upon the use of English."[46] Taken as a "rectification" of this statement, Conrad might indeed be claiming that his English is not quite "English" in Clifford's British colonial sense.

It is the seafaring experience, as this defines both Conrad's sense of spoken English and the linguistic and literary medium of his written English, that makes Conrad's English not quite "English" in the sense that Clifford implies when he writes of Conrad's "sympathies" with "men of British breed." The space of the sea in Conrad's work is certainly a place that privileges a particular English seafaring ethos. Indeed at times that English ethos is invoked through a rhetoric of English nationalism that sounds very similar to the jingoistic rhetoric that characterized the "new imperialism" of the 1890s (and reached its height during the 1897 Diamond Jubilee celebrating the sixtieth year of

Queen Victoria's reign). Perhaps the most famous example is the frame narrator's encomium to the River Thames at the beginning of "Heart of Darkness," in which he praises the "greatness" of "all the men of whom the nation is proud, from Sir Francis Drake to Sir John Franklin, knights all, titled and untitled—the great knights-errant of the sea."[47] The passage is cited as an epigraph to Niall Fergusson's *Empire*,[48] aptly illustrating that book's attempt to defend British imperialism as a force for good and as a model for the United States in the twenty-first century. Missing from Clifford's characterization of Conrad's "sympathies"—and strikingly absent from Fergusson's book, too—is a recognition of the way that rhetoric is undermined by Marlow's narrative voice ("Knights? Yes, but it is like a running blaze on a plain, like a flash of lightning in the clouds"[49]). Conrad sometimes deliberately simplifies the English identity of the seafaring ethos he invokes, but even given his tendency (as Najder notes[50]) to underrepresent in his fiction the multiracial makeup of the ships on which Conrad himself served, it is impossible to grasp the significance of the English seafaring ethos without measuring it in relation to the notably multiracial crews of the British merchant ships in his fiction (for example, in *The Nigger of the "Narcissus"* and *Lord Jim*). As Fredric Jameson points out in his influential reading of Conrad in *The Political Unconscious*, the "craft of the sea" in Conrad's fiction constitutes a complex distillation of real social experience and literary form, in which the hegemony of British imperialism is all at once realistically explored and ideologically contained: "the sea is both a strategy of containment and a place of real business."[51] This space of the sea, along with the English seafaring ethos it embodies, is also the medium of Conrad's English—all at once, as it were, Sir Hugh Clifford's "English race" and yet not quite English in that sense at all.

   The difference Conrad stages with Clifford over his adoption of—or by—"English" also concerns a significant difference over Clifford's claim to colonial authority over the Malay subject matter of Conrad's fiction. In staging the confrontation between himself, as impertinent non-native English speaker, and Clifford, the high colonial official, Conrad has Clifford "end by telling me...that as a matter of fact I didn't know anything about

Malays. I was perfectly well aware of this. I have never pretended to any such knowledge, and I was moved—I wonder to this day at my impertinence—to retort: 'Of course I don't know anything about Malays. If I knew only one hundredth part of what you and Frank Swettenham know of Malays I would make everybody sit up.' "⁵² The marked ambivalence of Conrad's acknowledgment and disavowal of Clifford's colonial authority reproduces almost precisely the terms of Conrad's initial reaction to Clifford's anonymous 1898 review criticizing Conrad's depiction of Malays. Defending himself against Clifford's accusations in a letter to his publisher, William Blackwood, he wrote in 1898: "Well I never did set up as an authority on Malaysia."⁵³

The difference is more sharply defined in 1898 than in 1919 and more sharply defined as a political, territorial difference between the region of Clifford's administrative authority—the British controlled Malay settlements ("Malaysia")—and the Dutch East Indies territories in which almost all of Conrad's "Malay" fiction is set. Although not directly linked to the question of Conrad's choice of English, this territorial difference has important implications for the way in which Conrad's English registers, from the very first, an ambivalence toward colonial authority. The fictional setting of "Sambir," in *Almayer's Folly*, as we have already seen, is located at the periphery of both British and Dutch colonial spheres of influence. The Malay world it depicts is, on the one hand, significantly different from the one Clifford knew. Its focus on a coastal Bugis community, not unlike the Bugis settlement of Patusan in *Lord Jim*, has led more careful critical commentators to note that Clifford's "Malays" are not necessarily the same people as Conrad's "Malays."⁵⁴ This difference of cultural perspective is made even clearer by the plot to restore a Bugis kingdom in *The Rescue*, Conrad's long-delayed third novel in the Malay trilogy, not completed until 1919 (the same year he issued his "rectification" of Clifford's statement). It would be misleading, however, to suggest that Conrad's "real Malays" are the Bugis people. Conrad's fictional communities are not, after all, premised on the same sort of attention to racial and ethnographic details that constitute Clifford's claim to knowledge of or authority over Malays. His "Sambir" and "Patusan" are not only communities formed by the historical and cultural diaspora of the Bugis people throughout the Malay Archipelago. The fictional model of those settlements presents a microcosm of the sort of imagined colonial community, shaped by multiethnic diasporas, that defines Conrad's particular peripheral vision of colonial history.

This peripheral vision is premised both on a difference of personal experience from Clifford and on a different cultural and historical grasp of the Malay Archipelago. In Conrad's initial response to Clifford's 1898 accusation that he "didn't know anything about Malays," Conrad had noted that "all the details" held up as "proof" of his ignorance "have been taken...from undoubted sources—dull, wise books."[55] As noted earlier, Conrad's "Patusan" not only suggests a detail drawn from Henry Keppel's *Expedition to Borneo of H.M.S. Dido*, one of the "dull, wise books" referred to in his 1898 letter; it also suggests an alternative reading of that book's historical record of British colonial intervention in the Malay Archipelago. This is not to suggest, however, that Conrad's fiction represents the perspective of the colonized peoples over against the authority of colonial administrators like Sir Hugh Clifford. Nonetheless, the ambivalence toward the form of "English" identification with British colonialism that surfaces in his mock diplomatic "rectification" calls attention to the ways in which Conrad situates his fiction deliberately at the conjuncture of volatile and antagonistic perspectives.[56] The imaginary "Sambir" of *Almayer's Folly*, "Patusan" of *Lord Jim*, central Africa of "Heart of Darkness," and "Costaguana" of *Nostromo* all project, on the one hand, communities that appear to be complex fictional correlatives of actual historical colonial settlements; and, on the other hand, complex dislocations of community on a local and a global scale.

The contrast between the Malaysian territories of Clifford's administrative experience and the Indonesian coastal communities of Conrad's fiction draws attention to the changing historical context within which Conrad's work as a whole emerged and at the same time foregrounds the linguistic significance of Conrad's English for registering that changing historical context. Between the mid-1890s, when Conrad began publishing, and 1919, when he issued his "rectification" of Clifford (and finally completed the serial version of *The Rescue*), there were enormous changes transforming both British-controlled Malaysia and the Dutch-controlled East Indies. These years saw an accelerated territorial and administrative consolidation of possessions that gave geographical and political shape to the territories of present-day Malaysia and Indonesia. These were the years of what is often characterized as liberal reform: the reorganization of the Residential system into the system of so-called indirect rule in British Malaysia; and, in the Dutch East Indies, the so-called Ethical policy of liberal reforms meant to dismantle the "culture system" of forced peasant labor on European plantations. These liberal reforms, however, were accompanied by a still more systematic form of economic, political, and administrative control over colonial territories, many of which—like "Sambir"—had until then only nominally been controlled by the respective British or Dutch authorities. While these reforms reflect the efforts of colonial administrators like Clifford to respond to the growing unrest with and resistance to colonial rule, they also register the growing unrest and resistance to which these reforms are an increasingly aggressive response.

Within the Malay-speaking communities under Dutch colonial control, one crucial aspect of anticolonial resistance was, as Benedict Anderson notes in his celebrated study of the rise and spread of nationalism, the emergence of the new language, Indonesian, from the *lingua franca* of Malay spoken throughout the Archipelago, that became the vehicle for imagining a new form of anticolonial nationalism and, ultimately, the official language of the new nation of Indonesia.[57] Conrad's English, by contrast to the emergence of Indonesian, would appear to embody the very opposite form of imagining community. Yet as the diplomatic rectification of Clifford suggests, if Conrad's English is hardly the language of anticolonial nationalism, it is not quite the language of colonial administration either. Rather, it is situated somewhere in between, a linguistic and literary medium peripheral to both the English and Dutch perspectives against which Indonesian anticolonial nationalism was being shaped from the *lingua franca* of Malay. Rooted linguistically, indeed, in the shipboard English of Conrad's early seafaring career, Conrad's English shares important linguistic and historical features with the *lingua franca* of Malay that formed the common language of communication and political contest between colonized and colonizer in the Malay-speaking communities of Conrad's "Sambir."

The fictional Malay community with which Conrad began his career as an English writer is located, historically, politically, and culturally, along the dividing line between forms of anticolonial national imagining and forms of neocolonial and imperial rule. Conrad's English was shaped by the contest between the global forces of decolonization and the aggressive resistance to decolonization that would characterize the twentieth century. Far from being settled, the history of this struggle remains evermore contested. In this sense the archive of colonial history belongs to the future. Colonial history is by no means a thing of the past. Its traumatic legacy will remain a determining feature of future readings of Conrad's work, not least because the unresolved power relations that bind Conrad's age to the era of decolonization have already projected a new "world order" more or less explicitly modeled on older forms of European colonialism and empire. So long as Conrad's famous title formulations, "heart of darkness" and "under western eyes," continue to register an uneasiness of geopolitical perspective in the aftermath of the so-called war on terror that has reformulated the "high imperialism" of the late nineteenth and early twentieth century for the twenty-first century, Conrad's work will likely remain an important guide for understanding past, present, and future forms of colonialism and imperialism.

NOTES

1. See Eric Hobsbawm, *The Age of Empire 1875–1914* (New York: Vintage, 1987).

2. See Ngũgĩ wa Thiong'o, *Moving the Centre: The Struggle for Cultural Freedoms* (Oxford: James Currey, 1993).

3. See Caroline Elkins, *Imperial Reckoning: The Untold Story of Britain's Gulag in Kenya* (New York: Henry Holt, 2005).

4. See Adam Hochschild, *King Leopold's Ghost: A Story of Greed, Terror, and Heroism in Colonial Africa* (Boston: Houghton Mifflin, 1998).

5. Christopher GoGwilt, "Pramoedya's Fiction and History: An Interview with Indonesian Novelist Pramoedya Ananta Toer," *The Yale Journal of Criticism* 9, no. 1 (1996): 147–64.

6. See Linda Dryden, *Joseph Conrad and the Imperial Romance* (New York: St. Martin, 2000) and Andrea White, *Joseph Conrad and the Adventure Tradition* (Cambridge: Cambridge University Press, 1993).

7. Ian Watt, *Conrad in the Nineteenth Century* (London: Chatto & Windus, 1980), 52.

8. See J. A. Hobson, *Imperialism: A Study* (Ann Arbor: University Michigan Press, 1965).

9. See V. I. Lenin, *Imperialism, The Highest Stage of Capitalism* (Peking: Foreign Language Press, 1975).

10. Joseph Conrad, *Almayer's Folly: A Story of an Eastern River*, ed. Jacques Berthoud (Oxford: Oxford University Press), 34.

11. Watt, *Conrad in the Nineteenth Century*, 168ff.

12. Joseph Conrad, "Heart of Darkness," in *"Heart of Darkness" and Other Tales*, ed. Cedric Watts (Oxford: Oxford University Press, 2002), 142.

13. Hobson, *Imperialism*, 252.

14. Lenin, *Imperialism*, 141.

15. Hobson, *Imperialism*, 252.

16. See Benita Parry, *Conrad and Imperialism: Ideological Boundaries and Visionary Frontiers* (London: Macmillan, 1983).

17. Hobson, *Imperialism*, 257.

18. See for example Stephen Ross, *Conrad and Empire* (Columbia, Mo.: University of Missouri Press, 2004), which draws in part from the argument of Michael Hardt and Antonio Negri, *Empire* (Cambridge, Mass.: Harvard University Press, 2000).

19. See note in Conrad, *Almayer's Folly*, 216.

20. See Hans Van Marle and Pierre Lefranc. "Ashore and Afloat: New Perspectives on Topography and Geography in *Lord Jim*," *Conradiana* 20, no. 2 (summer 1988): 109–35.

21. Henry Keppel, *The Expedition to Borneo of H. M. S. Dido for the Suppression of Piracy, with extracts from The Journal of James Brooke, Esq.* (New York: Harper & Brothers, 1846), 267ff.

22. Robert Hampson, *Cross-Cultural Encounters in Joseph Conrad's Malay Fiction* (Basingstoke: Macmillan, 2000), 100.

23. Conrad, "Heart of Darkness," 208.

24. Joseph Conrad, "An Outpost of Progress," in *"Heart of Darkness" and Other Tales*, 11.

25. Conrad, "Heart of Darkness," 151.

26. See Patrick Brantlinger, *Rule of Darkness: British Literature and Imperialism, 1830–1914* (Ithaca, N.Y.: Cornell University Press, 1988).

27. See J. Hillis Miller, "Should We Read 'Heart of Darkness'?" In *Conrad in Africa: New Essays on* Heart of Darkness, ed. Attie M. De Lange, and Gail Fincham, and Wiesław Krajka (Boulder, Colo.: Social Science Monographs, 2002), 21–40.

28. Chinua Achebe, "An Image of Africa: Racism in Conrad's 'Heart of Darkness,'" in *Hopes and Impediments: Selected Essays* (New York: Doubleday, 1989), 10.

29. Hannah Arendt, *The Origins of Totalitarianism* (New York: Harcourt, 1985), 185.

30. Ibid., 195–97.

31. Ibid., 190.

32. Rob Nixon, *London Calling: V. S. Naipaul, Postcolonial Mandarin* (Oxford: Oxford University Press, 1992), 91.

33. Arendt, *Origins of Totalitarianism*, 186.

34. Ibid., 185.

35. Homi Bhabha, "Signs taken for wonders: Questions of ambivalence and authority under a tree outside Delhi, May 1817" in *The Location of Culture* (London: Routledge, 1994), 102–122.

36. Conrad, "Heart of Darkness," 189.

37. See also Asako Nakai, *The English Book and Its Marginalia: Colonial/Postcolonial Literatures After* Heart of Darkness (Amsterdam: Rodopi, 2000).

38. Conrad, "Heart of Darkness," 207.

39. Homi Bhabha, *The Location of Culture* (London: Routledge, 1994), 108.

40. Sara Suleri, *The Rhetoric of English India* (Chicago: University Chicago Press, 1992), 152.

41. See Giorgio Agamben, *Homo Sacer: Sovereign Power and Bare Life*, trans. Daniel Heller-Rozen (Stanford: Stanford University Press, 1998) and Judith Butler and Gayatri Spivak, *Who Sings the Nation-State?: Language, Politics, Belonging* (London: Seagull, 2007).

42. For an overview, see Paul B. Armstrong's Norton Critical Edition of "Heart of Darkness" (4th ed. [New York: W. W. Norton & Co., 2006]).

43. Conrad refers to Clifford's unsigned review, "The Trail of the Book-Worm: Mr. Joseph Conrad at Home and Abroad," *The Singapore Free Press* (30 August 1898): 3.

44. Joseph Conrad, "Author's Note" to *A Personal Record*, in *The Mirror of the Sea and A Personal Record*, ed. Zdzisław Najder (Oxford: Oxford University Press, 1988), iii.

45. Ibid., iv.

46. Hugh Clifford, "The Genius of Mr. Joseph Conrad," in *Joseph Conrad: Third World Perspectives*, ed. Robert Hamner (Boulder, Colo.: Three Continents Press, 1990), 15.

47. Conrad, "Heart of Darkness," 137.

48. See Niall Fergusson, *Empire: The Rise and Demise of the British World Order and the Lessons for Global Power* (New York: Basic Books, 2004).

49. Conrad, "Heart of Darkness," 139.

50. Zdzisław Najder, *Joseph Conrad: A Life* (Rochester, N.Y.: Camden House, 2007), 99.

51. Fredric Jameson, *The Political Unconscious: Narrative as a Socially Symbolic Act* (Ithaca: Cornell University Press, 1981), 210.

52. Conrad, "Author's Note" to *A Personal Record*, iv.

53. Conrad to William Blackwood, 13 December 1898, in *The Collected Letters of Joseph Conrad*, ed. Laurence Davies et al., 9 vols. (Cambridge: Cambridge University Press, 1983–2007), 2: 130.

54. See, for example, G. J. Resink, "The Archipelago Under Conrad's Eyes," in his *Indonesia's History Between the Myths* (The Hague: W. Van Hoeve, 1968), 307–23, Christopher GoGwilt, *The Invention of the West: Joseph Conrad and the Double-Mapping of Europe and Empire* (Stanford: Stanford University Press, 1995), Hampson, *Cross-Cultural Encounters*, and Agnes S. K. Yeow, *Conrad's Eastern Vision: A Vain and Floating Appearance* (New York: Palgrave Macmillan, 2009), esp. 14ff.

55. Conrad to Blackwood, 13 December 1898, in *The Collected Letters of Joseph Conrad*, 2: 130.

56. For a rather different reading of this conjuncture, see John Marx, *The Modernist Novel and the Decline of Empire* (Cambridge: Cambridge University Press, 2005); and see also Yeow, *Conrad's Eastern Vision*.

57. See Benedict Anderson, *Imagined Communities: Reflections on the Origin and Spread of Nationalism* (London: Verso, 1991).

Conrad and Modernism

Andrea White

I am *modern,* and I would rather recall
Wagner the musician and Rodin the
Sculptor who both had to starve a little
in their day—and Whistler the painter
who made Ruskin the critic foam at
the mouth with scorn and indignation.
They too have arrived. They had to suffer for being "new."

> —Conrad, from a letter to his
> publisher, William Blackwood, 31 May
> 1902

We see in [Conrad's] experimentation
literary realism's vanishing point.

> —Patrick J. Whitely, *Knowledge and*
> *Experimental Realism in Conrad,*
> *Lawrence, and Woolf*

If modernism has an origin, Conrad is
arguably it.

> — Rishona Zimring, "Conrad's
> Pornography Shop"

Although "origins" is a contested and complex category, this
essay will attempt to demonstrate how the works of Joseph
Conrad figure in the beginnings of what we think of as Anglo-
American literary modernism and how our knowledge of this
historical phenomenon and a deeper understanding of Conrad's

works are complementary pursuits. As both inheritance and innovation, his fiction learns from and contributes to several concerns central to early twentieth-century writing. These concerns include innovative / experimental narrative strategies that respond to epistemological skepticism and explore consciousness; the new scene of writing and publishing in the urbanized, commercial settings of the early twentieth century; and concerns with self and other—in terms of nation, culture, race, class, and gender—in a world whose insular metropolitan assumptions were being challenged increasingly from within and without.

This essay will not rehearse in depth the contributing factors to the sense of crisis that underlay in various and varying ways European and Anglo-American culture from 1880 to 1930. Darwin's pronouncements had deeply unsettled the late Victorian faith in humanity's central place in the created universe and contributed to the disillusionment of the period generally. The world-weariness and sense of decline and degeneration that informed the *fin-de-siècle* were deepened in England particularly by doubts incurred by the Boer War and its pyrrhic victory, by a devastating world war, by the social unrest caused by labor disputes, by issues of women's suffrage and Irish independence, and by the growing sense of London itself as the center of a decaying empire. All worked to dismantle the Victorian belief in progress and to contribute to the skepticism of certain currents of early twentieth-century writing that came to be thought of as "modernist."

The Contemporary Scene of Writing

Józef Teodor Konrad Korzeniowski was an anomaly in the turn-of-the-century English scene of writing, and his works rested a bit uneasily among those of many of his Edwardian contemporaries. A "foreigner," as he was constantly being reminded, Conrad brought something new to English letters. In fact, this un-Englishness was a central feature of "English" modernism; as "all Europe contributed to the making of Kurtz,"[1] so Polish, American, and Irish voices entered and transformed early twentieth-century English writing. Conrad's polyglot, multinational background as

well as his former twenty-year career in the British merchant service contributed to his being "not just a canonical British writer"
but "part of global literature in English" who brought the impress
of European thought and literature—particularly that of Poland
and France—to English fiction.[2] While the Polish novel was still
in its early stages of development, and therefore of little use to
the apprentice novelist, Poland's oral tradition was part of his
unique and complex inheritance. Flaubert also had a great deal to
tell him about the possible shape a modern novel could take, and
Maupassant—as Ford Madox Ford, Conrad's early collaborator
would later report—told both of them everything they needed
to know about writing as a kind of impressionism. However, as
Ian Watt observed, Conrad's admiration for Maupassant had its
limits; particularly, Conrad found "too narrow as a view of life"
the determinism of the French writer's "naturalist perspective."[3]
Nor did he have a model in either Flaubert or Maupassant, Watt
contended, for what he wanted to do: "to express his sense of the
distance that existed between private perception and public meaning, and a more absolute disjunction between the interior experience of the individual and all the accepted assumptions of the
world outside as they were normally expressed in language and
in literature."[4] Conrad also cited Turgenev as an important shaping influence in spite of his lifelong antagonism toward things
Russian, an inheritance of his upbringing in Russian-dominated
Poland, and the loss of both his parents to Russian despotism. In
fact, Conrad was among those early modernists who directly benefited from Constance Garnett's recent translations into English
of Tolstoy, Turgenev, Dostoyevsky, and Chekhov. Virginia Woolf
would later assert the great influence of the Russians on the moderns in their psychological insights, their "understanding of the
soul and heart," and their "inconclusiveness,"[5] concerns central
to modernist literature.

However, Conrad was susceptible to the influences of contemporary currents of English writers as well, particularly the pronouncements of Walter Pater and Henry James about the art of
prose renderings of consciousness, the great subject of modernist
writers. Conrad's works—which demonstrate a theory of mind that
will be extended in the next decade's writers under the influence

of Freud's writings—reveal the impress of Pater's thinking; in fact, for both James and Conrad and for later modernists as well, Pater resonated with their own understanding of the subjective nature of experience. In his conclusion to *The Renaissance* (1873), Pater wrote: "Experience, already reduced to a swarm of impressions, is ringed round for each one of us by that thick wall of personality through which no real voice has ever pierced on its way to us, or from us to that which we can only conjecture to be without. Every one of those impressions is the impression of the individual in his isolation, each mind keeping as a solitary prisoner its own dream of a world."[6] Pater here articulates a growing skepticism about a knowable external world unmediated by a perceiving self.

The consequent concerns facing the artist—how to represent an endlessly varied reality and how to create meaning in a darkening world that seemed oblivious to human desire—initially found expression in the subjective writing of literary impressionism. Occupying a midpoint between romantic unities and modernist fragmentation, impressionism was an important chapter in modernism's genealogy, according to Jesse Matz.[7] As a narrative response to epistemological uncertainty, it is at the heart of Conrad's as well as later modernists' work. Conrad's preface to *The Nigger of the "Narcissus"* (1897), as well as Henry James's "The Art of Fiction" (1884) and Virginia Woolf's "Modern Fiction" (1925), all reveal the influence of Pater's thoughts on their aesthetic theories. Conrad's preface "serves as a preface to modernist fiction in English," according to David Smith.[8] Michael Levenson agrees: it can be read "as an entrance ... into the general situation of early modernism ... as a representative text," for in it Conrad's subjectivist perspective is made clear.[9] Pater's understanding of "the thick wall of personality" that stood between an individual and the world is Conrad's and can be seen in his fictions that articulate a skepticism about the absolute knowableness of the external world.

Rendering Consciousness

Even before Ford made his retroactive pronouncements in the 1913 essay "On Impressionism," Pater, James, and Proust were discussing the artist's need to render, to make the surface impressions on a center of consciousness reveal depths. If the only authority was the self, then narrative art must relinquish the omniscient narrator, or seriously destabalize its reliability, and represent experience through individual points of view, employing such strategies as inner monologue, stream of consciousness, and free indirect discourse to narrate the individual's experience of the world. Consequently, the writer's emphasis will fall necessarily on the effect of events on characters rather than on the events themselves, rendered from those individual points of view rather than told by an all-knowing narrator who can objectively report on an external world. This impressionism, while a narrative consequence of skepticism and a critique of conventional narration, worked to render subjectivity. As Ford wrote, it employed "all the devices of the prostitute" to create an illusion of reality, but a psychological or spiritual reality.[10] The artist seeks truth, as Conrad's preface maintains—he attempts to bring "to light the truth" and thereby "to make you *see*"—however, it is the truth of his own subjective apprehension of the universe that must supplement the truth of the sensually perceived surface of objective reality.[11] That surface truth is never abandoned by Conrad, Levenson asserts, but it is insufficient.[12] The workings of consciousness and the rendering of an inner life are serious undertakings of Conrad's novels, novellas, and stories and work to distinguish his writing from that of many of his Edwardian contemporaries while anticipating the fictional concerns and narrative strategies of the next decade's modernists.

This subjectivity was experienced as a separateness, and as Levenson argues, the sense of another character's fundamentally unknowable otherness is a central feature in modernist texts.[13] The artistic endeavor itself was a solitary one, as Conrad's preface asserts: "the artist descends within himself, and in that lonely region of stress and strife, if he be deserving and fortunate, he finds the terms of his appeal."[14] Each one of those impressions that experience is reduced to, according to Pater, "is the impression of the individual in his isolation, each mind keeping as a solitary prisoner its own dream of a world."[15] "We live, as we dream—alone," Marlow tells his listeners aboard the "Nellie" in

"Heart of Darkness" (1899),[16] thus anticipating many other modernist narrators. "How did one know one thing or another thing
about people, sealed as they were?" Lilly Briscoe cries toward the
end of *To the Lighthouse* (1927).[17] In Conrad's *Nostromo* (1904), even
at the moment of Decoud's and Nostromo's common endeavor,
it is their separateness that is insisted upon:

> Each of them was as if utterly alone with his task. It did
> not occur to them to speak. There was nothing in common
> between them but the knowledge that the damaged lighter
> must be slowly but surely sinking. In that knowledge, which
> was like the crucial test of their desires, they seemed to have
> become completely estranged, as if they had discovered in the
> very shock of the collision that the loss of the lighter would
> not mean the same thing to them both. This common dan-
> ger brought their differences in aim, in view, in character, and
> in position, into absolute prominence in the private vision of
> each. There was no bond of conviction, of common idea....[18]

What receives the emphasis here is not the external event, the
fact of the sinking lighter, but that the event has such a different meaning for each man even while engaged in his common
pursuit.

While Ford maintained that the goal of his and Conrad's
impressionism was to render "the material facts of life without comment and in exact language," Conrad's relationship to
impressionism was complex. Always concerned with recording
the material facts of life, the visible surfaces, he found those facts
insufficient for his purposes of revealing deep and complex motivations. From the beginning, in his first published story, "The
Idiots" (1896), he not only records visual surfaces but attempts
to interpret them as well, to give meaning, from a situated narrator's point of view:

> The sun was shining violently upon the undulating surface
> of the land. The rises were topped by clumps of meager
> trees, with their branches showing high on the sky as if they
> had been perched upon stilts. The small fields, cut up by
> hedges and stone walls that zigzagged over the slopes, lay in

rectangular patches of vivid greens and yellows, resembling the unskillful daubs of a naïve picture. And the landscape was divided in two by the white streak of a road stretching in long loops far away, like a river of dust crawling out of the hills on its way to the sea.[19]

Here the narrator does comment; meaning is conferred, as is often the case in Conrad's descriptive writing, through a series of similes, the reflections of a first person, and limited narrator. As Hugh Epstein points out in his discussion of Conrad's early impressionism, "Moments of pure sensation are, in themselves, meaningless; and if life really is no more than a succession of perceived moments, it cannot be a shared story: we are fundamentally alone." And, he continues, it is characteristic of Conrad, refusing to be pinned down by any formula, to oppose a narrator who actively seeks to confer meaning on what he sees to "a philosophy of mere contingency and solipsism to which [Conrad's] pessimism was prey.... Meaning is a matter of human dreams and illusions that impose themselves upon the visible world: Conrad's tales become the story of that imposition."[20]

In his discussion of *The Nigger of the "Narcissus"* and its intermittent shifting point of view from third to first person, Levenson discusses the tension within impressionism that Conrad's early work engages. While the artist's task is to make the reader see and thus pay close attention to the visible world and render it carefully with *les mots justes*, who within the fiction can see into another's mind, "sealed as they were"? The third-person narrator in *The Nigger of the "Narcissus,"* Levenson argues, "provides the precision of physical detail but hesitates to penetrate the individual psyche," while the first person can indulge in "moral and psychological speculation." The shifts, Levenson continues, "reveal the pressures upon an omniscience no longer confident that it knows all."[21]

Paradoxically, or perhaps consequently, Conrad's work, more than that of later modernists, often enacts a tension between that suspicion of our aloneness, of our separateness and solitude on the one hand, and a cherished, often idealized, solidarity on the other. Many of his works are concerned with the nature of community and with the relationship between the individual and the group, whether it be a ship's crew or humanity itself. As an early modernist who absorbed the full brunt of late Victorian skepticism, of Paterian subjectivity, and of Nietzschean doubt, and for whom writing itself was a lonely endeavor, Conrad must have felt the value of a solidarity that connects us to others, all too aware of the "thick wall of personality" that divides and separates us. Characteristically, Conrad's response is ambivalent. For example, as William Deresiewicz argues about *The Nigger of the "Narcissus,"* even though community is that novel's purported subject, "Much of the plot concerns, not unity and solidarity, but division and conflict. The men of the fo'c'sle, the common seamen, chafe at and finally almost mutiny against the uncompromising rule of the ship's officers."[22]

How to speak, then, from this uncertain vantage point, how to make readers, in all their separateness, see and share the modernist vision of moral complexity, of "irreconcilable antagonisms"? These are the problems facing modernist writers such as Conrad. In considering the ways in which Conrad's fictions addressed these challenges of narrating the new in its initial stages, we can better understand the second decade of modernism as practiced by such writers as James Joyce and Woolf. While these currents of influence and intertextuality were contemporaneous, rather than strictly linear, Woolf in particular learns from and continues the impressionism Conrad earlier helped to initiate. Her pronouncements repeat the basic tenets articulated by Conrad, particularly in his preface and in much the same language, as we shall see. In her 1924 essay, "Mr. Bennett and Mrs. Brown," Woolf insisted that the tools of the Edwardian writers—Arnold Bennett, John Galsworthy, and H. G. Wells—were not those of the Georgians. "For us those conventions are ruin, those tools are death,"[23] and here she is explicit that the old tools comprised the involved, omniscient narrator, the prescriptive plot and predictable chronology, and the undeserving concern with rendering the transient materiality of experience rather than its enduring spirit. While this argument justifies and explains her fictional strategies of achronology and inner monologues and Joyce's use of stream of consciousness, the seeds for these concerns and techniques can be found in Conrad's early work.

Erich Auerbach concludes *Mimesis* (1946), his study of the representation of reality in Western literature, with a passage from Woolf's *To the Lighthouse*. In his discussion, he points to her use of "multipersonal representation of consciousness, time strata, disintegration of the continuity of exterior events, shifting of the narrative viewpoint" as well as the exterior event's loss of hegemony as culminations of techniques and concerns she inherited and that mark her as "representative of her generation."[24] In her polemical essays "Mr. Bennett and Mrs. Brown" and "Modern Fiction," she discusses these "new tools" that modern writers need to make use of, and, in so doing, she echoes in significant ways the pronouncements of Conrad's preface. In "Modern Fiction," when Woolf upholds the "spiritual" writers—Thomas Hardy, Conrad, W. H. Hudson, and Joyce—and argues for the significance of their more psychological realism rather than the transient, material verisimilitude of Bennett, Galsworthy, and Wells, the language sounds familiar: "Life is not a series of gig lamps symmetrically arranged; but a luminous halo, a semi-transparent envelope surrounding us from the beginning of consciousness to the end. Is it not the task of the novelist to convey this varying, this unknown and uncircumscribed spirit, whatever aberration or complexity it may display, with as little mixture of the alien and external as possible?"[25] In Conrad's 1899 novella, "Heart of Darkness," the frame narrator describes Marlow's art of fiction: "The yarns of seamen have a direct simplicity, the whole meaning of which lies within the shell of a cracked nut. But Marlow was not typical (if his propensity to spin yarns be excepted) and to him the meaning of an episode was not inside like a kernel but outside, enveloping the tale which brought it out only as a glow brings out a haze, in the likeness of one of these misty halos that, sometimes, are made visible by the spectral illumination of moonshine."[26] In both cases, an omniscient narrator who can report the world objectively is challenged. We can only know imperfectly through the distorting "thick wall of personality." We hear, in Woolf's insistence upon the enduring "spiritual," an echo of Conrad's assertion in his preface that art must preserve the enduring and essential. The world of appearances, so apparently stable to the "materialists," is revealed in Conrad's fiction as undependable and ultimately unknowable. In *Lord Jim* (1900), it is Marlow, a subjective narrator indeed, who tells us of the shock this realization gave him, when he, on the basis of Jim's appearance—"appealing at sight to all my sympathies"[27] —would have trusted Jim—and would have been wrong: "I tell you I ought to know the right kind of looks. I would have trusted the deck to that youngster on the strength of a single glance, and gone to sleep with both eyes—and, by Jove! It wouldn't have been safe. There are depths of horror in that thought. He looked as genuine as a new sovereign, but there was some infernal alloy in his metal."[28] Trusting appearances assumes the solidity of a knowable external world, while the truth is that we can only know Jim through Marlow's imprecise apprehensions and attempts to narrate them, as well as through the eyes of other witnesses whose narrations Marlow reports. Even in fictions such as *Nostromo* and *The Secret Agent* (1907), in which the presence of an omniscient authorial narrator is felt, that authorial function is complicated by "other narrative devices such as irony and variations of distance."[29] For example, in *Nostromo*, there is less distance between the omniscient narrator and Decoud than between the narrator and the other characters, and although Decoud's thoughts are usually narrated with less irony, the narrator's treatment of him is inconsistent. In these works as well as in *Lord Jim,* at the very turn of the century, Conrad records the shift from inherited certitudes and values to modernist uncertainty.

In addition to the destabilized omniscient narrator, other narrative strategies were employed, by Conrad and by later modernists as well, to convey "this varying, this unknown and uncircumscribed spirit." If fiction must render the myriad impressions of an event on a subjective narrator, the experiencing of the event will be foregrounded, rather than the event itself which has surrendered the claim to any exterior completeness, as Auerbach observed. The explanation for the external event that serves to release the inner thought is necessarily delayed. For example, what came to be called "delayed decoding" placed the emphasis on a character's experiencing of reality. Ian Watt noticed that, as a way of "giving direct narrative expression to the way in which the consciousness elicits meaning from its perceptions," delayed decoding presented "a sense impression and [withheld] naming it or explaining its meaning until later,"[30] thus foregrounding the workings of consciousness trying to grapple with experience and make some sense of it.[31] Ford had been impressed with Stephen Crane's use of this technique—although not yet named—to describe the muzzle of a revolver a character was faced with: "He saw a steel ring directed at him."[32] Just so, Marlow's decoding is delayed when he "had to look at the river mighty quick because there was a snag in the fairway. Sticks, little sticks, were flying about, thick; they were whizzing before my nose, dropping below me, striking behind me against my pilot-house."[33] While an omniscient narrator could have reported that arrows were being shot from innumerable bows at the men on the boat, it takes several moments for Marlow to comprehend the cause of the event: "Arrows, by Jove! We were being shot at!"[34]

Even from the time of his first novel, *Almayer's Folly* (1895), Conrad employed this narrative strategy. In his introduction to the novel, Owen Knowles argues that, like so much of Conrad's fiction, it is largely retrospective. As such, the novel "involves a continuous exercise in 'backward' reading," not only Almayer's, as he needs to move through several mistaken explanations for events that occur, but our own as well, "highlighting the need for simple judgments to be replaced by more complex ones," as well as emphasizing the act of interpretation rather than the events themselves.[35] Instead of relating these conclusions as *faits accomplis*, in the manner of a traditional omniscient narrator, the modernist narration involves us in the often-flawed interpretive process of a situated narrator from his or her particular and limited point of view.

How, then, are we to *see*, given an unreliable and often erratic narrator and modernist skepticism about knowledge itself? A central focus of Conrad's fictional experimentation was the narrator who could provide that close attention to the visible world and interpret it from distinguishable points of view, but who could only make conjectures about other characters, "sealed as they were"; thus Conrad's many storytellers: the frame narrator of "Heart of Darkness," the "I" of "Karain" (1897), Dr. Kennedy of "Amy Foster" (1901), and the professor of languages in *Under*

Western Eyes (1911). His great invention, however, was Marlow, that English *homme moyen*, who narrates "Heart of Darkness," "Youth" (1898), *Lord Jim*, and *Chance* (1914). Marlow describes what he sees and experiences but questions as much as he asserts about the African jungle or Kurtz or Jim. In fact, much of what we learn about a character is shaped by the intermittent narratives of several points of view. Most famously, Marlow must interview Brierly's mate, the French lieutenant, Chester and Robinson, Stein, Jewel, and others to help shape his—and our—view of Jim. Thus in this modernist production as well as the ones to follow, the reliable single point of view is destroyed, and the storyteller himself and his framing, subjective presence in the narrative are foregrounded.

Modernist Treatment of Space and Time

When Woolf claimed in her essay "Mr. Bennett and Mrs. Brown" that on or about December 1910 everything changed, she could well have had in mind the aesthetic rebellion mounted by the postimpressionist exhibit brought to London in 1910 by Roger Fry. Among the featured artists were Van Gogh, Gauguin, and Cézanne, all of whom had grown impatient with impressionism and what they felt was its neglect of emotion. Cézanne especially wanted to accord equal weight to the eye and to the imagination, to the surface appearance, but also to the emotions it gave rise to, echoing Conrad's own concern with rendering the workings of consciousness, the latent content of a character's consciousness suggested by the palpable surface reality as reported by several points of view. Cézanne's incipient cubism, which so influenced Picasso and Braque, no longer promoted a verisimilitude seen from a single point of view. Rather it necessitated an observer actively engaged in the painting's several suggested points of view. In his articles attacking the Salon jury that had rejected the paintings of Cézanne and others in the 1863 Salon des Refusés, Émile Zola, Cézanne's friend and fellow art theorist, argued that "a work of art is a corner of nature seen through a temperament."[36] Writing in 1914, an art critic observed that the Postimpressionists currently at work were signaling "a return to the art that is the antithesis of Impressionism—the art of the imagination." And, he continued, the "art that is at hand [Cubism] is a highly *subjective* art as distinguished from the highly *objective* art of the Impressionists and Realists."[37]

According to Stephen Kern, "the multiplication of points of view in painting had an impact far beyond the world of art. It created a new way of seeing and rendering objects in space and challenged the traditional notion of its homogeneity."[38] While this study cannot treat in depth the interconnectedness of modernist arts, it serves our present purpose to notice the ways in which consciousness is always changing in modernist texts and that reality is always perceived differently by different observers at different times. Such is *Ulysses'* Leopold Bloom's realization as well. Thoughts of "parallax" and its implications recur to him, and us, throughout his day in Dublin in 1904. Multiple points of view characterize all of Conrad's fiction and had done so from well before 1910, although he came by his aversion to the monologic, to the single point of view a bit differently, perhaps, from his contemporaries and successors. Because of his background and history as a Pole, subject to Russian imperialism and subsequent loss of parents, he distrusted it not simply on theoretical grounds but as another form of autocracy. His use of a multivoiced discourse attempted to make us *see* while enacting the very difficulty of doing so; it became the chief focus of his experimentation and can be seen in his early use of the third-person narrator in *Almayer's Folly* and *An Outcast of the Islands* (1896), as well as in the first-person narrators of "The Idiots," "The Lagoon" (1897), "Karain," and others. The divided narration of *The Nigger of the "Narcissus"* seemed to point up problems, the solution to which was his most important narrator, Marlow, who will shortly make his appearance in "Heart of Darkness." But his experimentation continued in *Nostromo* with its profusion of narrators, in *The Secret Agent's* sardonic narrator, and in the professor of languages, the chief narrator of *Under Western Eyes,* the title of which indicates the limitations of a single, Eurocentric point of view. Modernist writers' consciousness of literary artfulness led to their continual search for the appropriate form, from work to work and sometimes within the same text. *Ulysses* (1922), for example, restlessly shifts from chapter to chapter, experimenting with narrative strategies that become increasingly interested in recording consciousness with little or no help from an informing narrator.

Related to the uses of multiple points of view and delayed decoding was the modernist treatment of time, about which, as Auerbach noticed, "there is something peculiar."[39] Here Henri Bergson's ideas about time's heterogeneity—as well as those of Einstein whose special theory of relativity was published in 1905—inform modernist narrative literature and allow the rendering of a psychological time that moves differently from clock, or public, time.[40] Unlike scientific, clock time, which can be measured in discrete units, psychological time moves with irregularity and is experienced as "duration" or as "a flow of interpenetrating moments,"[41] reflecting Henri Bergson's assertion that consciousness "is continually swelling with the duration which it accumulates: it goes on increasing—rolling upon itself, as a snowball on the snow."[42] In other words, "the present is swollen with the past."[43] Thus Auerbach explains the inordinate time it takes Woolf's narrator to articulate Mrs. Ramsey's thoughts as she holds the brown stocking up to her son's leg to measure it; "the road taken by consciousness is sometimes traversed far more quickly than language is able to render it." The effect is to reduce "the hegemony of the exterior event" occurring as it does in public time and to foreground the musing consciousness of Mrs. Ramsey.[44] Thus Marlow can tell Jim's story, which might take us several days to read, in a single evening to a colonial verandah of cigar-smoking listeners. Conrad's sense, here and elsewhere, of the gap between "private perception and public meaning"[45] will characterize second-generation modernist writers as well, particularly William Faulkner.

In order to render time's heterogeneity and the conflict between private and public time authentically, modernist writers found linear, strictly chronological plots problematic. According to Ford, neither "real stories, nor lives follow an orderly sequence so to seem real, stories must proceed in 'a very rambling way.'" A tenet of their impressionism, Ford continued, that the novelist needed to first get the character "in with a strong impression, and then work backwards and forwards over his past,"[46] resulted in frequent achronology. And indeed, to the consternation of readers then and now, Conrad's texts are often characterized by severe achronology, by events that are projected proleptically and recalled analeptically: for example, the abrupt prolepsis in *The Secret Agent,* from the orderly progression of the first three chapters in which we learn of Verloc's assignment to stage an outrage of some sort, to chapter 4 in which the event—the bomb outrage—has already occurred and comes to us, and to Ossipon, as a headline the newsboys are crying in the streets. In a subsequent chapter, the time shifts again to events that must have taken place sometime between the third and fourth chapters. In fact, it is of this novel that Kern comments: "Of all the assaults on the authority of uniform public time that appeared in the imaginative literature of this period, the most direct was the assignment to blow up the Greenwich Observatory. Conrad could not have picked a more appropriate anarchist objective."[47]

Along with questioning the possibility of a mean time—at Greenwich, or anywhere else—the general question of authority was challenged: of a benevolent Divinity, of a patriarchal order, of an imperial center or an all-knowing narrator. The authority of language itself to represent the world was also treated with wariness by most modernist writers. Not only did an epistemological skepticism underlie modernist texts then, but a crisis of representation was felt as well, the suspicion that experience was unrepresentable in language. Certainly as a polyglot, writing in his third language, Conrad famously complained of the impossibility of making language mean with precision. Marlow's attempts to describe Kurtz or Jim to his listening audiences often break down in conjectures, omissions, and sentences that trail off into indeterminate darkness. Thus Conrad's deep respect for the scrupulous use of sea language as used by mariners and frequently abused, he argued, by irresponsible journalists, and Marlow's great relief, in the tumult of his Congo experience, to come upon a tattered volume—*An Inquiry into some Points of Seamanship*—which he handles "with the greatest possible tenderness."[48] Although he can't interpret the drums he hears echoing in the far-off jungle or understand the African crew's "restraint" or his own confounding responses to the unintelligibility that surrounds him, he has no trouble comprehending this writer's explanations of chains and currents; there are facts this sea language corresponds to, facts Marlow respects. But more generally, meaning is opaque, and language can only intimate; meaning doesn't inhere but can only be suggested. "Words," as the professor of languages admits, "are the great foes of reality."[49] William Bonney, remarking on the "radical uncertainty of language found in Conrad's work, instances Marlow's unsuccessful attempts to describe Kurtz's eloquence; "as the description gets under way in all its conflation of antitheses Marlow is clearly able to describe nothing according to traditional forms of definition.... In such passages Conrad's texts demonstrate their modernity."[50] "How can I make you see," Marlow grumbles to his audience on board the Nellie, as well as to us. Even though the artist's task is to "make you *see*," his fiction repeatedly enacts the difficulty, even the impossibility, of doing so.

Modernist Difficulty: The Reader's Role

This experimentation and interest in rendering consciousness, often without the help of an informing, reliable omniscient narrator, assumed an active reader. In fact, T. S. Eliot's famous 1921 pronouncement—"it appears likely that poets in our civilization, as it exists at present, must be *difficult*"—has led later critics to understand all of modernist art as having been "formed on an aesthetics of difficulty."[51] Certainly, the ambiguities, the use of often-conflicting points of view, none of which carried absolute authority, the gaps and elliptical speech, and the uncertainties of time necessitated a participative reader who would act as a collaborator in constructing meaning. As Owen Knowles points out in his introduction to *Almayer's Folly*,[52] Conrad expects an active reader from his first novel's first paragraph: "'Kaspar! Makan!' The well-known shrill voice startled Almayer from his dream of splendid future into the unpleasant realities of the present hour. An unpleasant voice too. He had heard it for many years, and with every year he liked it less. No matter; there would be an end to all this soon." We won't understand that "Kaspar" is Almayer's first name or that "Makan" is a call to dinner, in Malay, or that the voice is that of his wife. We learn that a tension exists for Almayer between the dismal present and the splendid future, but for the rest we must wait watchfully and be the active reader this writing calls for, one who can deduce from the suggestions of the writer's impressions presented, who is comfortable listening to half statements, conjectures, and conflicting versions of events rather than being assured of Truth through declarative statements and triumphant endings. Reading itself is imaged as a predicament and is foregrounded in much modernist fiction. So many of Conrad's texts narrate their characters' inability to read what should be telling signs. For so many characters, the decoding is infinitely decoded; Secret Agent Verloc never reads his wife aright, a fatal incomprehension. Marlow is always aware of his listeners' inability to see, to understand what he's trying to explain. In "An Outpost of Progress" (1897), Kayerts and Carlier misread the novels and newspapers left at their outpost of "progress" on the African river, completely missing the point of their utter difference from, rather than likeness to, the heroic adventurers described therein.

Producing "Modernism": The Critic's Role

This new, active role for the reader was resisted by many, and reviewers complained about the ways in which Conrad's work put pressure on the reader, often demonstrating their own reluctance to be collaborative, active readers. In response to *The Nigger of the "Narcissus,"* a critic grumbled that the "uncompromising nature of his methods debar him from attaining a wide popularity." In response to *Lord Jim*, "it can't be read in a half doze." Of "Youth," "it would be useless to pretend that [it] can be very widely read." Of *Nostromo*, because of "Mr. Conrad's retrospective habit . . . many readers will never survive the novel." *The Secret Agent* was faulted for "defying all laws of construction: it races backwards and forwards with lordly disregard of time."[53] The critical accusation that modernism was "difficult" became general by 1915, but at first, Leonard Diepeveen argues, the charge of "difficulty" was aimed at individuals—like Conrad.[54] These complaints continued throughout his career from reviewers and critics who played an active role in determining readers' responses to the work. In fact, a study of literary periods reveals both their constructedness and the extent to which criticism—both contemporary with and subsequent to the literature it considers—produces literary values, canons, and periods. Modernists weren't the first writers to understand the importance of critical guidance in creating an audience for a new unsanctioned endeavor and in self-defense set out to provide that guidance themselves and to educate their readership accordingly. Wordsworth undertook the task himself of explaining and justifying his poetic innovations in his preface to *Lyrical Ballads* (1800); Henry James also used his prefaces to point out aspects of his fiction readers had missed;[55] Eliot, hoping to demystify the response of many to *The Waste Land* (1922), affixed his own explanatory notes to a second edition. Woolf, in her many book reviews and essays, articulated an aesthetic that helped justify her experimental fictions. Other modernist writers solicited critics to do the work for them. Because readers and critics could discern no pattern or plot in *Ulysses*, Joyce drew up an outline of the novel, which he made available to commentators on his work; in Edmund Wilson's opinion, readers could never have known how to read the novel without the scheme Joyce had so helpfully provided.[56]

Conrad also sensed the innovative nature of his fiction, and besides writing prefaces for his early work, as well as his Author's Notes, explaining and justifying his aesthetic undertaking, he coached Richard Curle, his friend and literary executor, in his preparation of *Joseph Conrad: A Study*[57] and had even more of a hand in guiding Curle's review of the Uniform Edition in 1923.[58] Certainly his recommendations to editors and publishers as to how volumes should be composed also expressed his desire to frame his work in particular ways. The critics' complicity in making the reader see what the new work was about was crucial; in the process, these nonfictional pronouncements created aesthetic hierarchies and the literary period known as modernism.[59]

These pronouncements were made in book reviews, essays, prefaces, letters, and memoirs, and in such journals and literary reviews as *The Savoy, New Age*, the *English Review, Criterion, Poetry and Drama,* and the *Little Review,* the "'engines' of modernism," as Tim Armstrong refers to the many little avant-garde magazines of the period.[60] They spoke to one another and carried on arguments among themselves and did so vis-à-vis the more conservative journals and reviews such as the *Times Literary Supplement*, the *Academy*, *Blackwood's*, and *The Athenaeum*. As journal editors (Eliot and Ford) and as publishers themselves (Woolf), they affected criteria and shaped the canon that came to be known as modernist. Woolf, Rebecca West, Dorothy Richardson, and Katherine Mansfield were all prolific book reviewers who articulated their aesthetic in everything they wrote. As editor of the *English Review*, and in his various nonfictional books, Ford Madox Ford set forth his theories of fiction. Ezra Pound, arriving in London in 1908, added a sense of urgency to the ongoing conversations, insisting that modern writers needed to "make it new." Eliot concurred, at length, in various essays in his own journal, *Criterion*, and elsewhere. Joyce, E. M. Forster, and D. H. Lawrence, in their various critical writings, all made their case for the art of fiction.

This outpouring of critical writing, practical and theoretical and, for the most part, combative, addressed itself in modernism's early phases to a felt vacuum. Ford had complained that for the writers of his generation, no "critical guidance" had been available.[61] The absence of this critical guidance or of any serious conversations about the art of prose fiction figured as the central argument of Henry James's "The Art of Fiction," itself a rejoinder to Walter Besant's published lecture, "The Art of Fiction."[62] In his essay, James takes issue with Besant's prescriptive ideas about the subjects of novels and their need for propriety, and he faults Victorian criticism generally for being overly moralistic. He derides people like Besant for whom "art means rose-coloured window-panes, and selection means picking a bouquet for Mrs. Grundy,"[63] that fictional but tyrannical and censorious arbiter of Victorian morality. Nor should the novelist be bound to a conclusive, happy ending, James argues: "for many, the 'ending' of a novel is like that of a good dinner, a course of dessert and ices."[64] Rather, James argues here, the writer should be free to select his subject and should be judged, not on the basis of what he presents, but on his success in doing what he attempted to do. Moreover, the novel, now come of age, should be "discutable" and treated as a serious art form. It should not be susceptible to such strictures as at present, he complained, dominated the critical scene: that only virtuous and aspiring characters should be represented, endings should be happy, there should be a "distribution at the last of prizes, pensions, husbands, wives, babies, millions, appended paragraphs, and cheerful remarks"; they should be "full of incident and movement" so that the reader isn't "distracted from this pleasure by any tiresome analysis or 'description.'"[65] Thus Conrad entered an argument already launched, the terms defined, and the lines drawn. His prefaces, particularly his early prefaces to *Almayer's Folly* and to *The Nigger of the "Narcissus,"* continue in many ways the critical conversations James initiated. They constitute an epistemological and aesthetic challenge to earlier conceptions of the artist's task while echoing Pater and anticipating Woolf's theories of art. As Conrad looks back to James, so Arthur Symons looks back to Pater, writing in 1896 that it was reading Pater that made him first aware that prose also could be a fine art.[66] Symons, poet and editor of *The Savoy,* had accepted Conrad's first story, "The Idiots," hearing the new note it sounded, its suggestive descriptions and its treatment of time and formal complexities. Similarly Conrad looks back to Flaubert for initiating this understanding of the art of fiction, impressed by Flaubert's concern with craftsmanship, with his poetry-like prose, his "ascetic...devotion to his art."[67]

Even though these pronouncements were not monolithic and varied from each other in important ways, they all constituted an ideological, social, and aesthetic response to the felt crisis of modernity, and they all had in common the conviction that the role of the artist in modern society was a crucial one, that he alone could impose at least a provisional order on the chaos that was the modern world. Ford recalled, in his characteristically hyperbolic fashion, that he and Conrad "agreed that the writing of novels was the one thing of importance that remained to the world and that what the novel needed was the New Form."[68] For these early twentieth-century writers generally, art filled the void of challenged authority, not in the Arnoldian sense of preserving "the best that has been said and thought,"[69] not as guardians of tradition or as final pronouncements, but as provisional truths. In their own disparate ways, these writers imaged the artist as embattled and solitary in a demotic, commercialized world, as a creator, a maker and shaper, a skilled workman, free to record his impressions of any subject in any way. That a sense of embattlement drove these pronouncements and manifestos is evidenced, for example, in Conrad's *The Secret Agent*. When Vladimir instructs Verloc as to a bomb attack's target, he suggests the Greenwich Observatory as the most effective: "The sacrosanct fetish of today is science.... Art has never been [the public's] fetish. [A bomb in the National Gallery is] like breaking a few back windows in a man's house.... There would be some screaming of course, but from whom? Artists—art critics and such like—people of no account. Nobody minds what they say."[70] Here Conrad evinces his own anxiety about the role of the artist in an increasingly commercial world beholden to science and the other gods of progress. This passage suggests that a fissure had opened up between an art increasingly subject to the demands of a growing commodity culture and the more serious, often iconoclastic crafting these writers were self-consciously undertaking. *The Savoy* published its last number in December of 1896 after only eight issues and increasing insolvency. In the epilogue of that last issue, Symons wrote that *The Savoy* had failed because "of the too meager support of our friends."[71] He had initiated the magazine to continue, and rival, the aesthetic project of *The Yellow Book,* which was languishing, partially as a result of Oscar Wilde's trial but also because of the stiff competition presented by the proliferation of six-penny illustrated magazines; the English public, Symons and others associated with the Decadent movement of the 1990s concluded, was not ready for art. They argued for the artist's freedom, subject neither to Mrs. Grundy, nor to the public's desire for happy, conclusive endings, nor to the censor. In his first issue of the *English Review* in 1907, Ford proclaimed that his new journal wouldn't be an "entertainment" that would cater to popular tastes and avoid unpleasantness; rather it would be for adults and would publish that which maintained a high standard of literary values even if objectionable to popular taste. In that first issue, he published—along with pieces by James, Conrad, Galsworthy, Hudson, and Wells—a formerly censored ballad by

Hardy, "The Sunday Morning Tragedy," that spoke of a young girl's death from a botched abortion, an unsuitable subject to Mrs. Grundy's way of thinking.[72]

Initial Reception

The impressionistic plots of character rather than of action weren't universally well received at the time, nor was the focus on consciousness or the demands on the reader always appreciated, as has been noted. Frank Kermode refers to the resistance with which these early modern novels were reviewed when he asserts that they constituted "scandals of the Edwardian avant-garde."[73] That this was contested territory that needed to be justified and explained is made evident by some writers/critics of the day who demonstrated their resistance to this early experimentation and innovative interest in rendering levels of consciousness. R. A. Scott-James, writing in 1908 about "The Psychological Novel," wasn't particularly enthusiastic about what he referred to as the new works' "self-consciousness,"[74] objecting to the "extremes" of psychological analysis he found there.[75] There was general resistance as well to modernism's "unreadability," its inconclusiveness and "emptiness at the center where meaning should be."[76] Although Scott-James found room to praise Conrad—"Mr. Conrad is not a mere 'descriptive writer.' He is an originator in that he has learnt to apply the modern spirit of self-consciousness to the panorama of nature [in *The Mirror of the Sea*]"[77]—Conrad ran headlong into some currents of the leading literary criticism of the day.

Those critics and readers wanting nosegays for Mrs. Grundy were as disappointed with Conrad's early fiction as with Hardy's late work, finding *Almayer's Folly* "dreary" and "dull" and marred by "plentiful circumlocution."[78] They objected specifically to its impressionism. One reviewer, noticing that the story was "rather told by suggestion than in asserted fact," objected to the sense that the narrator seemed to be "muttering the story to himself. It is indeed hard to follow, and the minor characters are very hard to distinguish till the story is well advanced. The action drags . . . it is too slow moving for the interest of volatile European readers."[79]

But those who rejected the story's modernist features—its interest in psychology and in the foregrounding of consciousness rather than external action—seem to have been miscued by the Bornean setting and consequently misread the novel as exotic, local-color writing, of which there was an abundance at the time, most of it quite congratulatory of the white hero's civilizing mission. Others responded unfavorably to its "outlandish foreign setting" and its lack of "impressive white men."[80] One reviewer, ostensibly reacting to the method and the matter of the novel could only hope that it wouldn't initiate "a torrent of Bornean fiction."[81]

But many welcomed it as something new and worthy: "we have been struck with the book, and know nothing quite like it of recent years," one reviewer exclaimed. "It breaks fresh ground in fiction," another exclaimed. "The story is powerfully imagined," was the opinion of another. Most readers noted the "atmosphere," and a few understood the qualities of the "local color" that made this writing different from the adventure and exotic fiction of the day, the integration of setting with character. The scenery "mingles with [the characters] to the end that one may know they would not have been what they were had the white fogs not risen nightly from the river."[82] Another writer concluded his review with this praise: "in the novelty of its local color, in the daring originality of its dramatic force, in the fresh disclosure of new scenes and characters, in the noble and imaginative handling of life's greatness and littleness, *Almayer's Folly* has no place in the prevalent fiction of the hour, which, like a flooded stream, sweeps past us into oblivion."[83]

That literary boundaries are best discerned retroactively is apparent when we consider these various strains of critical response. Someone like H. G. Wells, whose own fiction with its direct narration and interest in realism appears old-fashioned, was an early appreciator of Conrad. In his unsigned review in *Saturday Review*, 15 June 1895, Wells notes the "gloom" of the tale that many other reviewers objected to but finds the gloom "relieved by the rare love-story ... and flashes of humour. ... It is exceedingly well imagined and well written, and it will certainly secure Mr. Conrad a high place among contemporary story-tellers."[84] While *Almayer's Folly* was published to mixed reviews, Wells—

one of modernism's whipping boys—liked what he read and distinguished it from the fiction of the day as "a work of art."

Changing Views

Modernism continues to take shape differently, depending on which decade of the twentieth century one is writing from. Even from our vantage point in the twenty-first century's first decade, we can concur with the general agreement that the years 1880–1930 were experienced as a period of crisis and that the art produced during this time was revolutionary. The literary artists of this period we have come to think of as modernist wrote with an awareness of crisis that itself shifted and deepened. Crises of authority—political, social, and aesthetic—various struggles, and unrest took various forms that now can be seen differently depending on the shifting critical and cultural vantage points of the twentieth and twenty-first centuries. Modernism was a complicated response to the modern world and took several forms: epistemological, aesthetic, and social. Like all writing, these texts were subject to the various pressures of the early twentieth-century's literary market and the constraints of editors, publishers, and critics and must be read within the political and social climate of the day. While the aesthetic response—the new forms and experimental narrative strategies as expressions of epistemological skepticism—was the focus of most comment and criticism until the 1960s, literary scholars and critics started noticing the ways in which the fiction of modernism also constituted social criticism. In 1958 Albert Guerard admits of his earlier 1947 view of Conrad, "in the political area I undervalued Conrad because I found so few concrete references to the specific issues and conflicts of his time. It has taken the full aftermath of the second world war to make me recognize the political insights of *Nostromo, The Secret Agent,* and *Under Western Eyes* and their pertinence for our own time."[85] That *Almayer's Folly* was revolutionary and took aim at such issues as imperialism wasn't as clearly on view until such criticism as Guerard's. With works such as Irving Howe's *Politics and the Novel* (1957), Eloise Hay's *The Political Novels of Joseph Conrad* (1963), and Avrom Fleishman's *Conrad's Politics* (1967),

Conrad was opened to a different sort of attention. While a contemporary reviewer of "Heart of Darkness" defended the novella against those who might suspect that "Mr. Conrad makes attack upon colonization, expansion, even upon Imperialism,"[86] here assuring his readers that its subject is our common emotions, to most readers now, it clearly questions the "fantastic invasion" of Europeans in Africa.

Although Conrad, "as a middle-European of gentry status[,] was obsessed with the burden of history,"[87] readers and critics took most of the later moderns at their word about their break from the past, their intention to "make it new," and their impersonal aloofness from the kinds of current social and political concerns the elder Edwardians concerned themselves with. But the critical writing of the 1960s and the postcolonial, cultural, and gender studies of the later twentieth century have revealed the moderns as politically and socially engaged with the issues of their day. In that light, Alex Zwerdling first argued for Woolf's antipatriarchal stance toward gender inequities, a view of Woolf common today. In his 1986 study, he set out to answer the question, "Why has Woolf's strong interest in realism, history, and the social matrix been largely ignored? Why has it taken us so long to understand the importance of these elements in her work?"[88] Part of the answer is the "enormous body of unpublished material after 1972 and Quentin Bell's biography," and part is our own angle of vision as twentieth- and twenty-first-century readers and our shifts in critical attention. Thus as both Woolf and Joyce are read now for their antiwar sentiments, and Mansfield's stories are read anew, her "cry against corruption" taking on a more political weight, so we have come to read Conrad's first Malay novels as entering the literary scene not only as Flaubertian heirs and modernist innovations, but as subversions of genres and critics of empire.

To us now in the early twenty-first century, tempered as our readings have been by post-colonial critiques of Conrad's work, it comes as a surprise perhaps to learn of his apprehension about being misread from a rather different angle, one in which he defends his unfashionable understanding of the commonality of the earth's peoples, rejecting the commonly presumed superiority of "civilized" over "savage." In 1894, Conrad wrote a preface to his first novel that acknowledged his awareness of a central critical current his work opposed.[89] And that novel, *Almayer's Folly*, did insert itself uneasily in the contemporary scene. The Arnoldian critical tradition of viewing literature as a guardian of culture and as a bearer of evolutionary progress still pertained when the novel was published in 1895. Conrad was aware of this attitude from an essay he read in 1893 on the basis of which he felt that its author at least would find his first novel "decivilised." The article entitled "Decivilised" appeared in 1891 in the January 24 issue of *National Observer*. It was written by Alice Meynell, admired as a poet and a critic by many, among them Vita Sackville-West.[90] Representative of a major late Victorian current of thinking, she subscribed to the evolutionary view that saw the "primitive" as lower on the evolutionary ladder, a state to which the civilized shouldn't regress. Writing under the influence of James G. Frazer and other proponents of Victorian evolutionary thought that argued that art—literature in particular—should aid in the continuing improvement of the species toward superior civilization, she opposed some of the colonial literature of the day that emphasized newness rather than continuity and argued that the critic's task was to be watchful for retrograde literature that would decivilize. As David Leon Higdon points out, she "values continuity because she finds in it a measure of the best and a keeper of civilized values."[91] The major conflict here lies in her claim for "change, progress, and evolving man, while Conrad...speaks for what is permanent, common, and enduring."[92] As he wrote in his Author's Note to the novel, "And there is a bond between us and that humanity so far away....I am content to sympathise with common mortals, no matter where they live, in houses or in huts, in the streets under a fog, or in the forests behind the dark line of dismal mangroves that fringe the vast solitude of the sea."[93] Conrad appears to have read Meynall's article in its 1893 reprinting in *The Rhythm of Life*, so he knew what he was up against. Upon reading it, Conrad wrote to Hugh Chesson, Unwin's reader, as to how he might best represent the novel in notices the publisher put out that would deflect the kind of criticism registered in Meynell's writing. "Civilized story in savage surroundings," he suggested. His point in the "Author's Note" he then wrote focuses on man's commonality, his similarities: "Their hearts—like ours—must endure the load of the gifts from Heaven: the curse of facts and blessing of illusions, the bitterness of our wisdom and the deceptive consolation of our folly."[94] Interestingly, that ship's master the novelist John Galsworthy met on board the *Torrens* was already aware of the contested field he considered entering, getting ready—however unconsciously—to embark on his next career.

But it was increasingly difficult for early twentieth-century writers to subscribe to the evolutionary view's enthusiasm for civilization and progress as first the Boer War and then over a decade of unrest inflicted wounds on that optimism, argued for by Meynell and others: labor disputes, Irish unrest, increasingly vocal suffrage issues, anxieties about decline and degeneration, imperialist politics, and the devastation of the First World War. While postwar texts are generally haunted by the trauma of the years 1914–1918, Conrad's fiction of that period registers less surprise and disillusionment. To a skeptical mind familiar with the conflicts inherent to both imperialism and nationalism, the war was more inevitable than surprising to him. Of his later works, *The Shadow-Line* (1917) can be seen to register something of the war's initial shock, however, deepened by his own son's involvement at the French front. But "the horror," a recognition of what lies beyond the veneer of civilization, had always been his awareness. That London could once more become the dark abyss as the center of a decaying empire is a conviction his works attest to.

This essay can only gesture toward and limn the contours of the multiple ways in which Conrad's work participated in and contributed to Anglo-American modernism. His relationship to it was complicated, and his work's concerns—we are coming to see— were multiple. One in particular, gender uncertainty, has only recently become visible due to contemporary theories of gender and sexuality. Current feminist and gender criticism is noticing the ways in which the ambiguities take shape differently in modernist texts: Leopold Bloom as "the new womanly man," Woolf's androgency, Mansfield's anti-patriarchal rumblings and suggestions of lesbian love, Lawrence's *blutbrüderschaft*, Forster's muted homosexuality, the defensively misogynstic Marlow of *Chance,* the homosexual anxiety many have read in the Marlow of "Heart of Darkness," and the violent misogyny of *Victory's* Gentleman Jones. New readings now explain these as possible reactions to the "pressures exerted" by the New Woman novels of the 1890s and the direct challenge to male authority those novels presented.[95] New critical lenses reveal what has lain unexposed and unnoticed.[96]

The assumption of this essay, as of this series, is that literature participates in the cultural conversations that so shape our experience, our sense of the world, and its representations in prose fiction. Conrad's relationship to modernism was and continues to be complex, informed by contemporary events and currents of thought about culture and art. Nor can this essay escape its time and place but must necessarily comprise retrospective views, written from an early twenty-first-century standpoint.

NOTES

1. Joseph Conrad, "Heart of Darkness," in *Youth and Two Other Stories* (Garden City, N.Y.: Doubleday, Page & Co., 1923), 117.

2. J. Hillis Miller, "Foreword," in *Conrad in the Twenty-First Century: Contemporary Approaches and Perspectives,* ed. Carola M. Kaplan, Peter Lancelot Mallios, and Andrea White (New York: Routledge, 2005), 2.

3. Ian Watt, *"Almayer's Folly:* Introduction," in *Essays on Conrad* (Cambridge: Cambridge University Press, 2000), 52.

4. See Veeder, 184.

5. Virginia Woolf, "Modern Fiction," in *The Common Reader* (New York: Harcourt, Brace & World, 1925), 157–58.

6. Walter Pater, "'Conclusion' to *The Renaissance,*" in *Walter Pater: Three Major Texts,* ed. William E. Buckler (New York: New York University Press, 1986), 218.

7. Jesse Matz, *Literary Impressionism and Modernist Aesthetics* (Cambridge: Cambridge University Press, 2001), 2.

8. David Smith, *Conrad's Manifesto: Preface to a Career, The History of the "Preface" to* The Nigger of the *"Narcissus" with Facsimiles of the Manuscript* (Northamton, Mass.: The Gehenna Press, 1966), 9. For more on the publishing history of the preface, see Smith.

9. Michael H. Levenson, *A Genealogy of Modernism: A Study of English Literary Doctrine 1908–1922* (Cambridge: Cambridge University Press, 1984), 2.

10. Ford Madox Ford, "On Impressionism," in *Critical Writings of Ford Madox Ford*, ed. Frank MacShane (Lincoln: University of Nebraska Press, 1964), 54.

11. Joseph Conrad, "Preface" to *The Nigger of the "Narcissus,"* in *The Nigger of the "Narcissus": A Tale of the Sea* and *Typhoon* (London: J. M. Dent & Sons, 1923), vii, x.

12. Levenson, *Genealogy of Modernism*, 21.

13. Michael Levenson, *Modernism and the Fate of Individuality: Character and Novelistic Form from Conrad to Woolf* (Cambridge: Cambridge University Press, 1991), 102f.

14. Conrad, "Preface" to *The Nigger of the "Narcissus,"* viii.

15. Pater, "'Conclusion' to the *The Renaissance*," 218.

16. Conrad, "Heart of Darkness," 82.

17. Viriginia Woolf, *To the Lighthouse* (New York: Harcourt, 2005), 54.

18. Joseph Conrad, *Nostromo*, ed. Keith Carabine (Oxford: Oxford University Press, 1984), 295.

19. Joseph Conrad, *Tales of Unrest*, ed. Anthony Fothergill (London: Everyman, 2000), 45.

20. Hugh Epstein, "'Where He Is Not Wanted': Impressionism and Articulation in 'The Idiots' and 'Amy Foster,'" *Conradiana* 23, no. 3 (autumn 1991): 220, 222.

21. Levenson, *Genealogy of Modernism*, 8.

22. William Deresiewicz, "Conrad's Impasse: *The Nigger of the 'Narcissus'* and the Invention of Marlow," *Conradiana* 38, no. 3 (fall 2006): 206.

23. Virginia Woolf, "Mr. Bennett and Mrs. Brown," in *The Captain's Death Bed and Other Essays* (New York: Harcourt Brace Jovanovich, 1950), 110.

24. Eric Auerbach, *Mimesis: The Representation of Reality in Western Literature"* (Princeton: Princeton University Press, 2003), 546.

25. Woolf, "Modern Fiction," 154.

26. Conrad, "Heart of Darkness," 48.

27. Joseph Conrad, *Lord Jim*, ed. Robert Hampson (London: Penguin, 1986), 100.

28. Ibid., 76.

29. Jakob Lothe, *Conrad's Narrative Method* (Oxford: Clarendon Press, 1989), 207.

30. Ian Watt, *Conrad in the Nineteenth Century* (Berkeley: University of California Press, 1979), 175.

31. As early as 1924 Ramon Fernandez, in his article "The Art of Conrad," which appeared in *La Nouvelle Revue Française* shortly after Conrad's death, described this phenomenon. Although he hadn't come up with the term "delayed decoding," he did notice that Conrad "devotes himself to seizing things as they come into being, in their formative stages, and so to speak on the hither side of their definition. What I mean is that we experience them before it's possible to define them, to give them a name." *Joseph Conrad: A Critical Symposium*, ed. R. W. Stallman, trans. Charles Owen (East Lansing: Michigan State University Press, 1960), 10.

32. Ford, "On Impressionism," 67.

33. Conrad, "Heart of Darkness," 44.

34. Ibid.

35. Owen Knowles, "Introduction," in *Almayer's Folly* by Joseph Conrad, ed. Owen Knowles (London: J. M. Dent, 1995), xxxviii.

36. As quoted in John Rewald, *Paul Cézanne*, trans. Margaret H. Liebman (London: Spring Books, 1950), 46.

37. Arthur Jerome Eddy, *Cubists and Post-Impressionism* (Chicago: A. C. McClurg & Co., 1914), 90.

38. Stephen Kern, *The Culture of Time and Space: 1880–1918* (Cambridge, Mass.: Harvard University Press, 1983), 140.

39. Auerbach, Mimesis, 537.

40. Kern, *The Culture of Time*, 16.

41. Ann Banfield, "Remembrance and Tense Past," in *The Cambridge Companion to The Modernist Novel*. Ed. Morag Shiach (Cambridge: Cambridge University Press, 2007), 48.

42. As quoted in Anne Fernihough, "Consciousness as a Stream," in *The Cambridge Companion to the Modernist Novel*, 68–69.

43. Ibid., 69.

44. Auerbach, *Mimesis,* 537.

45. Watt, *"Almayer's Folly*: Introduction," 58.

46. Ford Madox Ford, *Joseph Conrad: A Personal Remembrance* (London: Duckworth & Co., 1924), 137.

47. Kern, *The Culture of Time,* 16.

48. Conrad, "Heart of Darkness," 99.

49. Joseph Conrad, *Under Western Eyes*, ed. Jeremy Hawthorn (Oxford: Oxford University Press, 1983), 11.

50. William W. Bonney, *Thorns & Arabesques: Context for Conrad's Fiction* (Baltimore: Johns Hopkins University Press, 1980), 203.

51. Leonard Diepeveen, *The Difficulties of Modernism* (New York: Routledge, 2003), xv.

52. Knowles, "Introduction" in *Almayer's Folly*, xxxix.

53. Ibid., 29.

54. Diepeveen, *The Difficulties of Modernism*, xiii.

55. William Veeder and Susan M. Griffin, eds., *The Art of Criticism: Henry James on the Theory and the Practice of Fiction* (Chicago: University of Chicago Press, 1986), 396.

56. Edmond Wilson, *Axel's Castle: A Study in the Imaginative Literature of 1870–1930* (New York: W. W. Norton & Co., 1931), 211.

57. See Richard Curle, *Joseph Conrad: A Study* (London: Kegan Paul, Trench, Trübner, 1914).

58. Conrad to Curle, 14 July 1923, in *The Collected Letters of Joseph Conrad*, ed. Laurence Davies *et al.*, 9 vols. (Cambridge: Cambridge University Press, 1983–2007), 8: 130–31. See also Richard Ambrosini, *Conrad's Fiction as Critical Discourse* (Cambridge: Cambridge University Press, 1991), 53–55.

59. For a more extended treatment of the role literary criticism and the new professionalism played in producing "modernism," see Diepeveen, *The Difficulties of Modernism*.

60. Tim Armstrong, *Modernism: A Cultural History* (Cambridge: Polity, 2005), 53.

61. Ford, "On Impressionism," 47.

62. "The Art of Fiction" is the title of an essay drafted in 1881 by Thomas Hardy and of productions in 1884 by Besant, James, and Andrew Lang, evidence of the topic's importance in contemporary conversations. See Veeder and Griffin, *The Art of Criticism*.

63. Veeder and Griffin, *The Art of Criticism*, 177.

64. Ibid., 169.

65. Ibid., 168–69.

66. Arthur Symons, "Walter Pater: Some Characteristics," *The Savoy* 8 (December 1896): 33–41, especially 34, 36, and 41.

67. Joseph Conrad, *A Personal Record* (London: J.M. Dent & Sons, 1923), 3.

68. Ford, *Joseph Conrad*, 30.

69. A. Dwight Culler, *Poetry and Criticism of Matthew Arnold* (Boston: Houghton Mifflin, 1961), 245.

70. Joseph Conrad, *The Secret Agent*, ed. Peter Lancelot Mallios (New York: The Modern Library, 2004), 26–27.

71. Arthur Symons, "A Literary Causerie: By Way of Epilogue," *The Savoy* 8 (December 1896): 92.

72. In a letter dated 15 October 1907, Hardy commiserated with Edward Garnett about the power of the Censor, who was still, unfortunately, alive and well:

> Last week a poem of mine, which I thought almost too obtrusive in its moral, was declined by one of our chief editors on the sole ground that his periodical was "read in families." Yet the subject of the poem, which gave no details, is read by all families in newspaper reports with full details continually. And a ballad of mine called "A Trampwoman's Tragedy" which appeared in a foreign review, had been declined by English editors for the same reason. The subject of that ballad, too, would be read aloud in any family circle with modern details in a newspaper.

The Collected Letters of Thomas Hardy, ed. Richard Little Purdy and Michael Millgate, 7 vols. (Oxford: Clarendon Press, 1978–88), 3: 278. A year later, responding to Ford's request to publish "The Sunday Morning Tragedy," Hardy wrote: "The Editor of the review, who returned it, merely said that he would have personally liked to print it, but that his review circulated amongst young people. Of course, with a larger morality, the guardians of young people would see that it is the very thing they ought to read, for nobody can say that the treatment is other than moral, & the crime is one of growing prevalence, as you probably know, & the false shame which leads to it is produced by the hypocrisy of the age" (3: 331).

73. Frank Kermode, "Forward," in *Ford Madox Ford's Modernity*, ed. Robert Hampson and Max Saunders (Amsterdam: Rodopi, 2003), 2.

74. R. A. Scott-James, *Modernism and Romance* (London: John Lane, 1908), 86f.

75. Ibid., 109.

76. Armstrong, *Modernism*, 62.

77. Scott-James, *Modernism and Romance*, 234.

78. Norman Sherry, ed., *Conrad: The Critical Heritage* (London: Routledge and Kegan Paul, 1973), 51.

79. Ibid., 58.

80. Ibid., 60.

81. Ibid., 51.

82. Ibid., 50.

83. Ibid., 60.

84. Ibid., 53.

85. Albert J. Guerard, *Conrad the Novelist* (Cambridge, Mass.: Harvard University Press, 1958), xi.

86. Sherry, *Conrad: The Critical Heritage*, 135.

87. Frederick R. Karl, *Joseph Conrad: The Three Lives* (New York: Farrar, Strauss and Giroux, 1979), 656.

88. Alex Zwerdling, *Virginia Woolf and the Real World* (Berkeley: University of California Press, 1986), 15.

89. This preface, or "Author's Note," although completed by January 1895, was not published until the Doubleday, Page "Sun-Dial" edition of 1921. For more on this, Conrad's first critical essay, see David Leon Higdon, "The Text and Context of Conrad's First Critical Essay," *The Polish Review* 20, nos. 2–3 (1975): 97–105.

90. Higdon, "The Text and Context," 101.

91. Ibid., 102.

92. Ibid., 105.

93. Conrad, *Almayer's Folly*, 3–4.

94. Ibid., 4.

95. Levenson, *Modernism and the Fate of Individuality*, 188f.

96. For some recent work that benefits directly from recent feminist and gender studies, see: Lisa Rado, ed. *Modernism, Gender, and Culture: A Cultural Studies Approach* (New York: Garland Publishing, 1997); Marianne DeKoven, *Rich and Strange: Gender, History, Modernism* (Princeton: Princeton University Press, 1991); Bonnie Kime Scott, ed., *The Gender of Modernism: An Anthology* (Bloomington: Indiana University Press, 1990); Susan Jones, *Conrad and Women* (Oxford: Clarendon Press, 1999); Andrew M. Roberts, *Conrad and Masculinity* (New York: St. Martin's Press, 2000); Jeremy Hawthorn, *Sexuality and the Erotic in the Fiction of Joseph Conrad* (London: Continuum, 2007); and Richard Ruppel, *Homosexuality in the Life and Work of Joseph Conrad: Love Between the Lines* (New York: Routledge, 2008). In addition, the following should also be consulted: Carola M. Kaplan's

"Beyond Gender: Deconstructions of Masculinity and Femininity from 'Karain' to *Under Western Eyes*," in Kaplan, Mallios, and White, eds., *Conrad in the Twenty-First Century*, 267–79; Nina Pelikan Struss's "The Exclusion of the Intended from Secret Sharing in Conrad's *Heart of Darkness*" in *Joseph Conrad's* Heart of Darkness: *A Casebook*, ed. Gene M. Moore (Oxford: Oxford University Press, 2004), 197–217; Ruth Nadelhaft's "A Feminist Perspective on *Heart of Darkness*," in *Joseph Conrad's Heart of Darkness* by D. C. R. A. Goonetilleke (London: Routledge), 92–100; and Johanna Smith's "'Too Beautiful Altogether': Patriarchal Ideology in *Heart of Darkness* in *Heart of Darkness: A Case Study in Contemporary Criticism*, Ross C. Murfin, ed. 2nd ed. (Boston: Bedford Books, 1996), 169–84.

Illustrated Chronology

1857: Józef Teodor Konrad
Korzeniowski (Joseph Conrad) is
born in Berdyczów, Ukraine, on
December 3.

1862: Conrad's father, Apollo
Korzeniowski, is exiled to Vologda,
Russia.

Conrad's childhood home

Conrad in 1863

1865: Conrad's mother, Ewelina Bobrowska Korzeniowska, dies of tuberculosis while in exile.

Apollo Korzeniowski

Ewelina Bobrowska Korzeniowska

1869: Having been allowed to return to Poland, Apollo Korzeniowski dies of tuberculosis contracted during his exile.

1874: Conrad goes to Marseilles, France, to study to become a sailor.

1875: Conrad begins his career as an apprentice aboard the *Mont-Blanc*.

1877: Conrad serves aboard the *Tremolino*, which may have been engaged in gunrunning.

Scene from Marseilles

1878: Depressed, Conrad attempts suicide, although it is let out that he was wounded in a duel. Later,

Conrad in 1874

because of problems with papers for working in France, Conrad joins the British Merchant Marine service instead.

1880: Conrad passes his officer's examination.

1881: Signs on as second mate aboard the *Palestine*. (This experience will serve as the basis for "Youth.")

1884: Conrad signs on as second mate of the *Narcissus*. (This would become the basis for *The Nigger of the "Narcissus."*) Conrad passes his examination for first mate.

1886: Conrad passes his master's examination for a captaincy and becomes a British citizen.

Conrad's Certificate of Discharge from the Riversdale

Conrad in 1882

Conrad's chart for the Gulf of Siam

Conrad's Master certificate

1888: Conrad assumes command of the *Otago*.

The Otago

1889: Conrad begins writing *Almayer's Folly*.

1890: Conrad signs on with a Belgian trading company to work on *Roi des Belges* on the Congo River. (This experience will be the basis for "Heart of Darkness.")

1893: Conrad becomes friends with John Galsworthy on a return voyage from Australia aboard the *Torrens*, upon which he was serving as first mate.

1894: Conrad finishes his tour of duty aboard the *Adowa* and

Conrad and other sailors aboard the Torrens

unknowingly leaves his profession at sea forever. He becomes friends with Edward Garnett.

The Torrens

1895: *Almayer's Folly* is published.

1896: *An Outcast of the Islands* is published, Conrad becomes friends with H. G. Wells, and he marries Jessie George. Conrad begins *The Rescue*, which he will not finish until 1920.

1897: *The Nigger of the "Narcissus"* is published, and Conrad meets and becomes friends with Henry James, R. B. Cunninghame Graham, and Stephen Crane.

1898: *Tales of Unrest* and "Youth" are published. Conrad becomes friends with Ford Madox Ford [Hueffer], and his first son, Borys, is born.

1899: *Heart of Darkness* is published. *Tales of Unrest* receives the *Academy* award.

Manuscript page from "Heart of Darkness"

1900: *Lord Jim* is published, and James B. Pinker becomes Conrad's literary agent.

1901: *The Inheritors* (written with Ford Madox Ford) is published.

1902: *Youth and Two Other Stories* is published.

1903: *Typhoon and Other Stories* is published. *Romance* (written with Ford Madox Ford) is published.

1904: *Nostromo* is published. Conrad writes a one-act play, *One Day More,* based upon "To-morrow."

Conrad in 1904

1905: "Autocracy and War" is published. Conrad receives a £500 grant from the Royal Bounty Fund.

1906: *The Mirror of the Sea* is published. Conrad's second son, John (named after John Galsworthy), is born.

1907: *The Secret Agent* is published.

1908: *A Set of Six* is published. Conrad receives £200 from the Royal Literary Fund.

1911: *Under Western Eyes* is published.

UNDER WESTERN EYES

BY

JOSEPH CONRAD

"*I would take liberty from any hand as a hungry man would snatch a piece of bread.*" . . .
MISS HALDIN

METHUEN & CO. LTD.
36 ESSEX STREET W.C.
LONDON

Title page for the first edition of Under Western Eyes

A SET OF SIX

BY

JOSEPH CONRAD

*Les petits marionnettes
Font, font, font,
Trois petits tours
Et puis s'en vont.*
NURSERY RHYME.

METHUEN & CO.
36 ESSEX STREET W.C.
LONDON

Title page for the first edition of A Set of Six

1910: Conrad completes *Under Western Eyes* and suffers a complete physical and emotional breakdown. Conrad receives a £100 Civil List Pension.

1912: *Some Reminiscences* (*A Personal Record*) and *'Twixt Land and Sea* are published.

1914: *Chance* is published, and Conrad achieves public fame and financial security. Conrad becomes friends with Bertrand Russell. He travels to Poland with his family and is caught behind Austrian lines at the outbreak of the First World War.

1915: "Poland Revisited," *Within the Tides*, and *Victory* are published. Conrad's son Borys enlists in the army.

1916: Conrad tours naval bases and goes on maneuvers aboard the HMS *Ready*.

1917: *The Shadow-Line* is published.

1918: Conrad takes up *The Rescue* again. Borys suffers shell shock.

1919: *The Arrow of Gold* is published. Conrad writes a stage adaptation of *The Secret Agent*.

1920: *The Rescue* is published. Conrad begins writing *Suspense*. Conrad writes *Laughing Anne*, a stage adaptation of "Because of the Dollars."

1921: *Notes on Life and Letters* is published. Conrad translates Bruno Winawer's play *The Book of Job* from Polish into English.

1923: *The Rover* and "Geography and Some Explorers" are published, and Conrad travels to America on a promotion tour.

1924: Conrad continues to work on *Suspense*. He declines the offer of knighthood and later suffers a heart attack and dies, leaving his novel *Suspense* unfinished.

Conrad's last home Oswalds

Conrad in 1923

1925: *Tales of Hearsay* and *Suspense* are published.

1926: *Last Essays* is published.

Conrad's grave

Chronology of British, Russian, Polish and French History

1762: Catherine II becomes Empress of Russia.

1772, 1793, 1795: Poland is partitioned between Russia, Prussia, and Austria.

1796: Paul I becomes Tsar of Russia.

1801: Alexander I becomes Tsar of Russia.

1812: Russia is invaded by France but weathers the invasion and emerges victorious and as the premier power on land in Europe. (This event is the basis for "The Warrior's Soul.")

1825: Nicholas I becomes Tsar of Russia.

1830: Polish insurgents revolt against Russian rule. The insurrection is not put down until almost a year later. Severe reprisals follow. (This event forms the basis for "Prince Roman.")

1853: Russia enters The Crimean War of 1853–1856 and ultimately is defeated.

Prince Roman Sanguszko, prominent member of the 1830 Polish uprising

1855: Alexander II becomes Tsar of Russia.

1863: Polish insurgents again revolt against Russian rule. The insurrection is not put down until near two years later. Again, severe reprisals follow.

1867: The Second Reform Act was passed in England and extended voting rights to a larger section of the population.

1868: William Gladstone first becomes prime minister of England.

1870: The Third Republic begins in France.

1874: Benjamin Disraeli becomes Prime Minister of England.

1876: The Land and Freedom Party, which sought social reforms, is formed in Russia.

1879: The People's Will wing of the Land and Freedom Party is formed with the specific intent of carrying out terrorist activities against the Russian government.

1881: Alexander II is assassinated by members of The People's Will. Alexander III becomes Tsar of Russia.

1882: The Married Women's Property Act is passed in England, which allows married women to own property independent of their husbands.

1884: The Third Reform Bill further extended voting privileges in England.

1891: In Russia, a famine across the land reinvigorates revolutionary activity against the Russian government.

1893: The Second Irish Home Rule Bill passes the House of Commons but is defeated in the House of Lords.

1894: Nicholas II becomes Tsar of Russia.

1899: The Second Boer War breaks out; it and would not end until 1902.

1901: Queen Victoria dies. King Edward VII ascends to the English throne.

1904: Vyacheslav Konstantinovich Plehve, Russian Minister of the Interior, is assassinated by members of the Socialist-Revolutionary Party. (This event will become the basis for *Under Western Eyes*.)

1905: The Bloody Sunday Massacre occurs in St. Petersburg, setting off a yearlong revolution in Russia.

1910: Edward VII dies. He is succeeded by George V.

1914: Archduke Franz Ferdinand is assassinated in Sarajevo, and the First World War breaks out. Third Irish Home Rule Act is passed but not acted upon until after the war when it was replaced by the Fourth Irish Home Rule Act in 1920.

1916: The Easter Rebellion occurs in Dublin.

1917: The Russian Revolution occurs, overthrowing the monarchy.

1918: The First World War ends. Representation of the People Act in England extends voting privileges to most women over thirty.

1919: Poland achieves its independence from Russia, Germany, and Austria-Hungary.

1920: League of Nations comes into being. Fourth Irish Home Rule Act is passed and establishes the division between southern and northern Ireland.

1922: The Republic of Ireland is formed.

Bibliographic Essay

Conrad Commentary Past and Present

John G. Peters

During the first twenty years of Conrad's writing career, the vast majority of commentary on his works appeared in the form of book reviews. There was the occasional critical essay and the occasional review that branched out beyond the particular book at hand, and these reviews and essays form the basis for later commentary on Conrad's life and works. The first important commentary was Sir Hugh Clifford's unsigned review of four of Conrad's books, "The Trail of the Book-Worm: Mr. Joseph Conrad at Home and Abroad" (1898). Clifford praises strong descriptions and literary style but also questions Conrad's understanding of Malays, suggesting that his Malay characters and Malay customs do not resemble their real-life models very closely. A similar essay is Edward Garnett's unsigned review of *Tales of Unrest*, "Academy Portraits: Mr. Joseph Conrad" (1898), which is actually a commentary on all of Conrad's work to that point and argues that Conrad focuses on the relationship between humanity and the universe at large. Over the next fifteen years, other similar commentaries would occasionally appear in addition to the usual reviews of Conrad's works.

The first extended commentary on Conrad's works was Richard Curle's *Joseph Conrad: A Study* (1914). Curle is the first to investigate Conrad's romantic realism (a topic that would appear in much of the early commentary on Conrad) and also considers Conrad's use of irony and fixed ideas. Curle's study was followed quickly by the first excellent study of Conrad's works in Wilson Follett's *Joseph Conrad: A Short Study* (1915). Follett's insightful analysis of Conrad (of which Conrad himself seemed to approve) looks at Conrad's indifferent universe and the place of individuals therein. He notes Conrad's emphasis on solidarity as a means of combating the ultimate isolation of the individual in an indifferent universe. Furthermore, Follett argues for the affirming rather than negating effect of Conrad's skepticism. Other extended studies published during Conrad's lifetime, such as Ruth M. Stauffer's *Joseph Conrad: His Romantic-Realism* (1922) and Ernst Bendz's *Joseph Conrad: An Appreciation* (1923), have occasional insights but fail to advance Conrad studies in any significant way. Two important biographical works appeared during this period: Ford Madox Ford's *Joseph Conrad: A Personal Remembrance* (1924) and G. Jean-Aubry's *Joseph Conrad: Life and Letters* (1927), which is a biography and compilation of many of Conrad's letters. Until the recently completed Cambridge University Press edition of Conrad's collected letters, Jean-Aubry was the main source for much of Conrad's correspondence. Similarly useful has been Ford's reminiscence. Although notoriously suspect in many details, it is nevertheless particularly important for its discussion of the development of Conrad's literary methodology. Next to Follett's book, Gustav Morf's *The Polish Heritage of Joseph Conrad* (1930) is the most important commentary of this period. In this book, Morf reads Conrad's literary career through the lens of his Polish past. Strongly influenced by psychoanalytic theory, Morf reads Conrad's works as an attempt to come to terms with his abandoning Poland when he left his homeland for a life at sea. Although Morf sometimes carries his conclusions too far, his work was quite influential on those commentators to follow him.

Soon after Conrad's death, his literary reputation fell into a precipitous decline. In early 1930, both Richard Curle, in his "Joseph Conrad and the Younger Generation," and Granville Hicks, in his "Conrad Five Years After," noted this decline. It would not be until the 1940s that Conrad's reputation would begin to rise again and not until the 1950s would Conrad take his place among the greats of twentieth-century British literature. During this period of decline, several important studies would appear to help recover Conrad's literary reputation. The first of these was R. L. Mégroz's *Joseph Conrad's Mind and Method* (1931), which argues, among other things, for a more significant role for women in Conrad's works than had typically been assumed. Mégroz also discusses Conrad's narrative methodology and the plotting of his tales, as well as the realism of his descriptive passages. Another important work of this period was Edward Crankshaw's *Joseph Conrad: Some Aspects of the Art of the Novel* (1936). In this work, Crankshaw considers the means by which Conrad achieved the effect he does in his fiction and contends that Conrad's work is a unified whole. David Daiches's commentary on Conrad in his *The Novel and the Modern World* (1939) was another important step in rescuing Conrad's literary reputation. Daiches sees Conrad as less concerned with humanity in their relationship with their social environment than with humanity in their natural environment. Daiches also argues that Conrad seeks to render phenomena objectively but to sympathize with that rendering and that he often places competing philosophical ideas next to one another, particularly those ideas that point to both affirmation and negation of human existence.

John Dozier Gordan's book *Joseph Conrad: The Making of a Novelist* (1940) begins a new phase in Conrad commentary in that it is the first modern book of commentary. With the exception of Daiches's commentary, most of what preceded Gordan was heavily influenced by the *belles lettres* tradition, even those commentaries that provided useful analysis were not immune to praising rather than analyzing to one degree or another. Beginning with Gordan's book, this tendency declined significantly. In particular, Gordan is especially good at identifying the history of Conrad's composition. The first extended textual analysis of Conrad's works, Gordan's book considers Conrad's writing process, as well as the sources for Conrad's works. M. C. Bradbrook's *Joseph Conrad: Poland's English Genius* (1941) is of primary importance in its being the first extended commentary on what would eventually become known as the "achievement and decline theory" of Conrad's literary career, in which she argues that after a period of strong productivity Conrad's later works exhibit a decline in literary quality. This would become an important theory that still has numerous adherents today. Morton Dauwen Zabel's lengthy introduction to *The Portable Conrad* (1947) was particularly important in its effect in recovering Conrad's literary reputation. Zabel contends that Conrad's narrative methodology is connected to the complex moral, philosophical, and psychological issues he considered. Zabel also comments on the psychological struggles of Conrad's characters and argues that the issue of honor is particularly important in Conrad's works. While Gordan's book is the first book of modern Conrad commentary, Albert J. Guerard's *Joseph Conrad* (1947) is the first major commentary on Conrad's works. Guerard focuses on Conrad's psychological and philosophical investigations and comments on Conrad's meaningless universe and its meaning for human existence. Guerard also expands upon Bradbrook's view of Conrad's achievement and decline. F. R. Leavis's *The Great Tradition* (1948) followed with an extremely important and influential commentary on Conrad's works. Leavis includes Conrad's work in the great tradition of moral realism in the novel and famously complained about Conrad's overuse of adjectives in some of his early works, particularly in "Heart of Darkness."

After the work of such commentators as Zabel and Leavis had served to recover Conrad's reputation, the work of Robert Penn Warren, Douglas Hewitt, Thomas C. Moser, and others would solidify the recent recovery of Conrad's literary reputation and would lay the groundwork for future commentary on Conrad's works. In 1950, Warren wrote an important introduction to Conrad's *Nostromo*, and, although it is directed toward this novel, Warren's comments also broaden to Conrad's work in general. In this piece, Warren argues that Conrad consistently looks into the inner life of human beings in order to arrive at truth. In addition, Warren suggests that Conrad recognized that values and ideas are illusory while also recognizing the necessity of maintaining such illusions in order to make life livable. Hewitt's *Conrad: A Reassessment* (1952) also helped solidify Conrad's reputation as a major figure in twentieth-century British literature. Hewitt argues that the setting and structure of Conrad's works reinforce his investigations into the psychological and moral wrestling of his characters and reveal the complexity of human existence. Furthermore, Hewitt contends that the ideas of courage, fidelity, and codes of conduct are primary issues in Conrad's works. Paul L. Wiley's *Conrad's Measure of Man* (1954) is primarily of importance as the first extended rebuttal to the growing strength of the achievement and decline theory of Conrad's literary career, in which he argues that rather than a decline in Conrad's abilities his later works reveal Conrad considering different aspects of human experience. Irving Howe's *Politics and the Novel* (1957) is important as the first major commentary on Conrad's politics. In his chapter on Conrad, Howe argues that Conrad was a political conservative who rejected revolutionary ideas. The two most important works of this period, however, were Moser's *Joseph Conrad: Achievement and Decline* (1957) and Guerard's *Conrad the Novelist* (1958), and both, though somewhat dated, remain important today. While other commentators had initiated the achievement and decline theory, Moser codified it and provided extended commentary for the causes of what many have seen as a decline in the literary quality of Conrad's later works. In particular, Moser argues that Conrad's inability to depict romantic love effectively and his emphasis on that issue in his later works lead to their declining quality. He also saw in Conrad's later works a lack of engagement with examples of fidelity and betrayal, which he suggests permeate Conrad's best works. Furthermore, Moser argues that issues of morality are at the heart of Conrad's earlier works but that these are replaced by the idea of Chance in his later works. In contrast to Moser's book, Guerard does not so much put forward a general theory of Conrad's works as he does present solid readings of Conrad's works (although he does concur with the achievement and decline theory). Guerard tends to focus on the moral challenges of Conrad's characters, as well as their attempts to come to a knowledge of themselves. He also discusses extensively Conrad's impressionism and narrative technique in general as evoking a feeling of detachment and evasiveness in Conrad's works that leads to their unique effect upon the reader. Shortly thereafter, Jocelyn Baines published what would become for many years the definitive biography of Conrad. His *Joseph Conrad:*

A Critical Biography (1959) is a literary biography and had the benefit of some previously unavailable sources, including some Polish sources being translated into English. Baines reads Conrad's life through his works and vice versa, while providing extensive documentation for his conclusions, and because of his skepticism toward Conrad's own comments about his life he avoids some of the misinformation that had appeared in previous biographies.

With Conrad's literary reputation firmly established, commentary on his works could move in other directions, and so from the 1960s critics began to pursue other issues in Conrad's works; some of these come out of earlier commentary, while others take up new frontiers of critical investigation. Among the most important additions to Conrad commentary to appear during this time were books on Conrad's politics by Eloise Knapp Hay and Avrom Fleishman. Hay's *The Political Novels of Joseph Conrad* (1963) views Conrad as something of a political conservative but not in the same way Howe had viewed him. According to Hay, although Conrad rejected revolutionary movements in his works and was suspicious toward democratic movements in general, much of this attitude arises from his skepticism toward political alternatives as a whole. Fleishman's *Conrad's Politics* (1967) takes a different approach to Conrad's politics. He argues instead for a liberal tradition after the order of the organicist tradition, in which individuals have political and social ties not through voluntary social contracts but rather through inherent ties of heredity, culture, and community. In addition to politics, commentators investigated various other topics during this period. Donald Yelton's *Memesis and Metaphor* (1967), for instance, considers the symbolic and metaphoric aspects of Conrad's works, particularly in light of the works of Flaubert and the French symbolists, resulting in plastic and musical imagination that is revealed in the fusing of the visual and evocative in Conrad's works. In a different direction, Edward Said, in his *Joseph Conrad and the Fiction of Autobiography* (1966), argues that Conrad rewrote his life in his fiction, particularly in his short fiction. Said suggests that Conrad uses that process of writing as a way to impose reason and intellect upon the world in order to face the chaos of existence. John A. Palmer's *Joseph Conrad's Fiction* (1968) is important primarily as another early challenge to the achievement and decline theory, in which he argues for a continually maturing progress in Conrad's fiction that concluded with the moral affirmation of Conrad's later works. Perhaps the most important work to be published during this time, however, was Norman Sherry's *Conrad's Eastern World* (1966), in which he uncovers many of the sources and references for Conrad's works set in Southeastern Asia. This book remains a useful reference for Conrad scholars.

The 1970s continued this trend of a multiplicity of topics engaging Conrad scholars. Among the more useful studies of this period is H. M. Daleski's *Joseph Conrad: The Way of Dispossession* (1977). In this book, Daleski argues that the possession of the self is one of the primary issues in Conrad's fiction. He contends that possession of the self is necessary in Conrad's world but that only by letting go of the self can one come to a true awareness of the self. Jacques Berthoud's *Joseph Conrad: The Major Phase* (1978) is book that does not so much project a consistent theory behind Conrad's works as it provides strong readings of some of Conrad's most frequently studied writings. Berthoud considers Conrad's works in light of Conrad's own views on art, focusing particularly on the ideas of vision and insight. Another important commentary of this period is Jeremy Hawthorn's *Joseph Conrad: Language and Self-Consciousness* (1979). For Hawthorn, language is a crucial aspect of Conrad's works, as it brings about the relationship between the subjective and the objective. In addition to these important commentaries, Ian Watt's *Conrad in the Nineteenth Century* (1979) appeared during this period and has become one of the landmarks of Conrad commentary. Watt employs a pluralistic approach to Conrad's fiction, considering it in light of biography, history, intellectual history, and formalism. The result is a collection of readings that cannot easily be categorized but nevertheless significantly enlightens those works, particularly in his discussion of impressionism and symbolism in Conrad's fiction. The most important work of this period in terms of influence, however, is Chinua Achebe's essay "An Image of Africa" (1977), in which he accuses Conrad of racism in his portrayal of Africans in "Heart of Darkness" and concludes that the novella cannot therefore be considered a great work of literature. This single essay has engendered numerous responses, both concurring and disagreeing, and continues to be commented upon regularly, as it ushered in the discussion of Conrad's relationship to issues of colonialism that continues today.

During the 1980s, Conrad and colonialism became a point of focus for Conrad scholars, including John A. McClure's *Kipling & Conrad: The Colonial Fiction* (1981) and Benita Parry's *Conrad and Imperialism* (1983). McClure argues that Conrad criticized the colonial myth of the benevolent Westerners bringing light into the dark non-Western world, finding little value in the colonial effort. In contrast, Benita Parry investigates the various means by which she argues that Conrad accepts imperialist assumptions concerning non-Westerners, while also arguing that Conrad both affirms and critiques colonialism. In addition to an expanded investigation into Conrad's relationship to colonialism, post-structuralist theory began to take on an increasingly important role in Conrad criticism. One of the first of these commentaries was William W. Bonney's *Thorns & Arabesques: Contexts for Conrad's Fiction* (1980). Bonney suggests a tension exists in Conrad's works that constructs and deconstructs elements in these works, especially the idea of Romance. Fredric Jameson's discussion of Conrad's *Nostromo* and *Lord Jim* in his *The Political Unconscious* (1981) also proceeds from post-structural tenets, though intermixed with Marxist thought. Jameson focuses on romance and reification in Conrad's works, contending that Conrad's fiction marks a fault line in modern literature, in which previously hidden cultural and literary structures are revealed. Another important commentary of this period is Aaron Fogel's *Coercion to Speak: Conrad's Poetics of Dialogue* (1985), which is specifically influenced by the ideas of Mikhail Bakhtin, and Fogel investigates how characters speak to one another and how they coerce one another to speak in Conrad's works.

Other significant studies to appear during the 1980s include Zdzisław Najder's biography *Joseph Conrad: A Chronicle* (1983), Cedric Watts's *Joseph Conrad: A Literary Life* (1989), Daniel R. Schwarz's *Conrad: Almayer's Folly to Under Western Eyes* (1980), and Jakob Lothe's *Conrad's Narrative Method* (1989). Najder's was the most important biography on Conrad and only his revised version,

Joseph Conrad: A Life (2007), has superceded it. Because of his access to materials in Polish, French, and English and his strict reliance on documentation, Najder has been able to provide a more accurate and complete chronicle of Conrad's life, with minimum speculation. Watts's biography is particularly useful because it focuses on the Conrad's life in relationship to the publishing world and literary marketplace. Schwarz, somewhat like Berthoud and Watt, does not work so much from an overarching idea concerning Conrad's works as he much as he considers each work individually, the reading arising from each specific work as opposed to a broad theoretical matrix, although there is an underlying implication of Conrad espousing humanist values in his fiction. Finally, as the title suggests, Lothe focuses on Conrad's narrative methodology. He draws upon narratology, structuralism, and other contemporary literary theory to reject the notion that content in Conrad's works precedes form.

Criticism during the 1990s tended to augment and, in many cases, improve upon the developments of the 1980s. For example, Andrea White's *Joseph Conrad and the Adventure Tradition: Constructing and Deconstructing the Imperial Subject* (1993) considers the adventure tradition of the nineteenth century and argues that Conrad admired the discoveries and accomplishments of the adventure tradition, while also rejecting much of the imperialist ideology that usually accompanied that tradition. Similarly, Christopher GoGwilt's *The Invention of the West: Joseph Conrad and the Double-Mapping of Europe and Empire* (1995) goes to the origins of colonialism and argues that the concept of a unified West was a social construct that the West employed to justify Western rule of the non-Western world. GoGwilt contends that Conrad both affirms and rejects the West's constructed view of itself. Bruce Henricksen's *Nomadic Voices: Conrad and the Subject of Narrative* (1992) is a good example of the continued influence of poststructuralist theory in Conrad studies. In this useful book, Henricksen looks at Conrad's fiction with the theories of Lyotard and Bakhtin in mind, as he responds to Fogel's *Coercion to Speak*, suggesting that Conrad's works evolve from a monologic mode to a polyphonic mode, *The Nigger of the "Narcissus"* being an example of the monologic end of the spectrum and *Under Western Eyes* being an example of the polyphonic end. Post-structuralist theory also informs Daphna Erdinast-Vulcan *Joseph Conrad and the Modern Temper* (1991). In this work, she argues that Conrad responded to modernism and contends that Conrad's world view bears similarities to Nietzsche's, and she further suggests that Conrad is continually involved in a conflict between a desire to believe in values and an inability to believe in those very values.

Along with studies influenced by post-colonial and post-structuralist theories, a number of other interesting studies appeared during this time. For example, Joyce Piell Wexler's *Who Paid for Modernism?: Art, Money, and the Fiction of Conrad, Joyce, and Lawrence* (1997) looks at Conrad's conflicted attitude toward writing for art and writing for money. Wexler contends that Conrad always sought to reach a wider audience while maintaining artistic standards. In a different direction, Richard Ambrosini's *Conrad's Fiction as Critical Discourse* (1991) considers Conrad's literary theory and suggests that he works from a coherent literary theory based upon such issues as work, idealism, fidelity, precision, and effect. Approaching Conrad's works through the lens of psychology, Robert Hampson, in his *Joseph Conrad: Betrayal and Identity* (1992), relies in part on the psychology of R. D. Laing to suggest an evolution of the self in Conrad's fiction, in which the isolated self moved toward the socialized self and to the sexualized self during his literary career. Another area that began to garner attention during this period was gender studies in relationship to Conrad's works. Ruth Nadelhaft's *Joseph Conrad* (1991) begins the emphasis on gender issues as they appear in Conrad's works. Employing feminist theory, Nadelhaft looks at Conrad's works, arguing that, unlike most commentators had assumed, women play a more prominent role in his works than had previously been thought. In addition, Nadelhaft argues that typically the antifeminist and misogynistic attitudes that occasionally appear in Conrad's works are often a result of Conrad's narrators' views and that when one separates Conrad from his narrators there is often a great deal of sympathy for the plight of women in his novels. Similarly, Susan Jones's *Conrad and Women* (1999) agrees that women are more important in Conrad's works than many have assumed. Jones argues that various women in Conrad's life had a crucial influence on his writing career, that women were often significant characters in Conrad's fiction, and that Conrad's reading public consisted predominantly of women in his later writings.

In the new millennium, Conrad criticism has moved in a variety of directions. Post-colonialism and post-structuralism have continued to be influential on the commentary, but a number of other interesting studies have also appeared. Robert Hampson's *Cross-Cultural Encounters in Joseph Conrad's Malay Fiction* (2000) continues the interest in the relationship between Conrad and the colonial world. Working from post-colonial, post-modern, and New Historicist theories, Hampson argues that Conrad's Malay works come out of a Western cultural construct of the Malay world but also out of Conrad's own experience in the Malay Archipelago, and Hampson suggests that Conrad was aware of this Western construct and often deconstructed this cultural construct in his fiction. In a somewhat different direction, Stephen Ross, in his *Conrad and Empire* (2004), looks at the idea of Conrad and imperialism and discusses the issue more in terms of globalization than solely imperialism itself. Ross contends that imperialism is a product of globalization and argues that Conrad's fiction investigates the way that global capitalism replaces the traditional concept of nation-state and how such a transformation affects the individual in Conrad's works. Important studies influenced by post-structuralist theory include Michael Greaney's *Conrad, Language, and Narrative* (2002) and Con Coroneos's *Space, Conrad, and Modernity* (2002). Greaney works from ideas by Derrida and Bakhtin in his investigation of the relationship between speech and writing in Conrad's fiction. Greaney argues that Conrad employs a story-telling mode in his early Malay fiction that evolves into Marlow's narratives, in which there is a tension between authentic and inauthentic language. This mode in turn evolves into the narrative of Conrad's political fiction, which employs the techniques of high modernism. Somewhat differently, Coroneos is influenced by Foucault's thinking as he looks at the connections between space and modernity in Conrad's works.

Nadelhaft's and Jones's emphasis on gender issues has continued into this decade. For instance, Lissa Schneider, in her *Conrad's Narratives of Difference* (2003), considers Conrad's works from a feminist perspective, arguing that femininity and gender appear in Conrad's fiction by way of female imagery and allegory and through feminine narrative strategies. Moving in a different direction of gender studies is Andrew Michael Roberts's *Conrad and Masculinity* (2000), in which he argues that masculinity is culturally constructed and that Conrad both represents and questions images of a culturally constructed masculinity. More recently, Jeremy Hawthorn, in his *Sexuality and the Erotic in the Fiction of Joseph Conrad* (2007), argues that sexuality and the erotic appear with much greater frequency and significance in Conrad's works than has typically been thought by most commentators, while Richard J. Ruppel's *Homosexuality in the Life and Work of Joseph Conrad: Love Between the Lines* (2008) argues that homosexuality and homoeroticism appear frequently in Conrad's life and works.

In addition to post-colonial, post-structural, and gender studies, a number of other studies have appeared in various other directions. For instance, Martin Bock's *Joseph Conrad and Psychological Medicine* (2002) looks at Conrad's life and works through the lens of pre-Freudian medical psychology. Specifically, he considers the physical and mental illnesses from which both Conrad and his characters suffered and contends that Conrad's works chronicle various mental illnesses. Furthermore, Bock argues that the ideas of restraint, seclusion, and water that are connected to these mental illnesses arise out of contemporary psychological and medical ideas of that time. My own book, *Conrad and Impressionism* (2001), considers Conrad's works in relationship to impressionist epistemology and suggests that this epistemology appears in Conrad's narrative techniques and results from Conrad's radical skepticism. Somewhat more recently, Richard J. Hand's *The Theatre of Joseph Conrad* (2005) argues for the value of Conrad's dramatic forays. Hand considers Conrad's drama in light of contemporaneous melodrama, as well as symbolism, Grand Guignol, expressionism, and even theater of the absurd. Another look at an understudied topic is Stephen Donovan's *Joseph Conrad and Popular Culture* (2005). Donovan argues for a complex relationship between Conrad and popular culture, suggesting that despite Conrad's scorn of popular culture his works actually abound in references to popular culture. Yet another useful recent book is Allan H. Simmons's *Joseph Conrad* (2006). Simmons places recent feminist, post-colonial, and post-structuralist readings of Conrad within their historical and biographic context and argues that Conrad was aware of contemporary social and political issues, such as feminism and imperialism, and consistently addressed these in his works.

There would appear to be no abatement in the development of Conrad studies. Today, as has been true since the earliest commentary, the depth of Conrad's works seems to lend them to a variety of critical approaches, and it would seem that Conrad's works will continue to receive considerable and increasing attention.

PRIMARY WORKS

Conrad, Joseph. *Almayer's Folly: A Story of an Eastern River*. London: T. Fisher Unwin, 1895.

————. *An Outcast of the Islands*. London: T. Fisher Unwin, 1896.

———— *The Nigger of the "Narcissus": A Tale of the Forecastle*. London: William Heinemann, 1897. (First American edition entitled *The Children of the Sea*)

————. *Tales of Unrest*. London: T. Fisher Unwin, 1898.

————. *Lord Jim: A Tale*. Edinburgh and London: William Blackwood and Sons, 1900.

————. *Youth: A Narrative and Two Other Stories*. Edinburgh and London: William Blackwood and Sons, 1902.

————. *Typhoon and Other Stories*. London: William Heinemann, 1903.

————. *Nostromo: A Tale of the Seaboard*. London and New York: Harper & Brothers, 1904.

————. *The Mirror of the Sea: Memories and Impressions*. London: Methuen & Co., 1906.

————. *The Secret Agent: A Simple Tale*. London: Methuen & Co., 1907.

————. *A Set of Six*. London: Methuen & Co., 1908.

————. *Under Western Eyes*. London: Methuen & Co., 1911.

————. *Some Reminiscences*. London: Eveleigh Nash, 1912. (First American edition entitled *A Personal Record*)

————. *'Twixt Land and Sea: Tales*. London: J. M. Dent & Sons, 1912.

————. *Chance: A Tale in Two Parts*. London: Methuen & Co., 1914.

———. *Victory: An Island Tale.* London: Methuen & Co., 1915.

———. *Within the Tides: Tales.* London: J. M. Dent & Sons, 1915.

———. *The Shadow-Line: A Confession.* London: J. M. Dent & Sons, 1917.

———. *The Arrow of Gold: A Story between Two Notes.* London: T. Fisher Unwin, 1919.

———. *The Rescue.* London: J. M. Dent & Sons, 1920.

———. *Notes on Life and Letters.* London: J. M. Dent & Sons, 1921.

———. *The Rover.* London: T. Fisher Unwin, 1923.

———. *Suspense.* London & Toronto: J. M. Dent & Sons, 1925.

———. *Tales of Hearsay.* London: T. Fisher Unwin, 1925.

———. *Last Essays.* London & Toronto: J. M. Dent & Sons, 1926.

Conrad, Joseph, and Ford M. Hueffer. *The Inheritors: An Extravagant Story.* London: William Heinemann, 1901.

———. *Romance: A Novel.* London: Smith, Elder & Co., 1903.

———. *The Nature of a Crime.* London: Duckworth & Co., 1924.

Correspondence

Conrad, Joseph. *The Collected Letters of Joseph Conrad.* Ed. Laurence Davies et al. 9 vols. Cambridge: Cambridge University Press, 1983–2007.

Knowles, Owen, ed. *"My Dear Friend": Further Letters to and about Joseph Conrad.* Amsterdam: Rodopi, 2008.

Najder, Zdzisław, ed. *Conrad's Polish Background: Letters to and from Polish Friends.* Trans. Halina Carroll. London: Oxford University Press, 1964.

Najder, Zdzisław, and Joanna Skolik, eds. *Polskie Zaplecze Josepha Conrada Korzeniowskiego: Dokumenty Rodzinne, Listy, Wspomnienia.* 2 vols. Lublin: Wydawnictwo Gaudium, 2006.

Stape, J. H., and Owen Knowles, eds. *A Portrait in Letters: Correspondence to and about Joseph Conrad.* Amsterdam: Rodopi, 1996.

Biographies

Allen, Jerry. *The Sea Years of Joseph Conrad.* Garden City, N.Y.: Doubleday, 1965.

Baines, Jocelyn. *Joseph Conrad: A Critical Biography.* London: Weidenfeld & Nicolson, 1959.

Batchelor, John. *The Life of Joseph Conrad: A Critical Biography*. Oxford: Blackwell, 1994.

Conrad, Borys. *My Father: Joseph Conrad*. New York: Coward-McCann, 1970.

Conrad, Jesse. *Joseph Conrad and His Circle*. New York: E. P. Dutton, 1935.

———. *Joseph Conrad as I Knew Him*. Garden City, N.Y.: Doubleday, Page, 1926.

Conrad, John. *Joseph Conrad: Times Remembered* 'ojciec jest tutaj.' Cambridge: Cambridge University Press, 1981.

Curle, Richard. *The Last Twelve Years of Joseph Conrad*. Garden City, N.Y.: Doubleday, Doran, 1928.

Ford (Hueffer), Ford Madox. *Joseph Conrad: A Personal Remembrance*. Boston: Little, Brown, 1924.

Jean-Aubry. G. *The Sea Dreamer: A Definitive Biography of Joseph Conrad*. Trans. Helen Sebba. Garden City, N.Y.: Doubleday, 1957.

Karl, Frederick R. *Joseph Conrad: The Three Lives, A Biography*. New York: Farrar, Straus, Giroux, 1979.

Meyer, Bernard C. *Joseph Conrad: A Psychoanalytic Biography*. Princeton, N.J.: Princeton University Press, 1967.

Meyers, Jeffrey. *Joseph Conrad: A Biography*. London: John Murray, 1991.

Najder, Zdzisław. *Joseph Conrad: A Life*. Trans. Halina Najder. Rochester, N.Y.: Camden House, 2007.

Ray, Martin, ed. *Joseph Conrad: Interviews and Recollections*. Iowa City: University of Iowa Press, 1990.

———, ed. *Joseph Conrad Memories and Impressions: An Annotated Bibliography*. Amsterdam: Rodopi, 2007.

Retinger, J. H. *Conrad and His Contemporaries: Souvenirs*. London: Minerva, 1941.

Roditi, Édouard. *Meetings with Conrad*. Los Angeles: Press of the Pegacycle Lady, 1977.

Stape, J. H. *The Several Lives of Joseph Conrad*. London: William Heinemann, 2007.

Sutherland, J. G. *At Sea with Joseph Conrad*. London: Grant Richards, 1922.

Villiers, Peter. *Joseph Conrad: Master Mariner*. Dobbs Ferry, N.Y.: Sheridan House, 2006.

Watts, Cedric. *Joseph Conrad: A Literary Life*. New York: St. Martin's Press, 1989.

Bibliographies

Ehrsam, Theodore G. *A Bibliography of Joseph Conrad*. Metuchen, N.J.: Scarecrow Press, 1969.

Keating, George T., ed. *A Conrad Memorial Library: The Collection of George T. Keating*. Garden City, N.Y.: Doubleday, Doran, 1929.

Knowles, Owen. *An Annotated Critical Bibliography of Joseph Conrad*. New York: St. Martin's Press, 1992.

Smith, Walter E. *Joseph Conrad: A Bibliographical Catalogue of His Major First Editions, With Facsimiles of Several Title Pages*. [San Francisco]: [Privately Printed], 1979.

Teets, Bruce E. *Joseph Conrad: An Annotated Bibliography*. New York: Garland, 1990.

Teets, Bruce E., and Helmut E. Gerber. *Joseph Conrad: An Annotated Bibliography of Writings about Him*. De Kalb, Ill.: Northern Illinois University Press, 1971.

Wise, Thomas J., ed. *A Conrad Library: A Catalogue of Printed Books, Manuscripts and Autograph Letters by Joseph Conrad (Tèodor Josef Konrad Korzeniowski)*. London: Printed for Private Circulation, 1928.

Introductions

Gillon, Adam. *Joseph Conrad*. Boston: Twayne, 1982.

Karl, Frederick R. *A Reader's Guide to Joseph Conrad*. Rev. ed. New York: Farrar, Straus & Giroux, 1969.

Middleton, Tim. *Joseph Conrad*. New York: Routledge, 2006.

Peters, John G. *The Cambridge Introduction to Joseph Conrad*. Cambridge: Cambridge University Press, 2006.

Watts, Cedric. *A Preface to Conrad*. 2nd ed. London, Longman, 1993.

Conrad and Colonialism

Achebe, Chinua. "An Image of Africa." *Massachusetts Review* 18, no. 4 (winter 1977): 782–94.

Adams, David. *Colonial Odysseys: Empire and Epic in the Modernist Novel*. Ithaca, N.Y.: Cornell University Press, 2003.

Bongie, Chris. *Exotic Memories: Literature, Colonialism, and the* Fin de Siècle. Stanford, Calif.: Stanford University Press, 1991.

Brantlinger, Patrick. "*Heart of Darkness*: Anti-Imperialism, Racism, or Impressionism?" Criticism 27, no. 4 (fall 1985): 363–85.

Collits, Terry. *Postcolonial Conrad: Paradoxes of Empire.* New York: Routledge, 2005.

Darras, Jacques. *Joseph Conrad and the West: Signs of Empire.* Trans. Anne Luyat and Jacques Darras. London: Macmillan, 1982.

Dryden, Linda. *Joseph Conrad and the Imperial Romance.* New York: St. Martin's Press, 2000.

Firchow, Peter Edgerly. *Envisioning Africa: Racism and Imperialism in Conrad's* Heart of Darkness. Lexington: University Press of Kentucky, 2000.

GoGwilt, Christopher. *The Invention of the West: Joseph Conrad and the Double-Mapping of Europe and Empire.* Stanford, Calif.: Stanford University Press, 1995.

Goonetilleke, D. C. R. A. *Developing Countries in British Fiction.* Totowa, N. J.: Rowman and Littlefield, 1977.

Griffith, John W. *Joseph Conrad and the Anthropological Dilemma: "Bewildered Traveller."* Oxford: Clarendon Press, 1995.

Hamner, Robert D., ed. *Joseph Conrad: Third World Perspectives.* Washington, D.C.: Three Continents Press, 1990.

Hampson, Robert. *Cross-Cultural Encounters in Joseph Conrad's Malay Fiction.* New York: Palgrave, 2000.

Harris, Wilson. "The Frontier on Which *Heart of Darkness* Stands." *Research on African Literatures* 12, no. 1 (spring 1981): 86–93.

Hawkins, Hunt. "Conrad's Critique of Imperialism in *Heart of Darkness*." *PMLA* 94, no. 2 (March 1979): 286–99.

Henthorne, Tom. *Conrad's Trojan Horses: Imperialism, Hybridity, and the Postcolonial Aesthetic.* Lubbock: Texas Tech University Press, 2008.

Lee, Robert F. *Conrad's Colonialism.* The Hague: Mouton, 1969.

McClure, John A. *Kipling & Conrad: The Colonial Fiction.* Cambridge, Mass.: Harvard University Press, 1981.

Mongia, Padmini. "Narrative Strategy and Imperialism in Conrad's *Lord Jim*." *Studies in the Novel* 24, no. 2 (summer 1992): 173–86.

Parry, Benita. *Conrad and Imperialism: Ideological Boundaries and Visionary Frontiers.* London: Macmillan, 1983.

Ross, Stephen. *Conrad and Empire*. Columbia: University of Missouri Press, 2004.

Singh, Francis B. "The Colonialistic Bias of *Heart of Darkness.*" *Conradiana* 10, no. 1 (spring 1978): 41–54.

Sutherland, Lynn. *The Fantastic Invasion: Kipling, Conrad, and Lawson*. Carlton, Victoria, Australia: Melbourne University Press, 1989.

Watts, Cedric. " 'A Bloody Racist': About Achebe's View of Conrad." Yearbook of English Studies 13 (1983): 196–209.

White, Andrea. *Joseph Conrad and the Adventure Tradition: Constructing and Deconstructing the Imperial Subject*. Cambridge: Cambridge University Press, 1993.

Zins, Henryk, *Joseph Conrad and Africa*. Nairobi: Kenya Literature Bureau, 1982.

Conrad and Gender

Casarino, Cesare. *Modernity at Sea: Melville, Marx, Conrad in Crisis*. Minneapolis: University of Minnesota Press, 2002.

Colbron, Grace Isabel. "Joseph Conrad's Women." *The Bookman* 38, no. 5 (January 1914): 476–79.

Harpham, Geoffrey Galt. *One of Us: The Mastery of Joseph Conrad*. Chicago: University of Chicago Press, 1996.

Hawthorn, Jeremy. *Sexuality and the Erotic in the Fiction of Joseph Conrad*. London: Continuum, 2007.

Jones, Susan. *Conrad and Women*. Oxford: Clarendon Press, 1999.

Krenn, Heliéna. *Conrad's Lingard Trilogy: Empire, Race, and Women in the Malay Novels*. New York: Garland, 1990.

London, Bette. *The Appropriated Voice: Narrative Authority in Conrad, Forster, and Woolf*. Ann Arbor: University of Michigan Press, 1990.

Nadelhaft, Ruth L. *Joseph Conrad*. Atlantic Highlands, N. J.: Humanities Press, 1991.

Roberts, Andrew Michael. *Conrad and Masculinity*. New York: St. Martin's Press, 2000.

———, ed. *Conrad and Gender*. Amsterdam: Rodopi, 1993.

Ruppel, Richard. *Homoeroticism and Homosexuality in the Life and Fiction of Joseph Conrad: Love Between the Lines*. New York: Routledge, 2008.

Schneider, Lissa. *Conrad's Narratives of Difference: Not Exactly Tales for Boys*. New York: Routledge, 2003.

Snyder, Katherine V. *Bachelors, Manhood, and the Novel, 1850–1925*. Cambridge: Cambridge University Press, 1999.

Straus, Nina Pelikan. "The Exclusion of the Intended from the Secret Sharing in Conrad's *Heart of Darkness*." *Novel* 20, no. 2 (winter 1987): 123–37.

Strychacz, Thomas. *Dangerous Masculinities: Conrad, Hemingway, and Lawrence*. Gainsville: University Press of Florida, 2008.

Conrad and Philosophy

Armstrong, Paul B. *The Challenge of Bewilderment: Understanding and Representation in James, Conrad, and Ford*. Ithaca, N.Y.: Cornell University Press, 1987.

Bancroft, William Wallace. *Joseph Conrad: His Philosophy of Life*. Boston: Stratford, 1933.

Bohlmann, Otto. *Conrad's Existentialism*. New York: St. Martin's Press, 1991.

Coroneos, Con. *Space, Conrad, and Modernity*. Oxford: Oxford University Press, 2002.

Daleski, H. M. *Joseph Conrad: The Way of Dispossession*. London: Faber & Faber, 1977.

Johnson, Bruce. *Conrad's Models of Mind*. Minneapolis: University of Minnesota Press, 1971.

Lord, Ursula. *Solitude versus Solidarity in the Novels of Joseph Conrad: Political and Epistemological Implications of Narrative Innovation*. Montreal: McGill-Queen's University Press, 1998.

Miller, J. Hillis. *Poets of Reality: Six Twentieth-Century Writers*. Cambridge, Mass.: Harvard University Press, 1965.

Panagopoulos, Nic. *The Fiction of Joseph Conrad: The Influence of Schopenhauer and Nietzsche*. Frankfurt: Peter Lang, 1998.

Peters, John G. *Conrad and Impressionism*. Cambridge: Cambridge University Press, 2001.

Ressler, Steve. *Joseph Conrad: Consciousness and Integrity*. New York: New York University Press, 1988.

Roussel, Royal. *The Metaphysics of Darkness: A Study in the Unity and Development of Conrad's Fiction*. Baltimore, Md.: Johns Hopkins University Press, 1971.

Whiteley, Patrick J. *Knowledge and Experimental Realism in Conrad, Lawrence, and Woolf.* Baton Rouge: Louisiana State University Press, 1987.

Wollaeger, Mark A. *Joseph Conrad and the Fictions of Skepticism.* Stanford, Calif.: Stanford University Press, 1990.

Conrad and Morality

Cooper, Christopher. *Conrad and the Human Dilemma.* New York: Barnes & Noble, 1970.

Gekoski, R. A. *Conrad: The Moral World of the Novelist.* New York: Barnes & Noble, 1978.

Palmer, John A. *Joseph Conrad's Fiction: A Study in Literary Growth.* Ithaca, N.Y.: Cornell University Press, 1968.

Panichas, George Andrew. *Joseph Conrad: His Moral Vision.* Mercer, Ga.: Mercer University Press, 2005.

Saveson, John E. *Conrad, the Later Moralist.* Amsterdam: Rodopi, 1974.

——— . *Joseph Conrad: The Making of a Moralist.* Amsterdam: Rodopi, 1972.

Wiley, Paul L. *Conrad's Measure of Man.* Madison: University of Wisconsin Press, 1954.

Conrad and Psychology

Ash, Beth Sharon. *Writing in Between: Modernity and Psychosocial Dilemma in the Novels of Joseph Conrad.* New York: St. Martin's Press, 1999.

Berman, Jeffrey. *Joseph Conrad: Writing as Rescue.* New York: Astra Books, 1977.

Bock, Martin. *Joseph Conrad and Psychological Medicine.* Lubbock: Texas Tech University Press, 2002.

Dobrinsky, Joseph. *The Artist in Conrad's Fiction: A Psychocritical Study.* Ann Arbor, Mich.: UMI Research Press, 1989.

Guerard, Albert J. *Conrad the Novelist.* Cambridge, Mass.: Harvard University Press, 1958.

Hampson, Robert. *Joseph Conrad: Betrayal and Identity.* London: Macmillan, 1992.

Kirschner, Paul. *Conrad: The Psychologist as Artist.* Edinburgh, Scotland: Oliver & Boyd, 1968.

Morf, Gustav. *The Polish Heritage of Joseph Conrad.* London: Sampson Low, Marston, [1930].

———. *Polish Shades and Ghosts of Joseph Conrad.* New York: Astra Books, 1976.

Moser, Thomas C. *Joseph Conrad: Achievement and Decline.* Cambridge, Mass.: Harvard University Press, 1957.

Simons, Kenneth. *The Ludic Imagination: A Reading of Joseph Conrad.* Ann Arbor, Mich.: UMI Research Press, 1985.

Conrad and Narrative

Beach, Joseph Warren. *The Twentieth Century Novel: Studies in Technique.* New York: Appleton-Century-Crofts, 1931.

Cutler, Frances Wentworth. "Why Marlow?" *Sewanee Review* 26, no. 1 (January 1918): 28–38.

Davidson, Donald. "Joseph Conrad's Directed Indirections." *Sewanee Review* 33, no. 2 (April 1925): 163–77.

Fernández, Ramón. "The Art of Conrad." Trans. Anne Luyat. In *Conrad in France.* Ed. Josiane Paccaud-Huguet. Boulder: Social Science Monographs, 2006, 13–20.

Greaney, Michael. *Conrad, Language, and Narrative.* Cambridge: Cambridge University Press, 2002.

Hawthorn, Jeremy. *Joseph Conrad: Narrative Technique and Ideological Commitment.* London: Edward Arnold, 1990.

Henricksen, Bruce. *Nomadic Voices: Conrad and the Subject of Narrative.* Urbana: University of Illinois Press, 1992.

Jameson, Fredric. *The Political Unconscious: Narrative as a Socially Symbolic Act.* Ithaca, N.Y.: Cornell University Press, 1981.

Lothe, Jakob. *Conrad's Narrative Method.* Oxford: Clarendon Press, 1989.

Lothe, Jakob, Jeremy Hawthorn, and James Phelan, eds. *Joseph Conrad: Voice, Sequence, History, Genre.* Columbus: Ohio State University Press, 2008.

Paris, Bernard. *Conrad's Charlie Marlow: A New Approach to* Heart of Darkness *and* Lord Jim. New York: Palgrave Macmillan, 2005.

Pettersson, Torsten. *Consciousness and Time: A Study in the Philosophy and Narrative Technique of Joseph Conrad.* Åbo, Finland: Åbo Akademi, 1982.

Price, Antony. *"Chronological Looping" in* Nostromo. Kuala Lumpur: University of Malaya Library, 1973.

Senn, Werner. *Conrad's Narrative Voice: Stylistic Aspects of His Fiction.* Bern: Francke Verlag, 1980.

Wake, Paul. *Conrad's Marlow: Narrative and Death in "Youth," "Heart of Darkness,"* Lord Jim, *and* Chance. Manchester, England: Manchester University Press, 2007.

Walpole, V. *Conrad's Method: Some Formal Aspects. Annals of the University of Stellenbosch.* Kaapstad, South Africa: Nasionale Pers Beperk, 1930.

Watts, Cedric. *The Deceptive Text: An Introduction to Covert Plots.* Brighton, England: Harvester Press, 1984.

Conrad and Politics

Bantock, G. H. "Conrad and Politics." *English Literary History* 25, no. 2 (June 1958): 122–36.

Bhagwati, Ashok. *Politics and the Modern Novelist: Conrad's Conservatism.* Dehli, India: B. R. Publishing, 1991.

Fleishman, Avrom. *Conrad's Politics: Community and Anarchy in the Fiction of Joseph Conrad.* Baltimore, Md.: Johns Hopkins University Press, 1967.

Hay, Eloise Knapp. *The Political Novels of Joseph Conrad: A Critical Study.* Chicago: University of Chicago Press, 1963.

Howe, Irving. *Politics and the Novel.* New York: Meridan Books, 1957.

Rieselbach, Helen Funk. *Conrad's Rebels: The Psychology of Revolution in the Novels from* Nostromo *to* Victory. Ann Arbor, Mich.: UMI Research Press, 1985.

Rosenfield, Claire. *Paradise of Snakes: An Archetypal Analysis of Conrad's Political Novels.* Chicago: University of Chicago Press, 1967.

Schwarz, Daniel R. "Conrad's Quarrel with Politics in *Nostromo.*" *College English* 59, no. 5 (September 1997): 548–68.

Srivastava, Rajiv Kamal. *Novel and Politics: A Study of Joseph Conrad.* Patna, India: Novelty, 1998.

Conrad and His Sources

Busza, Andrzej. "Conrad's Polish Literary Background and Some Illustrations of the Influence of Polish Literature on His Work." *Antemurale* 10 (1966): 109–255.

Gordan, John Dozier. *Joseph Conrad: The Making of a Novelist.* Cambridge, Mass.: Harvard University Press, 1940.

Hervouet, Yves. *The French Face of Joseph Conrad.* Cambridge: Cambridge University Press, 1990.

Sherry, Norman. *Conrad's Eastern World.* Cambridge: Cambridge University Press, 1966.

——. *Conrad's Western World.* Cambridge: Cambridge University Press, 1971.

Tutein, David W. *Joseph Conrad's Reading: An Annotated Bibliography.* West Cornwall, Conn.: Locust Hill Press, 1990.

Other Useful Commentaries

Ambrosini, Richard. *Conrad's Fiction as Critical Discourse.* Cambridge: Cambridge University Press, 1991.

Andreas, Osborn. *Joseph Conrad: A Study in Non-Conformity.* New York: Philosophical Library, 1959.

Berthoud, Jacques. *Joseph Conrad: The Major Phase.* Cambridge: Cambridge University Press, 1978.

Billy, Ted. *A Wilderness of Words: Closure and Disclosure in Conrad's Short Fiction.* Lubbock: Texas Tech University Press, 1997.

Bonney, William W. *Thorns & Arabesques: Contexts for Conrad's Fiction.* Baltimore, Md.: Johns Hopkins University Press, 1980.

Bruss, Paul. *Conrad's Early Sea Fiction: The Novelist as Navigator.* Lewisburg, Penn.: Bucknell University Press, 1979.

Burgess, C. F. *The Fellowship of the Craft: Conrad on Ships and Seamen and the Sea.* Port Washington, N.Y.: Kennikat Press, 1976.

Clifford, Sir Hugh. "The Trail of the Book-Worm: Mr. Joseph Conrad at Home and Abroad." *The Singapore Free Press* (30 August 1898): 3.

Conroy, Mark. *Modernism and Authority: Strategies of Legitimation in Flaubert and Conrad.* Baltimore, Md.: John Hopkins University Press, 1985.

Cox, C. B. *Joseph Conrad: The Modern Imagination.* London: J. M. Dent & Sons, 1974.

Crankshaw, Edward. *Joseph Conrad: Some Aspects of the Art of the Novel.* London: John Lane, 1936.

Curle, Richard. "Conrad and the Younger Generation." *Nineteenth Century and After.* No. 635 (January 1930): 103–12.

Daiches, David. *The Novel and the Modern World*. Chicago: University of Chicago Press, 1939.

Donovan, Stephen. *Joseph Conrad and Popular Culture*. New York: Palgrave Macmillan, 2005.

Dowden, Wildred S. *Joseph Conrad: The Imaged Style*. Nashville, Tenn.: Vanderbilt University Press, 1970.

Erdinast-Vulcan, Daphna. *Joseph Conrad and the Modern Temper*. Oxford: Clarendon Press, 1991.

———. *The Strange Short Fiction of Joseph Conrad: Writing, Culture and Subjectivity*. Oxford: Oxford University Press, 1999.

Fogel, Aaron. *Coercion to Speak: Conrad's Poetics of Dialogue*. Cambridge, Mass.: Harvard University Press, 1985.

Follett, Wilson. *Joseph Conrad: A Short Study of His Intellectual and Emotional Attitude toward His Work and of the Chief Characters of His Novels*. Garden City, N.Y.: Doubleday, Page, 1915.

Garnett, Edward. "Academy Portraits: Mr. Joseph Conrad." *Academy*. No. 1380 (15 October 1898): 82–83.

Geddes, Gary. *Conrad's Later Novels*. Montreal: McGill-Queen's University Press, 1980.

Gillon, Adam. *The Eternal Solitary: A Study of Joseph Conrad*. New York: Bookman Associates, 1960.

Goonetilleke, D. C. R. A. *Joseph Conrad: Beyond Culture and Background*. New York: St. Martin's Press, 1990.

Graver, Lawrence. *Conrad's Short Fiction*. Berkeley: University of California Press, 1969.

Guetti, James L. *The Limits of Metaphor: A Study of Melville, Conrad, and Faulkner*. Ithaca, N.Y.: Cornell University Press, 1967.

Hand, Richard J. *The Theatre of Joseph Conrad: Reconstructed Fictions*. New York: Palgrave Macmillan, 2005.

Haugh, Robert F. *Joseph Conrad: Discovery in Design*. Norman: University of Oklahoma Press, 1957.

Hawthorn, Jeremy. *Joseph Conrad: Language and Fictional Self-Consciousness*. London: Edward Arnold, 1979.

Hewitt, Douglas. *Conrad: A Reassessment*. Cambridge: Bowes & Bowes, 1952.

Hicks, Granville. "Conrad after Five Years." *New Republic* 61 (8 January 1930): 192–94.

Hodges, Robert R. *The Dual Heritage of Joseph Conrad*. The Hague: Mouton, 1967.

Hoffman, Stanton de Voren. *Comedy and Form in the Fiction of Joseph Conrad*. The Hague: Mouton, 1969.

Hunter, Allan. *Joseph Conrad and the Ethics of Darwinism: The Challenges of Science*. London: Croom Helm, 1983.

Kaplan, Carola, Peter Lancelot Mallios, and Andrea White, eds. *Conrad in the Twenty-First Century: Contemporary Approaches and Perspectives*. New York: Routledge, 2004.

Knowles, Owen and Gene M. Moore. *Oxford Reader's Companion to Conrad*. Oxford: Oxford University Press, 2000.

Land, Stephen K. *Paradox and Polarity in the Fiction of Joseph Conrad*. New York: St. Martin's Press, 1984.

Leavis, F. R. *The Great Tradition: George Eliot, Henry James, Joseph Conrad*. New York: George W. Stewart, Publisher, [1948].

Lester, John. *Conrad and Religion*. New York: St. Martin's Press, 1988.

Mégroz, R. L. *Joseph Conrad's Mind and Method: A Study of Personality in Art*. London: Faber & Faber, 1931.

Mozina, Andrew. *Joseph Conrad and the Art of Sacrifice: The Evolution of the Scapegoat Theme in Joseph Conrad's Fiction*. New York: Routledge, 2001.

Murfin, Ross C., ed. *Conrad Revisited: Essays for the Eighties*. University: University of Alabama Press, 1985.

Nettels, Elsa. *James & Conrad*. Athens: University of Georgia Press, 1977.

Peters, John G., ed. *Conrad in the Public Eye: Biography/Criticism/Publicity*. Amsterdam: Rodopi, 2008.

Purdy, Dwight H. *Joseph Conrad's Bible*. Norman: University of Oklahoma Press, 1984.

Raval, Suresh. *The Art of Failure: Conrad's Fiction*. Boston: Allen & Unwin, 1986.

Said, Edward W. *Joseph Conrad and the Fiction of Autobiography*. Cambridge, Mass.: Harvard University Press, 1966.

Schwarz, Daniel R. *Conrad:* Almayer's Folly *to* Under Western Eyes. Ithaca, N.Y.: Cornell University Press, 1980.

———. *Conrad: The Later Fiction*. London: Macmillan, 1982.

Simmons, Allan H. *Joseph Conrad*. New York: Palgrave Macmillan, 2006.

Stallman, R. W., ed. *The Art of Joseph Conrad: A Critical Symposium*. East Lansing: Michigan State University Press, 1960.

Thorburn, David. *Conrad's Romanticism*. New Haven, Conn.: Yale University Press, 1974.

Warren, Robert Penn. "Introduction." *Nostromo* by Joseph Conrad. New York: Modern Library, 1951, vii–xxxix.

Watt, Ian. *Conrad in the Nineteenth Century*. Berkeley: University of California Press, 1979.

Watts, Cedric. *Conrad's* Heart of Darkness: *A Critical and Contextual Discussion*. Milano, Italy: Mursia International, 1977.

Wexler, Joyce Piell. *Who Paid for Modernism?: Art, Money, and the Fiction of Conrad, Joyce, and Lawrence*. Fayetteville: University of Arkansas Press, 1997.

Winner, Anthony. *Culture and Irony: Studies in Joseph Conrad's Major Novels*. Charlottesville: University Press of Virginia, 1988.

Wright, Walter F. *Romance and Tragedy in Joseph Conrad*. Lincoln: University of Nebraska Press, 1949.

Yelton, Donald C. *Mimesis and Metaphor: An Inquiry into the Genesis and Scope of Conrad's Symbolic Imagery*. The Hague: Mouton, 1967.

Zabel, Morton Dauwen. "Introduction." In *The Portable Conrad*. New York: Viking Press, 1947, 1–47.

Contributors

CHRISTOPHER GOGWILT is Professor of English and Comparative Literature at Fordham University. He is the author of *The Invention of the West: Joseph Conrad and the Double-Mapping of Europe and Empire* (1995) and *The Fiction of Geopolitics: Afterimages of Culture from Wilkie Collins to Alfred Hitchcock* (2000). He is currently completing a set of comparative studies of Joseph Conrad, Jean Rhys, and Pramoedya Ananta Toer, entitled *The Passage of Literature between English, Creole, and Indonesian Modernisms*.

MARK D. LARABEE is Assistant Professor of English at the United States Naval Academy. A recipient of the Bruce Harkness Young Conrad Scholar Award, he has published on Conrad in *Studies in the Novel*, *CEA Critic*, *Approaches to Teaching Conrad's "Heart of Darkness" and "The Secret Sharer"* (2002), and *Joseph Conrad: The Short Fiction* (2004). He was an Olmsted Scholar at the University of Lausanne, Switzerland; he holds the rank of Commander, U.S. Navy; and he has served at sea for many years. He is currently completing a book on representations of space and place in fiction of the First World War and is working on a new project on maritime globalization and literature.

JOHN G. PETERS is an Associate Professor of English at the University of North Texas and former President of the Joseph Conrad Society of America. He is author of *Conrad and Impressionism* (2001), which was named one of *Choice Magazine*'s Outstanding Academic Titles for 2001. He has also written *The Cambridge Introduction to Joseph Conrad* (2006) and is editor of *Conrad in the Public Eye: Biography/Criticism/Publicity* (2008). In addition to monographs, he is author of a number of scholarly articles on Conrad and other authors. He has also translated the Japanese poet Takamura Kōtarō's book *The Chieko Poems* (2007) and is currently completing a book on the history of the commentary on Joseph Conrad.

ALLAN H. SIMMONS is Reader in English Literature at St. Mary's University College, Twickenham, London. Author of *Joseph Conrad* (2006) and *"Conrad's Heart of Darkness"* for Continuum's "Reader's Guides Series" (2007), he edited the "Centennial Edition" of *The Nigger of the "Narcissus"* (1997) and co-edited *Lord Jim: Centennial Essays* (2000) and *Nostromo: Centennial Essays* (2004). He is General Editor of *The Conradian: The Journal of the Joseph Conrad Society (UK)* and Executive Editor of Rodopi's *Conrad Studies* series.

CEDRIC T. WATTS served in the Royal Navy before taking his BA (class 1), MA, and PhD at Cambridge University. He is currently Research Professor of English at the University of Sussex. His seventeen critical and scholarly books include seven devoted to Conrad, notably *Conrad's "Heart of Darkness": A Critical and Contextual Discussion* (1977), *A Preface to Conrad* (1982; 2nd edn., 1993), *The Deceptive Text* (1984), *Joseph Conrad: A Literary Life* (1989), *Joseph Conrad: "Nostromo"* (1990), and *Joseph Conrad: "The Secret Agent"* (2007). Cedric Watts, awarded the Ian Watt prize for excellence in Conrad scholarship, has edited eleven volumes of Conradian material, including *An Outcast of the Islands, The Heart of Darkness* (serial text), *Nostromo, The Secret Agent,* and *Victory, The Nigger of the "Narcissus"* and *Lord Jim, "Heart of Darkness" and Other Tales* and *"Typhoon" and Other Tales* (both for Oxford), and *Lord Jim.* His other works include *"Hamlet" and "Romeo and Juliet" Cunninghame Graham: A Critical Biography* (with Laurence Davies, 1979; digital rpt., 2008), *"Measure for Measure"* (1986), *Henry V: War Criminal? and Other Shakespeare Puzzles* (with John Sutherland; Oxford University Press, 2000), *Literature and Money* (1990), *A Preface to Keats* (1985), *A Preface to Greene* (1997), and *Thomas Hardy: "Tess of the d'Urbervilles"* (2007). Cedric Watts has also edited Hardy's *Jude* and seventeen Shakespearian plays.

JOYCE PIELL WEXLER is Professor and Chair of English at Loyola University Chicago. She is the author of *Who Paid for Modernism? Art, Money, and the Fiction of Conrad, Joyce, and Lawrence* (1997), *Laura Riding's Pursuit of Truth* (1979), and *Laura Riding: A Bibliography* (1981).

ANDREA WHITE teaches literature and critical theory at California State University, Dominguez Hills, where she is Professor of English and Coordinator of Graduate Studies. She is the author of *Joseph Conrad and The Adventure Tradition* (1993) and co-editor of *Conrad in the 21st Century* (2005). She has also written articles for various journals and collections such as *The Cambridge Companion to Conrad* (1996) and *Approaches to Teaching "The Secret Sharer" and "Heart of Darkness"* (2002) and presented at local and international conferences. She is a former President of the Joseph Conrad Society of America and is currently a trustee of that society, as well as Honorary Committee Member for Distinguished Overseas Members of the Joseph Conrad Society U.K.

Index